The Trumpet in the Hall

by the same author

WAVELL: Portrait of a Soldier
THE WATERY MAZE
RUPERT OF THE RHINE (Brief Lives)
THE BLACK WATCH AND THE KING'S ENEMIES
THE WILD GREEN EARTH
BEYOND THE CHINDWIN
RETURN TO BURMA

ETON PORTRAIT

THE RARE ADVENTURE (novel)

LOWLAND SOLDIER (verse)

BERNARD FERGUSSON

THE TRUMPET IN THE HALL
1930-1958

No longer hosts encountering hosts
Shall crowds of slain deplore:
They hang the trumpet in the hall,
And study war no more.

Scottish Psalter
Paraphrase XVIII

COLLINS
ST JAMES'S PLACE, LONDON

First Impression 1970
Second Impression 1970

ISBN 0 00 211825 4
Set in Monotype Garamond
© Bernard Fergusson 1970
Printed in Great Britain
Collins Clear-Type Press
London and Glasgow

To my wife Laura and my son Geordie

MAPS

I

On the eve of going to Sandhurst for the first time, I walked up the hill through the woods to say good-bye to Old Miss Happle. She lived in a but-and-ben in a group of three or four houses known as the Poundland, looking out across the valley. From my earliest youth we had made regular pilgrimages to call on Old Miss Happle, and it was unthinkable that I should take this next momentous step in my life without her blessing.

She had been bedridden for years. She talked in an old-fashioned Scotch which has disappeared long since, and was a repository of local lore and old songs; but she was in fact descended from one Jacob Happell, who had been engaged as a man-servant in Germany by some Scotsman doing his Grand Tour in the 1750s, and had eventually settled on Kilkerran. On this particular day she was not very communicative; but she followed up her farewells with a letter I still have, which conveys something of her character and also reveals the misgivings which people of her background and generation had about life in the Army. It ends up: –

Mind you mind the Book; mind you are a Fergusson of Kilkerran; and don't get gambling with your officer friends.

Younger sons of Scottish landed families have been joining the Army for a long time past. If you look at Army Lists for fifty years each side of 1800, you will find a host of Scotch names even in the English regiments of the line: there weren't enough Scotch regiments, Lowland or Highland, to accommodate all those who wanted to go soldiering. My father and grandfather were the first heads of the family to become regular soldiers, although one eldest son, who died before he succeeded, had left school without his father's permission, to join the Army and fight against the rebels in the Forty-Five, and stayed on as a regular. Others had fought as and when political or personal reasons provoked them into doing so: one was killed at Pinkie, one had to go into exile after being involved in Montrose's fiasco, and the last to bear the name of Bernard had been engaged in an armed feud against some of his neighbours. But for five generations before my grandfather the head of the family had doucely, and not unprofitably, followed the law in Edinburgh, two days' ride across Scotland from Kilkerran; and for four they had represented their native Ayrshire in Parliament.

My grandfather, succeeding at the age of seventeen, was apparently not drawn to the law, and joined the Grenadiers. A few years later, his cousin and neighbour, Hunter Blair of Blairquhan, died in his arms at Inkerman; and my grandfather, while still in the Crimea, was elected in his place as member for Ayrshire. He left the Grenadiers, and spent the rest of his life either in Parliament or as a Colonial Governor – South Australia, New Zealand, Bombay – before being killed in an earthquake in Jamaica in 1907. My father also joined the Grenadiers and soldiered on for almost forty years: serving under Kitchener in Egypt and the Sudan before, at and after Omdurman, commanding the 5th Division at Mons and Le Cateau, and a Corps for the rest of the war. He retired as a full general in 1922, and two years later went off to be Governor-General of New Zealand, leaving my elder brothers at Oxford and Sandhurst respectively, and myself still in my first year at Eton.

When my parents returned, six years later, I was already at Sandhurst. I had spent most of my school holidays forty miles from Kilkerran with an uncle and aunt, who had a son in The Black Watch. Through him I had got to know many of its officers, and I viewed rather dismally the prospect of doing all my soldiering in or near London, which was the lot of the Brigade of Guards in those days, apart from an occasional sojourn in Egypt. I had written rather nervously to my father in New Zealand to ask if I might switch my allegiance from the Grenadiers. To my relief he agreed, saying that he had written to the Colonel of The Black Watch to put my name down, knowing that there was a long waiting list.

Thanks to the kindness of the English tenants who had taken a lease of Kilkerran during my parents' absence, I was able to spend a few days of every holidays there. No family can ever have loved their home more than we did ours; and every time I returned there I felt much as the men of The Black Watch did when in 1775 they landed back in Scotland after many years overseas, fell on their knees and kissed the ground. There is no record of our ever having lived anywhere else; we were related to many of our neighbours; my grandfathers were not only neighbours but first cousins; we knew every corner of the place, moorland and woodland, field and burn; some of the tenants had been on their holdings for more than two centuries. There was a great sense of permanence. My eldest brother still lives in the house, and his elder son and grandsons in a small house on the place; and although my own home now is twenty-five miles away in the next valley, I felt throughout my days of soldiering that life was really just a prolonged sortie from Kilkerran.

It was from the last of my visits to the English tenants, who were already beginning to pack up in anticipation of my parents' return, that I went to say good-bye to Nanny Hupple. A few days later, I kept a chilly rendezvous at Waterloo Station – it was January, 1930 – with five Eton friends, and rumbled apprehensively down the line to Camberley, a journey which was to become all too familiar. Three of the six were future Grenadiers, including Algy Grant of Monymusk, who was to be killed in Normandy in 1944, and Dickie des Voeux, to be killed at Arnhem three months later. Another was Patrick Campbell-Preston, destined like me for The Black Watch and to become by far my closest friend. Years later we were to marry sisters; he was to be my second-in-command and my successor in command in the Regiment; and eventually to die in 1960 from a heart condition, deriving directly from his ordeals as a prisoner of war. He escaped twice; was recaptured both times; and was decorated after the war for having been such a pillar of strength to his fellow prisoners throughout their darkest days. He was one of the few men I have known really well – Lord Wavell was another – whose character has seemed to me to be utterly without flaw.

Of those six, only one survives besides myself. It is commonly said, and with truth, that the casualties in the Second War were nothing like as heavy as those in the First; but my own contemporaries were hard hit. If I may be forgiven, just this once, for inflicting a catalogue of names, I can still recall the occupants of every room down our particular passage that first term at Sandhurst, since we were housed in strict alphabetical order. Blake, Royal Ulster Rifles, killed in Korea. Coke, King's Own Scottish Borderers, killed at Arnhem. Cooper, Cheshire Regiment, drowned as a glider pilot in the Sicily landings. Cotter, Lincolns, still alive. Crookshank, Indian Army, still alive. Crosthwaite, King's Own Scottish Borderers, died on active service in Italy. De Robeck, Durham Light Infantry, still alive. Douglas, Camerons, killed in North Africa. Fane, Coldstream, killed while leading his men into action in France, characteristically tooting on a hunting-horn. Fergusson. Frisby, Royal Hampshire Regiment like his father, and now a retired major-general. That makes six out of ten of us from that corridor alone who became battle casualties, and it makes me reflect, not for the first time, how lucky I have been to have kept a whole skin, more or less, so far.

I would have preferred to join the Army by way of a University. Most of my Eton friends were going to Oxford or Cambridge or, in one case, to Trinity College, Dublin; and when I stayed with Jo Grimond at Balliol or with Dermot McGillycuddy at T.C.D., I was thoroughly envious of their civilised, easy way of life, when they tired not only the sun but the moon with talking. But my father would not hear of it, and he was plumb right. At Eton I had sat several notional army exams, with actual entrance papers, and realised that they were well within my scope; and for the last two years had given myself an easy-osy time. A thorough toughening-up was what I needed, and Sandhurst in those days was certainly tough. The legendary "Boy" Browning of the Grenadiers, who had been Adjutant throughout my brother Simon's time, had gone on to conquer other fields; but the ghost of his voice, his omniscience and his omnipresence still haunted each coign and shadow of block and building, induced agoraphobia as you crossed the Square and inspired at all times a certain trembling of the knees. And the Under-Officers, although only a year older than ourselves, were almost as terrifying.

The only way to treat it all, I soon decided, was to forget that I had ever aspired to be an academic; to beat the non-academics at their own game; to see (but keep strictly to my own bosom) the funny side of it; and to kid myself that by some extraordinary mistake I had enlisted in the Foreign Legion like a member of the Geste family, and found myself in the Depot at Sidi-Bel-Abbès. This worked, and I found I could hold my own. I derived much encouragement from the old soldiers who acted as our servants, one to every eight cadets. My own, Piper, was a veteran of The Queen's Regiment in both the South African and the First World Wars: a gentle, respectable family man with a drooping moustache like the White Knight's, and a fund of tales about Boers and Boches, Buller and Bobs.

The drill I positively enjoyed. It was good to be one of a squad of fifty, or a Company of 150, or (when we had graduated to that honour) of the complete Battalion of 600, taking part in arms drill, or marching past in quick or slow time. I revelled with others in the music of the Military Band, playing such classic quick marches as *Old Panama* or slow ones like *The Colours*. What I hated most was Equitation (which, believe it or not, meant "riding") and Physical Training. Equitation was all right for those who hunted at home, and who, incidentally, were allowed one day off a week in winter to go hunting from Sandhurst: this in deference to the time-honoured theory that hunting gave the young officer "an eye for country." For me and my non-riding friends Equitation was hell, and the riding-serjeants had a contempt for us which they made no effort to hide. In their eyes, anybody with any pretension to be an officer and a gentleman should be able to ride, like the officers in the smart cavalry Regiments from which they came.

As for P.T., that was hell too. We would fall in outside our Company Building in our pink-and-white-striped blazers, white trousers, vests and cravats, socks and shoes below, funny little round pill-box hats on top, and blue shorts and towels tucked under our arms. Once in the Gym, we had to change in the twinkling of an eye and fall in again in three squads and two ranks for fifty minutes of torture. The greatest joy of Sandhurst was when the squat little Warrant-Officer in charge blew his whistle and we all froze in our places. He would then scream: "Towels: GO!" This was the signal for us to strip mother-naked, to scamper off to the showers – in and out, no time to linger or relax – dress again at Sandhurst pace, fall in and march back to the Company: aching in every limb, but thanking the Almighty that P.T. was over for another forty-eight hours at least.

Rough and rude as we often were, we Gentlemen Cadets – and I still relish the old-fashioned ring of the phrase, which some booby in the War Office abolished soon after the war broke out – had an element of the romantic in us, as all good soldiers must. There were few of us without close army connections already. I was impressed only lately, when reading a book about the Duke of Wellington, by the fact that many of the names of his officers in the Peninsula and at Waterloo were represented in my generation at Sandhurst: Fane, Luard, Paget, Vandeleur, and so on. We warmed to the history of individual Regiments, to which a generous amount of time was given in the Syllabus, as much as to any of the subjects we were taught. Why did The Glosters wear their cap-badges aft as well as fore? Why did The Royal Welch wear black flashes at the back of their collars? Why did The West Yorkshires have *Ça Ira* as their regimental march? Why was this Regiment called "Pontius Pilate's Bodyguard," and another the "Pompadours," and another the "Moonrakers," and another the "Dirty Half-Hundred"? We drank in such lore, and never forgot it.

On Band Nights the programme always ended, before *God Save The King*, with a regimental march. The Band worked its way religiously through the whole Army List, and as in those days there were many more Regiments than there are to-day, you were lucky if you heard your own during your mere eighteen months at Sandhurst. I am sure I was not the only one by a long chalk who felt moved when we stood to drink the loyal toast: 300 dedicated young men, half the College, aged eighteen or nineteen: all in uniform, all with aspirations to go into this Regiment or that, all committed to a career in the honourable profession of arms. All of us were of that brotherhood by choice.

My elder brother Simon had warned me that one of the most memorable things about Sandhurst was the playing of the Last Post on the bugle at night, and the four simple notes of its coda, Lights Out, ten minutes later. Indeed, throughout my twenty-eight years' service I was always to be moved by these: they gently expunged and exorcised such worries as the day might have brought. Among the Sandhurst buglers was one Priest, whom Simon had told me about. Portly and unmilitary in appearance, he never failed to cajole from his instrument a beautiful and faultless tone. "That's Priest to-night," one could say with certainty. He must be dead long since; but his Last Post still quavers into the darkness of my memory, and I can forgive him even his ruthless Reveille.

Gentlemen Cadets were not allowed cars in those days, and we covered a vast mileage on bicycles, both on duty and in our leisure hours. There were two other Presbyterians in my Company: Adam Gordon from Ross-shire (afterwards Highland Light Infantry), and Colin McVean from Argyll (afterwards Indian Army). We had to attend Church Parade in the morning, and the service with the Anglicans in the Chapel, which is surely the ugliest place of worship ever built by any religion; but on Sunday evenings we used to bicycle the seven miles to Aldershot and back, to St Andrew's Church of Scotland Garrison Church. Though crowded in the mornings in those days of compulsory Church Parades, and with two or three Scotch battalions in the garrison, the evening congregation never exceeded a dozen. Well brought up though we no doubt were, Adam and Colin and I would never have been so assiduous in attending the church of our fathers had it not been for the character of the chaplain. He was a splendid, dreamy, absent-minded, slow, corpulent, pasty-faced Gaelic-speaking Highlander called Ewen Maclean; and the sermons which he preached to his tiny flock of faithful in his beautiful voice are still memorable after forty years, though they sounded more like private ruminations. He would interpolate into the lessons, as though thinking to himself, illuminating comments on their matter. When he was reading of Judas's question: "*Why was not this ointment sold for 300 pence, and given to the poor?*" there was a long pause, and the deep Black Isle voice asked itself the question: "Whaat did he caare for the pooer?" He was to come into my life once again, seven years after I left Sandhurst.

In the course of time I became Senior Under-Officer of my Company; two of the other three had been at school with me, Algy Grant and Lyon Corbett-Winder. I felt very grand with the insignia of my rank on my sleeve: an intricate design in braid like that of an Austrian Hussar, running almost up to my elbow. I had staunch help from the four Junior Under-Officers and from Hawkins the excellent Company Serjeant-Major from the Coldstream; but I had a major worry: my bad eyesight. I had long worn spectacles for reading and shooting, but I could not bring myself to wear them in uniform. I had the old-fashioned idea, fully shared by my father, that they were un-military and unbecoming in a soldier. (Since then, of course, many distinguished soldiers from Alanbrooke down have worn them without a qualm.) For most purposes this didn't matter, but when it came to drilling the Company from a hundred yards away I was in trouble. Peer as I might, I couldn't see which foot they were on as they marched, or deduce the precise moment at which to give the executive word of command. With the inter-company drill competition, on which the betting in the Serjeants' Mess was always heavy, looming ahead, Hawkins implored me to swallow my pride and wear my spectacles, but I wouldn't. I schooled myself instead to learn the knack of saying to myself: "Left, Right, Left, Right," until I had a sort of sub-conscious metronome inside me. It was on my father's orders that I eventually took to an eye-glass before joining the Regiment, and soon got hardened to people looking askance at me on first acquaintance.

Passing-Out Day came at last. We marched past for the last time; the Sword of Honour was bestowed (by some oversight, not on me); we, the departing Senior Division, marched up the steps of the Grand Entrance to the strains of *Auld Lang Syne*, followed as tradition dictated by the Adjutant on his charger; and the great doors swung to behind us. The Adjutant now was Norman Gwatkin of the Coldstream, the only officer I have ever seen as smart as Boy Browning. He had been a wonderful friend and counsellor to us four S.U.O.s, contriving to make us feel in our innocence that we really were helping him run the place; and we were as sad to say good-bye to him as to anybody.

Leave came next, and the excitement of seeing one's name in *The Times* as being really commissioned into the Regiment, and shooting the moor for the last time for many years: this was 1931 and the Depression, and from now on the grouse-shooting would be let to tenants. There were several visits to the regimental tailors in Edinburgh, to try on uniform and be kitted up generally. At preparatory school, at public school, at Sandhurst, you get a fresh start each time; but when you join your Regiment you are joining it for good. To that extent your arrival is more of an ordeal, since you feel that a bad beginning may damn you for ever. To fortify each other, Patrick Campbell-Preston and I joined forces in London, just as we had done twenty months before, and travelled together down to Colchester where the 2nd Battalion was lying, from Liverpool Street, that most depressing of stations.

My start could hardly have been less auspicious. On my first morning I dressed with scrupulous care – I had never before worn the kilt, except in the privacy of the tailor's – and set off to find C Company Office, to which I had been ordered to report. Before I had covered thirty yards I encountered a smart personage wearing a Sam Browne belt and two rows of medal ribbons: he seemed to rate a salute, so I gave him one. He smiled and explained that he was in fact the R.S.M. He added: "And if I might presume to advise, Sir, I would go back to my quarters and put my spats on the correct feet!"

Having put that right, I reported to my company commander, Captain Gurdon (whose two sons were to serve under me in the Regiment years later), who said that he had nothing for me to do, and I'd better go back to the mess. There I met the Adjutant, who said: "What the hell are you doing here? Get back to your company!"

Despite that unpromising beginning, there couldn't have been a more welcoming family to join. We new boys were at once made at home in the mess, and within two weeks we had lunched or dined with every married officer. Patrick and I were appalled when we went to look up two Sandhurst friends who had joined an English Regiment in the same garrison, whose reception had been very different from ours, despite the fact that one of them had been born and brought up in that Regiment. It was a chilly evening, but they were cowering in the farthest corner of the ante-room from the fire, by which two other officers were sitting; and when they pressed the bell to order the refreshment which was what we had really come in search of, they did so in whispers. Patrick's ringing laugh, which was known – and indeed almost audible – all over Scotland, brought their forefingers to their lips as they glanced furtively towards the fireplace. We walked home – for it felt like home – across Abbey Fields thanking our stars that we belonged where we did.

I was happy from the outset, although woefully short of money. A Second-Lieutenant drew 9s. 10d. a day. Even if you neither smoked nor drank, your mess bill, including your share of entertainment and your subscriptions, gobbled it all up. We were not regarded as a "rich" Regiment, but even so there were at least three subalterns with private incomes of over £2,000 a year, and there was one married subaltern who kept a butler. The minimum private allowance one was required to have was £250 a year. As a special concession I had been allowed in with £150, and it was hard going; but nobody ever tried to embroil me in activities which I couldn't afford. After a few months I bought a very old open two-seater Singer car for £17 10s: it looked a bit provincial among the Lagondas and the Bentleys among which it nestled at night, but nobody minded. And I managed to persuade five brother officers to join me in buying a 3½-ton cutter for £65, a sum which we borrowed initially out of the Polo Fund – an unprecedented misappropriation to which no die-hard objected.

To me the consciousness of being in a rich tradition transformed even the most routine of military duties. Others might find it tedious to be Orderly Officer; I rather enjoyed the awareness of responsibility. I found it no hardship to stand shivering with the Orderly Serjeant in the driving rain of a winter's night, when at 10 p.m. precisely Last Post was sounded on the bugle, though perhaps not quite so well as Priest used to do it. Ten minutes later, a piper would play *Donald Blue* for Lights Out. Some time during the night one would turn out the Guard. The sentry would bellow: "Guarrd! Turrn Out!" and out the Guard would bustle, adjusting their equipment as they came.

We were expected to turn out ourselves, in any dress, even pyjamas, at 6.30 a.m. on the 15th of every month, to hear the Pipes and Drums play the Crimean Reveille, a medley of tunes of which the origin is forgotten, breaking from Slow Time into Quick, and from Quick back into Slow, with no word of command given; and burgeoning finally into the usual Reveille, the familiar *Hey, Johnnie Cope, are ye wakin' yet?* A curious choice, I have always thought, since two detached companies of the Regiment were involved in the disaster of Prestonpans, when the Jacobite Army caught Sir John Cope literally napping in a dawn attack, the occasion vaunted by this mocking tune.

And the ritual of the monthly Guest Night never palled,

beside which the Sandhurst Band Nights had been only the most shadowy of foretastes. For some reason we usually drank more than was good for us, but it was a matter of pride that one should carry one's drink like a gentleman, and for one's efficiency not to be remotely impaired the morn's morning, even though one's head be splitting like a walnut. Throughout dinner, the military band played muted music from next door, the pipers marched round the table while we drank port and liqueurs, and the Pipe-Major played his piobaireachd, finishing his crunluadh behind the Commanding Officer's chair. I wondered whether this might ever be my privilege. On the table were the massive silver centre-pieces and the huge ram's-head snuff-mulls, with their shaggy wool like Lloyd George's hair and their grotesquely twisted horns.

Afterwards there would be dancing: eightsome or sixteen-some reels followed by foursomes, and country dances like the Duke of Perth and Hamilton House. Each new officer had to satisfy the Adjutant concerning his proficiency in these, and it was galling for a young Highlander who had danced from his nursery days to the entire satisfaction of his proud family when his performance was judged not up to regimental standard. There were certain prescribed regimental steps to be mastered too. Undue shouting and skelloching in a reel was pronounced vulgar, and woe betide you if reports came back from the Northern Meeting or the Portree Gathering that you had been seen or heard doing something unbecoming in a reel.

I can still put a name and a face to most of my original platoon. With three of them I was to soldier much in the future, in peace and war alike. One was Corporal "Big Jim" Ewan, a huge humorous uncompromising man from Brechin who was usually wreathed in smiles, but who could unleash a rough tongue to shrivel a wrong-doer. Another was "Rob" Roy the platoon piper, probably the best in the Battalion, with a wide repertoire of piobaireachd even at that early age; he came of an old regimental family, and was supposed to be descended from that Private Roy in the Regiment whose greatcoat pillowed the head of the dying General Abercromby at Aboukir. And there was Peter Dorans, my soldier servant, who came off that cousin's estate where I had spent my holidays when my parents were in New Zealand: we were to be together ten years with a short break in the middle, and I owe him my life.

Three-quarters of the fun of all regimental soldiering derived from the Jocks. Most of them were either farm-servants from Perthshire or Angus, or miners from Fife, and they were a constant joy: sometimes exasperating, always stimulating. And they would stand by "the officer" through thick and thin.

Once, during the post-mortem on an exercise, the Commanding Officer found fault with my siting of a Lewis-gun, and sought confirmation from the section commander.

"You couldn't see the enemy from where you were, could you, Corporal Jack?" he said.

"Yes, Sir!" said Corporal Jack. "I could see'm fae the tap o's hcid tae the soles o's feet."

"Sorry, Fergusson," said the Colonel. "I take that back."

Afterwards, I asked him: "Just what exactly could you see from there?"

"No' a bliddy thing," said Jack cheerfully. He was killed in a lorry accident in Palestine a few years later, but my heart warms to him still.

Then there was the time the company pay blew away. My cousin Malcolm Wolfe Murray had driven me to the bank to collect it, and it was in the usual tartan bag, mostly in ten-shilling notes, amounting to two or three hundred pounds in all. By now we were stationed in Maryhill Barracks, Glasgow, long since demolished. Between the Company blocks and the officers' mess was a broad expanse of parade ground and foot-ball field. There was a high wind blowing; and as I got out of the car I picked up the bag by the wrong end, and all the notes fell out. Before you could say "Malcolm Wolfe Murray," the air was full of ten-bob notes scudding and scurrying down wind, and there was nothing left in the precious bag but a few half-crowns. From every window of every block the Jocks poured out and chased after the flying money, while I went in miserably to my company commander and told him what had happened. He looked at me grimly, and said: "Well, I wish you luck!" and I could sense my good friend the Colour-Serjeant, sitting behind the paying-out sheets waiting for the cash, also wishing me well. I reckoned that the sum involved would be just about a year's pay plus a year's private allowance combined.

A butcher's boy, delivering meat in the Barracks from a bicycle, brought me £12 10s. in muddy notes. One by one, the Jocks came back, each with a fistful of soiled or screwed-up paper: some had picked them off the windward wall of the officers' mess. Jocks from every company in the Battalion filed into the company office, and laid their findings on the table. The Colour-Serjeant smoothed them out and counted them. At last he stood up and saluted the Company Commander. "Every penny is accounted for, Sir," he said. And then the Jocks of C Company, many of whom were "married off the strength" – that is, drawing no marriage allowance and living in penury – came in one by one, and drew their pittances of ten bob or a pound apiece. There was and is no possible comment for me to make.

In March 1935, the Battalion still being in Glasgow, I went off for two years to be A.D.C. to Wavell. Archibald Percival Wavell had been gazetted Second-Lieutenant in the Regiment on the 8th May 1901, three days after his eighteenth birthday, and in time to see service in the South African War. His father had exchanged into The Black Watch from The Norfolk Regiment ten years earlier, to command the 2nd Battalion. His son, Archie John, was at this moment at Sandhurst, and also destined for the Regiment: destined also to lose a hand fighting in Burma, and to be killed fighting against the Mau Mau on Christmas Eve 1953. The future Field-Marshal had had no regimental service since his departure to be a student at Camberley in 1912, except for a few months in Silesia just after the war, when he came back with some exalted brevet rank for a short spell as a company commander. But his heart was as truly in the Regiment as anybody's; and I have always remembered him saying to me: "Never forget: the Regiment is the foundation of everything."

It was at about this time that the first assaults were being made upon the regimental system. There were considerable discrepancies throughout the Army, and the infantry in particular, in the rate of promotion of officers. In some regiments you could count on being a captain in eight or nine years; in others it might take eighteen or more. In The Black Watch we were averaging sixteen, and The Rifle Brigade was even slower. The best solution the War Office could dream up was a device called the "Group System": the phrase still "gars me grue." The idea was to link the various Regiments of the Line in bunches of five or six, within which there would be a common promotion roll for officers. This plan was actually put to all Regiments, by teams of three officers, each headed by a Brigadier, who were sent round to "sell" it: it was rejected outright by all except two, neither of which had the reputation of being "happy ships."

Years before, Lord Wolseley had written, in the final chapter of his memoirs: "Keep your hands off the Regiments, you iconoclastic civilians who meddle and muddle in Army matters: you are not soldiers, and you do not understand them." The odd thing about the Group System plan was that the idea was floated by people who presumably did look upon themselves as soldiers. It stank to me, as to most other people, as what the Army calls an "s.i.w.," or a "self-inflicted wound." I remember at this moment meeting an extremely nice Brigadier, who had been an ensign under my father thirty years before, and who had headed one of these missionary teams. He asked me why they had had such chilly hearings. I asked him respectfully how he would react if such a plan were to be suggested to the Brigade of Guards. He replied stiffly: "Of course, there would never be any question of that." I felt I had provoked a good answer.

For the time being, the snake was scotched but not killed; and after the war, to vary the metaphor, it was to spread like couch-grass, and had to be combated. Wavell, by then a Field-

Marshal and in the House of Lords, was a powerful agent in this, and fought until he died. But during the war the Adjutant-General's Branch seemed to go out of its way to mix up Regiments as much as it could. I remember how, in 1940, when I was Brigade Major to a brigade which consisted entirely of Highland Light Infantry, we got a signal telling us to expect a draft of 200 Royal Irish Fusiliers to reinforce one of our units. Jocks and Irish tend not to mix, and my heart sank; but when these men arrived, they all spoke with Yorkshire accents.

Being sent to Wavell as his first-ever A.D.C. was the greatest stroke of luck that ever befell me. We didn't have everything in common. He adored horses, and I loathed them; he loved golf, and I didn't play it. But when, on his death, my father wrote to me suggesting that I knew Wavell better than I knew him, my father, I suddenly realised that there was a good deal in it. Although nothing could ever supplant my father in my affection, I had seen far more of Wavell over the years between 1935, when I first joined him in the 2nd Division at Aldershot, and 1950, when he died. They only met once. My parents happened to be down in England, an event which happened rarely, as it was difficult to prise my father away from Kilkerran, from which by the exigencies of his life he had been separated so much. The Wavells invited them to luncheon at Aldershot, and in my dual capacity as son and A.D.C. I was on tenterhooks; and Wavell, of course, who by now was pretty well my god, was holding my father in awe. He had been a third-grade staff officer in the War Office on General Sir Henry Wilson's operations staff at the time of the "Curragh Incident," when my father was actually in command at the Curragh, and had expressed his vehement disapproval of Wilson's machinations in letters to his father at the time.* I have always been glad that my father and Wavell met at least this once. My father was then seventy, tall, straight as a spar, magnificent to look at, his career over, except for fifteen dedicated anonymous years, spanning the war, as Lord-Lieutenant of his county. Wavell was fifty-two,

*The Curragh Incident, pp. 146-7, 153-4, 196-7; Sir James Fergusson: Faber; 1964.

short, stocky, with a glass eye and a stubborn chin: impressive indeed to look at, but in a totally different way, and on the threshold of campaigns in which his name was to shine as illustriously as those of Marlborough or Wellington. Both were by nature reserved, but they hit it off, and corresponded thereafter from time to time. I am sure that it was this one encounter which encouraged Wavell to tell my father many years later in strictest confidence that the reason why he would not be hearing from me for some months to come was because I was going on a secret foray behind the Japanese lines, and also to conceal from him the reports – exaggerated, as in the case of Mark Twain – that I had been killed.

On Wavell's staff at Aldershot, in those momentous years of 1935 to 1937, while the Second War was looming, I got to know much of what was going on behind the scenes, and many of those who were soon to play important parts: Dill, Gort, Alanbrooke, Auchinleck, Freyberg, Alexander. Wavell's own brigade commanders were men with names which were soon to be famous: Victor Fortune (to be knighted for his prowess as a defiant prisoner of war); Arthur Smith (Wavell's Chief of Staff during those historic years in the Middle East); and "Jumbo" Wilson, afterwards Field-Marshal Lord Wilson of Libya, the most ungainly and unmilitary of figures who always talked through his nose. The Brigade Majors included Horrocks and Dempsey, both future distinguished commanders. Not even Wellington's A.D.C. in the Peninsular War, Fitzroy Somerset, was luckier than I was in this, or any other, respect.

By January 1937 I had sucked the job dry, and Wavell agreed that two years was long enough to spend as an A.D.C. The Battalion was due to go to Palestine in the autumn; and I left Wavell in March of that year in order to grow myself back into my roots before it sailed. I rejoined in Glasgow, but soon we went to Barry-Buddon Camp on the Angus coast near Carnoustie, where we began to rehearse our role for "internal security duties." We pretended as earnestly as we could to round up imaginary Arab gangs in the bents and grasses of the links and sand-dunes, which bore no more resemblance to the bleak hills of Judaea than to the mangrove-swamps of Malaya or the Mountains of the Moon. I think that it dawned on us then that four years in Glasgow had not been the best preparation for semi-active service; but we had not been long in Palestine before every Second-Lieutenant and every Lance-Corporal had had experience of being isolated and under fire in remote places. When the War broke out, everybody had been on the *qui vive* for two years; and I doubt if there was any better-trained battalion.

At the last Church Parade before we left Barry-Buddon Camp, to go on embarkation leave, the preacher was none other than Ewen Maclean, the pot-bellied, peely-wally, eloquent old Highlander whom I had so often "sat under" when at Sandhurst, and who was now Assistant Chaplain General at Scottish Command. The Battalion, less Roman Catholics, was present in full strength under the Commanding Officer, Alick McLeod, whose father, General Sir Duncan McLeod, had fifty years before been Colonel of the Regiment. We were packed like pilchards in the N A A F I Hut.

The moment came for the sermon. Maclean gave out as his text: *"What shall it profit the King if he clotheth himself in cedar?"* I asked myself what on earth he was going to make out of that. I might have known that he had something up the capacious sleeves of his gown, and so he had. It was no good being a King in a superb palace unless you were a good King. It was no good being a good Christian unless you were good at your job and your duty. (How many lesser preachers would have put that the other way round?) It was no good belonging to a Regiment like The Black Watch unless you mastered the craft of soldiering, faithfully performed the duties entrusted to you, and above all kept your temper and maintained your discipline when provoked: as we were bound to be provoked in the land to which we were being despatched on the business of The King and our countrymen, whom we would be representing.

He spoke in his fathom-deep voice, as though he were thinking aloud: just as he used to speak when I was seven years younger, and still a Gentleman Cadet. Then he moved on to a solemn charge. "The Black Watch will be courteous to women. The Black Watch will be kindly to men. The Black Watch will be merciful to prisoners. The Black Watch will be true to its history, as it has ever been. – We will now partake of the Sacrament."

And so we all did, if only for the reason that nobody dared to leave; and for once there was no great buzz of chatter when at last we skailed into the sunlight.

2

OUR destination was Jerusalem; but we were in for a surprise. While the Port Said tugs were taking charge of us, to nudge us in to our berth, the ship was boarded by a staff officer from Force Headquarters in Jerusalem who brought us fresh orders. During our two weeks at sea, the Arab troubles had bubbled up again. Andrews, the District Commissioner at Nazareth, had been shot and killed coming out of church, and similar incidents, obviously synchronised, had happened all over the country. Wavell, who was now C.-in-C. in Palestine, had delayed the departure of The Royal Sussex whom we were supposed to relieve, and we were to be switched to Sarafand, of which none of us had heard; the staff officer, under a bombardment of questions, told us that it was on the plain about ten miles east of Jaffa.

We reached Sarafand railway-station after a tedious, thirsty night crossing the Sinai Desert in a baking hot train. Colonel McLeod ordered us to change into the kilt so as to impress the populace of Sarafand as we marched in. There was much cursing as we unpacked our creased kilts from our kit-bags, with our shirt-tails flapping in a scorching desert wind; and Sarafand proved to be merely a military camp, part huts, mostly tents, with no populace to impress but The Wiltshire Regiment, an Ordnance Depot, a Royal Signals establishment and an Air Force Hospital. It was now noon, and extremely hot.

The Wiltshires had kindly prepared a breakfast for us which they thought would be to our barbarous taste: it consisted of porridge, made of Quaker Oats instead of meal, into which they had stirred sugar instead of salt. I had been saddled, among other things, with the job of messing officer, and I went from group to group of Jocks wringing my hands and begging them to make some show of eating the porridge, so as not to hurt the feelings of the Wiltshires: but in vain.

The present Palestine Garrison consisted of two brigades which divided the country between them: the northern with its headquarters at Haifa, the southern at Sarafand. We had been in the place for less than a week when I was sent for by Colonel McLeod, who said dismally that he had been called on to provide a subaltern as Brigade Intelligence Officer and that he was going to provide me. I was pretty unhappy, as I had only been back six months with the Battalion, and was enchanted to be commanding a platoon again, but the Colonel pointed out that it should be a fascinating job, and one in which I could be useful to the Battalion. I was sent to see the Brigade Commander, a tall, lugubrious, hook-nosed, red-faced Gordon Highlander called Laurence Carr who eventually became a lieutenant-general. He surveyed me, pronounced that I would "do", and I moved over the following day with my servant Farrar, a small ex-keeper from the Stewartry of Kirkcudbright whom Peter Dorans, now time-expired and working as a forester on Kilkerran, had selected as his replacement.

I hated saying good-bye to my platoon; I should have hated it even more if I'd known that it would be four years before I got back to the Regiment; but I was encouraged by the briefing given me by Brigadier Carr and his brigade major. My job, apart from keeping a lot of maps up to date, would be to reconnoitre every town and village in southern Palestine, to make myself known to the headmen, to assess each village's capacity for billeting, to make a rough sketch-map of each, and to report on every track: its probable "going" in dry or rainy season, and its potential sites for ambushes, whether laid by us or for us. I saw myself, as did so many young officers in those days, as a pseudo-Lawrence. The Brigadier clinched it all by saying: "I shall regard you very much as a keeper. If I find you in the kennels all the time, by which I mean these headquarters, I shall know you aren't doing your job. If I don't see you about the place, I shall assume you're on the moor, or in the coverts, or on the marshes, or after poachers. I shall expect to see you here most nights, but sometimes when you're well afield you won't be able to get back; you must let us know when that is going to be, and you must always let the brigade major know where you are going. Once a week you must stay back here to write a report and tell me what you've been up to."

My team back at base consisted of a corporal and a draughtsman, who kept the documents and drew the pretty pictures from my rough sketches; my transport of a single green-painted army Austin Seven, an admirable vehicle for the job, since we could lift it easily over ruts and boulders and out of mud. My team in the field was a driver; Farrar; a well-educated Christian Arab interpreter who preferred to go under the assumed name of "Mansour" for fear of being identified, and who taught me Arabic in his spare time; and myself. Sometimes, if I were going somewhere which might be tricky, but more often just to give toilers in the office a breath of fresh air, I would be accompanied by a few troops in a 15-cwt. truck as an escort, but in fact on the rare occasions when I could have done with an escort there wasn't one. After a week's handover from a captain in The Royal Sussex whom I was relieving, I was on my own. I got to know the Intelligence Officers in the various battalions – John Benson was ours – and the Intelligence staff at Force Headquarters in Jerusalem and elsewhere. The Jerusalem "I" staff included a major, and a couple of captains. One of these last was Orde Wingate, then aged thirty-four, speaking good Arabic of the Sudanese variety and learning Hebrew avidly. He was grim, unsmiling and far from forthcoming; but the fact that we were neither of us wholly conventional made us take stock of each other, and so began the association which was to become so close during the war.

Soon after the First War, Lord Trenchard with his usual persuasiveness had managed to sell to the powers in Whitehall his doctrine of "Air Control". The Army distrusted it, and with hindsight I am sure rightly, though Marshal of the Royal Air Force Sir John Slessor, for whom I have unlimited admiration, wrote in his book *The Central Blue* as late as 1956: "I doubt whether to-day any, even among those who were its most impassioned opponents, would seek to revive the old arguments against it."* Stripped to its essentials, the idea was that you built up a network of political intelligence officers who would learn their areas like the back of their hands and get on terms with the tribal leaders. If that failed the next step was to give a demonstration of the effectiveness of bombing from the air. If that in turn failed, you told the people to evacuate their villages, and then reduced them to rubble. Finally, as a last resort, you bombed to kill, but you hoped that in practice it would never come to that. What appealed most to the "powers" was the comparative cheapness of this system, which should save tying up a lot of troops.

Trenchard's system was first tried out in Iraq; and according to Sir John Slessor it was the hostility of Sir Henry Wilson, then C.I.G.S., to the system that caused the Army to refuse all support on the ground, so that the Iraq Levies had to be raised under R.A.F. auspices. Aden, Trans-Jordan and Palestine – the two latter being under the same High Commissioner – were also transferred to basic R.A.F. control; but when things got out of hand in Palestine the real need was for troops on the ground. Intelligence still remained basically in the hands of the Royal Air Force. They provided the senior Intelligence Officer at Force Headquarters, and half a dozen Special Service Officers in the rank of Flight-Lieutenant, each with his own area and each speaking first-class Arabic.

The actual running of the country was of course in the hands of the Civil Administration, though to hear us young officers talk you would never have guessed it. The High Commissioner since 1931 had been General Sir Arthur Wauchope, of the Regiment: a cousin of my mother's, and a complex character. He was a rich bachelor, though he died a comparatively poor man, having given away most of his fortune in benefactions in Palestine. Little thanks did he get from anybody. He was a

The Central Blue: Marshal of the R.A.F. Sir John Slessor; Cassell: 1956, p. 51.

tiny little man, wizened and untidy, with a passion for music, books, pictures, good wine and intellectual company. Although he was the last man in the world you would guess to be a soldier, he had been a tiger on the battlefield, and thrice severely wounded.

His first term of five years had been a success. His tragedy was that he was persuaded to take on for a second, and from that moment everything went wrong for him. I was young at the time, but I heard my elders and betters discussing it; and my reading of it is that he mistook the increasing and irreconcilable differences between the Jews and the Arabs for mere growing pains. The Jews thought, and the Arabs were sure, that he inclined to the Jews; I believe he was being strictly impartial between both, though he certainly loved the intellectual company the Jews afforded him.

There is an illuminating letter from Dill (Wavell's predecessor in Palestine) to Wavell, written in October 1936, which hits Wauchope's nail right on the head: –

Arthur Wauchope loves every stone of this country, he has worked himself to the bone for it – and it has let him down. . . . His forbearance knew no bounds and for it he got no thanks – it was merely held to be weakness. He hated the idea of Martial Law. He felt its operation would leave a sullen people with rebellion in their hearts. He is delighted that peace has come without having had to resort to stern measures. But the peace is only an armed truce. . . . As I see it, Arthur Wauchope loves greatly, administers with knowledge and imagination, but he does not rule.*

Wauchope's powers, legal, moral and physical, had ebbed, and the process was the more painful because, despite the seven years' difference in their age, he and Wavell had been on the closest terms of friendship for thirty years, ever since serving together in the 2nd Battalion in India in 1906. It was obvious that he must go, and go he did, though not until March 1938. That Battalion, which he had joined on first commissioning forty-two years before and had commanded in peace and war, mounted a farewell guard of honour for him. In his farewell

Wavell: *Scholar and Soldier*: John Connell: Collins: 1964, p. 188.

radio broadcast the night before, he had finished with the words: "Pray for the peace of Jerusalem: they shall prosper that love her." And so he vanished into obscurity, with one late flowering to comfort him: he was to be Colonel of the Regiment for the last six years of his life.

His successor was Sir Harold MacMichael from that unrivalled stud of administrators, the Sudan Political Service. I did not know him until later, but he was a man in a million. Between him and Wavell and Wavell's successors there was never a breath of disagreement. Some of the District Commissioners and Assistant District Commissioners had also come from the Sudan; others had been in Palestine ever since the end of the war.

Far and away our closest links were with the Palestine Police, with whom we quickly established an unshakeable alliance. They were often maligned, not least by British politicians who were backing one side or the other; there was an occasional black sheep among them; but they were a *corps d'élite*, and an honour to serve alongside. Sadly, their history has never been written, and now it could not be done: the material is lost. They had their origin in the Palestine Gendarmerie, set up just after the First War; and one survival of those days, Brigadier-General Angus McNeil, still lived in dignified retirement in a Druze village near Haifa, and continued to do so, as a very old man, right up to the 1948 war.

There was every sort and kind of person in the Force, including a handful of ex-Black-and-Tans, a fact made much of by the Force's political enemies in England. The two I remember, both fairly senior, were thoroughly decent men. Among the constables was an Irish peer who had been at Sandhurst; a theological student who thought that seven years in the *soi-disant* Holy Land might resolve some doubts which had beset him; some ex-soldiers who had enjoyed being stationed in the country; two Merchant Navy officers; and a rollicking line-shooter who afterwards wrote a series of books about his time in the Force, making himself the hero of everybody else's best stories, as well as several which he made up for himself.

The British element at that time was kept strictly to 700; selection was severe and a recruit's basic training lasted six months. Everybody knew about everybody, and *esprit de corps* was high. Expansion was to come, rapid and not enough controlled; but in those days they were a superb lot of men. I cannot recall how big were the Arab and Jewish contingents, although I got to know some of their officers well, especially in later years; the strain on their loyalty was great, but it was a long time before it became too great. The pity was that the deteriorating situation in the country had flooded above the level where it could be controlled by the ordinary sluices and floodgates of the forces of law as represented by the Police. Instead of the military being brought in as a last resort because the Police could no longer cope, the military too often became the first appearance of the iron fist. We were not as good at normal intervention as the Police were, for after all it was not our *métier*; and any salutary fear that "if you don't behave, the soldiers will be sent for," had been quickly dissipated when the population realised how gentle and unalarming we were. Gone were the days when the Turks ruled the whole country with a mere two squadrons of mounted gendarmerie. Any bother anywhere, and they would ride in and string up a random number of locals to their own olive-trees. If they could identify the miscreants, so much the better; if not, anybody would do. It used to happen that villagers with a feud against their neighbours would cross the boundary and perform some outrage against the Turks in that district, and then sit back gloating while their neighbours swung for it; but this trick was easily repaid in kind, and soon, in the old phrase, fell into desuetude. The Turks couldn't be bothered to trace out whys and wherefores. Whatever the ethics of the system, those two squadrons were ample for the job, and peace reigned from Dan to Beersheba.

By contrast, I remember with shame a senior British police officer reproaching me gently in his office one morning when I hadn't been in Palestine very long. He said: "It is all very well for you blood-thirsty young fellows coming out here looking for a scrap. You come out for two or three years, and – come on, confess it! – you rather look forward to being shot up in an ambush or something. But *I* am a Police Officer. *I* chose a profession in which I looked forward to maintaining law and order, to being the father of my people, to stop people from being murdered, to keep the peace, to encourage people to come and tell me what's up, so that I can look after them. Every time I get embroiled in a pseudo-military operation, it may be fun for you, but it's a major set-back for me. I have seen God knows how many battalions pass through Palestine during my time here; you soldiers come and go, but we police-men stay. This is only a passing and exciting phase in your life, but for me it's everything. For me, every change of battalion means that I have to start all over again, trying to teach you chaps what it's all about, and trying to stop you bitching what I am trying to build up. Every time I am seen in company with soldiers, I lose a bit of ground as a policeman, and I lose a bit more heart. I have nothing against you soldiers, though you're not much good in this country until you've learned your stuff, and then you're moved on; and I have to start all over again, trying to civilise the next lot. Oh, well."

I never forgot that *cri de coeur*, and it shaped my approach to the job more than anything else that was said to me.

The Palestine of 1937 was a compact country: "without the Negeb, about the size of Wales" was the stock thing one used to say. The Negeb was the long diamond-shaped area drooping south from Beersheba, inhabited only by Bedawin and therefore devoid of interest to the security forces. Communications were poor as compared with even ten years later, let alone with to-day. There were only two tarmac roads running north and south: the one from Haifa parallel with the coast to Jaffa-Tel Aviv and Gaza, which petered out into rough metalling before you reached Beersheba; and the other from Haifa through Nablus and Jenin to Jerusalem, Bethlehem and Hebron: this also deteriorated into track before it reached Beersheba. Then there were three laterals: Haifa – Nazareth – Tiberias; another that linked the coast road with Tulkarm and Nablus; and finally the busy one from Jaffa which skirted Sarafand and ran up through the Bab-el-Wad ("The Door of the Glen"), to climb the 3,000 feet to Jerusalem. This last was a beautiful road – especially in early spring, when the anemones and other wild flowers were at their best – with a series of zigzags called the Seven Sisters; but it was liable to be shot up from the heights on either side, and there were several innocent-looking villages along it with bad reputations. Of the other roads, a few were metalled, but you were condemned to frequent changes of gear when you used them; the others, particularly on the plain or in the foothills, turned to mud with even the minimum of rain, and quickly became impassable.

The main spine of hills from north to south resembles a fishbone, with valleys running off to east and west: those to the east run down through aridity to below sea-level: to the Sea of Galilee, the Jordan Valley and the Dead Sea; those to the west to the riches of the plain, where most of the Jewish colonies had been established. Those who were anti-Jewish lost no opportunity of pointing out that the Jews had no historic claim to the plain, which in biblical days had been Philistine; and that they seemed to be in no hurry to establish themselves on their traditional but comparatively infertile heights of Samaria and Judaea. The higher vertebrae of the spine rose to over 3,000 feet, the highest being about Hebron, where the small and long-established Jewish community had been exterminated by massacre in 1929. Imagine that a quarter of the way down the fishbone somebody has snapped it in two, and drawn the pieces apart to form rich valleys, the Wadi Beisan and others: one or two small vertebrae like Mount Gilboa have been left. This gap gives easy access from Haifa to the Jordan near Samakh, which appropriately enough means "fish." And talking of names, perched on a mountain high above Samakh are the ruins of a Crusaders' Castle with a name to beat all names: Kawkab-al-Hawa, "Star of the Wind."

My area comprised the southern half of all this. It took in Qalqiliya, a trouble-spot through which ran the main railway-line from Haifa to Egypt; it excluded the notorious "Triangle"

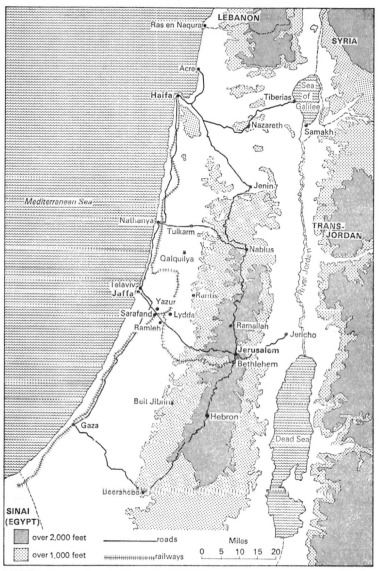

PALESTINE, 1937, Showing Principal Roads

of Nablus, Tulkarm and Jenin; and included "Kilo 41," the kilometre-stone on the Jerusalem-Nablus road with its block-house looking down into a sinister valley; and so down to the Jordan. Ramallah, Jerusalem, Bethlehem, Jericho, Jaffa, Tel Aviv, Hebron, Gaza, Beersheba were all mine: no mean wash-pot over which to cast out my shoe.

By the time we had been in Palestine a couple of weeks, the turbulence appeared to have died down, and Wavell ordained that the reliefs which he had postponed should take place. The country seemed quiet, and that wily old fox Haj Amin el Husseini, the Mufti of Jerusalem, with his red beard and his surprisingly blue eyes, had taken sanctuary in the sacred precincts surrounding the Dome of the Rock, which he knew we would never violate to arrest him. This was a personal disappointment to me, since I had a letter of introduction to him from T. E. Lawrence's old colleague Colonel S. F. Newcombe, whom I had got to know through Wavell: it remains un-presented to this day.

So the Battalion drove up in lorries to Jerusalem, and took over the hutted camp in the southern suburbs of the city, off the Bethlehem road; it was known as Talavera Barracks in those days, but was later re-christened "Allenby." They weren't bad quarters, though chilly in winter; and thanks to Haxton the veteran mess serjeant I was able to book a perman-ent room there for myself, which I could justify by having frequent business in Jerusalem. I was present at the hand-over from the Royal Sussex to The Black Watch; I remember it chiefly because one of their company commanders and one of ours had not met since they had been at Harrow together, and a reunion of Harrovians is always a boisterous occasion. I then drove back to Sarafand, had a bath, and changed into blue patrols for dinner. It had just been announced, and I was finishing my second pink gin, when the telephone rang. All hell had broken loose throughout the length and breadth of Palestine, and in my area in particular.

The Mufti had slipped out of his sanctuary, and these inci-dents, occurring simultaneously all over the shop, had obviously been arranged as diversions. There were many accounts about how he actually got away, and I am not sure which was the correct one: whether or not he was disguised as a woman; whether he got out through the Dung Gate or through Solomon's stables: whether he was smuggled over the hills or sailed in a boat from Jaffa. At all events, he turned up a few days later in the Lebanon, and soon afterwards, with the connivance of the French, established himself in a cosy villa at Juneh or Juniya, a few miles north of Beirut.

As I was answering the telephone, I saw through the window a great tongue of flame shoot up from Lydda Airport a couple of miles away: it was the fuel compound. I called for my Austin Seven and Farrar and the driver; but at once the telephone rang again to tell me that the Royal Sussex troop train had been blocked by rocks rolled down into the gorge through which the railway ran, and that they were being fired on from the hills above. I had no sooner rung off than yet another call came through, this time to say that the Haifa-Egypt Express had been de-railed near Qalqiliya, which by bad luck was in my area by about 400 yards. (When years later I was writing at Wavell's behest the history of the Regiment during those years, he pencilled in the margin of the galley-proofs against the phrase "Haifa-Egypt Express" the comment: "I presume you describe it thus on the principle of *lucus a non lucendo?*')

I remember little of the next forty-eight hours, except that they were crowded. I lived mostly off Arab bread and cheese bought at various food-shops; and my activities were ineffective. The fire at Lydda Airport burned itself out, the Royal Sussex cleared the rocks off the line and carried on to Egypt, and the train from Haifa somehow got itself back on the rails and resumed its pocketa-pocketa progress to Gaza and beyond. Somebody tipped us the wink that the derailment had been organised, as an extra-curricular activity, by the headmaster of the school at Rantis, a pretty little town in the Shephelah a few miles east of the railway; and I was despatched with an escort of the 60th Rifles from Tel Aviv to arrest him. "Bubbles" Barker (afterwards General Sir Evelyn, and himself to be

Commander-in-Chief in Palestine when I returned there after
the war) was the Commanding Officer, and he chose to accompany my escort. It was frankly rather fun to be arresting a headmaster in mid-lesson in front of his pupils, and I tried to
imagine myself doing it to Dr Alington, headmaster of Eton
throughout my time, and a man never at a loss in any situation.
But it was all too obvious that the prestige of the headmaster of
Rantis was soaring in the eyes of his assistants and his boys and
girls when I tapped him on the shoulder as he stood in front of
his blackboard, and bade him lay aside his chalk, and come
along with me. There was no real evidence against him, and
what little there was didn't stick. No doubt he got a civic
reception from Rantis on his return.

Another time I was told to blow up the house of an evil-doer
in a village near Lydda, in whose possession had been found a
quantity of illegal arms. This was a standard practice, about
which I was never very happy: it was all too easy to "plant"
stuff on somebody else, and whenever you found anything the
apparent owner always claimed that an enemy must have put
it there. With my sapper detachment and a platoon of infantry
for escort I went to the village, identified the house, and
evacuated everybody while the sapper subaltern prepared his
charges. It was a little place of not more then twenty houses,
but we had some bother in getting everybody out; the women
were ululating, the men cursing, the children more curious
than anything else. My men shepherded them to a position
about 200 yards away, where in due course the sapper subaltern joined me.

"I'm sorry to have been so long," he said, "but I thought
I'd put an extra seven pounds at each corner just to make sure.
Would you like to press the plunger?"

I accepted this honour, and did so. It became simultaneously
obvious that he had "made sure," all right. Stones and boulders
and an iron girder hurtled past our heads, and it was a miracle
that nobody was hurt. The sapper and I saw to our horror the
minaret of the mosque crumbling before our eyes and then
subsiding into the cloud of dust that engulfed the village. When

at last this cleared, the village was full of naked chickens running this way and that with their feathers blown off them,
and looking aggrieved. The sapper got a rocket, and the
Government paid full compensation for the damage to the
mosque.

Once I disgraced myself. There was a particularly sinister
village between Sarafand and Jaffa called Yazur; it had a dis-
affected population of over 2,000, and was surrounded by
a high wall, through which there were only two entrances.
Once again we were to blow up a house, a big one this time
belonging to an Arab notable against whom there was abundant
evidence of sabotage, and who had fled the country. Yazur
being such a tough nut, I was allotted a complete company of
the 60th as escort under "Puffin" Owen. I arranged to meet
them at the village along with the sapper detachment. I was
delayed by a puncture, and when I got there I found the
infantry lorries drawn up outside the village, and was told by
the drivers that Puffin had already taken his men inside. For
some reason neither Farrar nor Mansour were with me, so I
went in through the gate unescorted; only I knew which was
the house to be blown, though I had never been actually inside
Yazur before.

I found myself in a dark and narrow street, with a hostile,
growling crowd following me which grew with every minute.
Whenever I came to a fork and asked in Arabic: "Which way
did the soldiers go?" they always seemed to point down the
narrower and less inviting vennel, and I began to be certain
that they were edging me into a trap. Then one or two stones
began to fly, and I to lose my nerve. I pulled out my revolver,
and said: "The next stone that's thrown, I'll shoot that man
there," and indicated a chap in the front row who appeared
to have some authority: he blenched, turned, gave some rapid
orders I couldn't catch and the stones stopped. Meanwhile, I
was walking backwards, my revolver still in my hand, and my
tummy feeling very empty. It was in this undignified attitude
that I emerged, stern first, on to the *maidan*, a large open space
in the middle of the village where Puffin and his men were

drawn up. I put my revolver back in its holster, said "Hullo, Puffin!" rather sheepishly, and we got on with the job.

Whenever I hear people talk about "the massacre of Sharpe-ville" or similar incidents, "brutal shooting by police," and so forth, I always remember myself at Yazur, and withhold judgment. What I have read about Sharpeville suggests that it was the same sort of thing on a bigger scale: that a small party of African police under white officers became alarmed by the threatening attitude of a vast and hostile crowd, lost its nerve and began shooting. Once you let your men open fire, it is not easy to stop them; fear takes over and they carry on shooting for longer than necessary. If it is true that most of the victims at Sharpeville were shot in the back, this goes far to support my theory. It is much better to have one or two marksmen with you, and to give them and them alone definite orders whom and when to shoot. The unforgivable sin is to "shoot over the heads of the crowd", when the wrong person is likely to get hurt.

My first experience of shooting in earnest had happened a few weeks earlier. There is a fairly full account of the incident in Connell's *Wavell** taken mostly from Wavell's notes, and partly from my own version. In fact I was not "sent for," as Connell states: I was more or less on the spot. John Benson and I were in the Jaffa Gate Police Station, just inside the Old City, when we heard half a dozen shots a little to the south-ward. Running out, we hopped into my Austin Seven and drove down the hill towards the Birket-es-Sultan, a dried-up pool of water; the road runs along and below the City wall. There in the gutter on their faces lay two Jocks looking in-credibly boyish and pathetic; they had both been shot in the back, and as Connell quotes from my own account, their white neatly-Blancoed spats were stained with blood. I noticed how smartly burnished their black bayonet-scabbards were; side-arms were all they had. They had obviously been given no warning, since they had not even turned to face their attackers. I recognised them both as belonging to my late platoon:

*Wavell: *Scholar and Soldier*, p. 194: *Wavell, Portrait of a Soldier*, p. 45.

Private Milton and Private Hutchison, both of whose fathers had served in the Regiment before them.

John and I were joined simultaneously by a group of police from Jaffa Gate, and a party of Jocks under A. K. Hamilton, who had heard the shooting from the barracks. The police made us cordon off the road, pending the arrival of tracker dogs. Until then, they wouldn't let us touch the bodies, but it was all too evident that there was nothing to be done for them. The Jocks were angry and sullen; I myself couldn't believe that it had really happened: it seemed so unreal. Above us the ancient City wall was a back-drop; 400 yards away across the valley was the Scots Memorial Church; just round the corner was Aceldama, the field of blood. Twilight was coming.

The dogs arrived, under Inspector Adams, a former Perth-shire gamekeeper from Lord Forteviot's estate of Dupplin. He shewed them some empty cartridge-cases lying near the bodies. They sniffed them, and immediately began tugging at their leads, down the road towards where it turned across the valley to climb to the Scots Church; but instead of following the road, they crossed it on to the track that led to Silwan – Siloam of the Bible – three-quarters of a mile away. Adams at once checked his dogs: we knew where the murderers had gone, and that was all we needed to know for the moment.

That was an evening of conference and plan-making. By midnight I had had three separate interviews with Wavell: the first when I told him what had happened; the second when he sent for me to ask what mood the Jocks were in; and the third about 11 p.m. when I told him the details of the final plan. Connell says that Colonel McLeod saw Wavell late that evening, expressing fears that the Battalion might "break loose and take revenge." I have forgotten this, and I think it probable that my second meeting with Wavell was after that. The formed body that had come down to the Birket-es-Sultan under Hamil-ton had come from the stand-by company, and was perfectly disciplined; but it was true that a mob of off-duty Jocks had tried to break out of the main gate, where they had been success-fully harangued and halted by Findlay the R.S.M. I told Wavell that I was convinced there would be no trouble once the troops were properly fallen in and under the discipline of their officers; he took my word for it, and thank God I was right, though he says in his notes: "I must admit that I spent an unhappy night, as I knew I had taken a certain risk." It was all too obvious that he was worried: I never saw him shew anxiety, even in the major crises of the war, as much as on that evening.

Colonel McLeod gave out his final orders in the billiard-room of the Officers' Mess at Talavera. The lights had failed, and we were all in semi-darkness. Jock Munro, the Jerusalem Police Superintendent, and various other Police officers were present. Silwan was to be completely surrounded by dawn, and thereafter the police dogs would follow the trail they had already indicated into the village. Police guides would meet the various companies and lead them into position. We ate a cold buffet meal in the dining-room, had a drink, filled our flasks, drew our haversack rations, and joined our various parties. My rendezvous was in the walled garden of a monastery at Bethany, on the farthest side of the cordon, with one of the companies and a British Constable called Coton – one of the ex-Merchant Navy officers I have mentioned; there was no moon, and it took quite a time to get everybody into position without making a sound. Coton and I were to move down into the village as soon as it was light, to meet the dogs and their party as they came in up the track.

It seemed a very long wait until at last there came the familiar lightening of the sky in the east, and the sun bobbed up above the hills of Moab, a sight which never lost its beauty in my eyes. Coton and I emerged from behind our monastery wall, and saw the dogs straining at their leashes as they came up the track towards the village, with a posse of Police and a platoon of Jocks following, including the huge and unmistakable figure of John Benson. A dry stream-bed – the brook Kedron – divided the village in two, and the houses stood terraced on the steep slopes on either side. For some reason Coton and I separated, and I found myself moving along a terrace on the edge of the ravine. I had just got to an L-shaped house, of which the angle faced across the valley, when I heard a *ping*, and a great chunk of masonry fell from the house a couple of feet from my head; and I realised that for the first time in my life I was being shot at. Across the ravine, and less than 200 yards away, I could see Mungo Stirling and a parcel of Jocks; and I realised that whoever was firing at me must be on the same hill-side but below them, and presumably unaware that he was inside a cordon. By this time I was lying on my tummy and trying to spot my enemy. I yelled across at Mungo to "*do* something," and he and his men began skipping down the hill-side to try and find the sniper. He fired two more rounds at me, both wides, before he must have realised what was happening, and stopped; but Mungo's men never found him or his rifle. These must have been the shots which Wavell says in his notes that he heard; only one other was fired, which I will describe in a moment.

Freed from my uncomfortable perch, I reached the dog party in time to witness their identification. Still straining so that Adams and his colleague had their work cut out to hold them, they went unerringly into a house, stood up, and put their paws almost affectionately, as though they were playing a game, on the shoulders of two Arabs, whose guilt shewed in their faces. Within a few seconds their rifles also came to light, hidden under a pile of blankets. They suffered themselves to be led away without protest. The evidence of identification by dogs alone was not enough in itself to convict; but the reputation of the tracker-dogs, imported from Germany, was tremendous, and equated by the Arabs almost with sorcery, so that the defence almost always broke down under cross-examination in court.

Meanwhile, all the males of the village had been gathered to one end of it, while the houses were searched: though deference was paid to the rule that the householder must be present while his own house was gone through, to anticipate the usual complaint that whatever was found must have been "planted." The cordon was still in being, and nobody was allowed to pass in or out. Unfortunately one poor old man, driving a donkey in from the direction of Bethany, ignored repeated orders to stop; and Mungo said to one of his Jocks: "Put a shot across his bows." Something went wrong, and the Jock in fact shot him through the buttock: this was the other shot I have mentioned.

I was with Mungo at that moment, chaffing him for not having caught "my" sniper. None of us was as distressed as we should have been; the release from the long night's tension was finding us rather light-hearted. The old man, with his hand clutched to his behind, and his donkey were brought to Mungo's command post; and Mungo said to his medical orderly: "Now, Private So-and-so, do your stuff and shew off your medical training." All the Jocks crowded round. The medical orderly knew nothing about anything beyond administering a pill and dressing blisters; but he proceeded, with willing help, to tuck up the old man's night-gown and pull down his pants, while the old man protested and tried to protect his modesty. At last a neat little in-and-out bullet-hole was revealed in his wizened starboard buttock, purely a flesh wound; and the Jocks said to the orderly: "C'mon, now, Jock, dae yer stuff: whit ye're gaun tae dae about thon?"

The orderly, on his mettle, looked perplexed, and then reached for his one and only remedy, a bottle of iodine; impregnated a handful of cotton-wool with it, and applied it to the bullet-hole. The poor old man gave a scream, and jumped about nine feet in the air: it must have been agony. I am afraid the Jocks laughed, and one of them said: "Gar him loup again, Jock, gar him loup again!"

But my last memory of the old boy, in case anybody should think that we were being wantonly cruel, is of him sitting as comfortably as he could, and smiling, with the Jocks pressing food and cigarettes on him, and trying out their embryo Arabic on his puzzled ears, while his donkey cropped what little grazing it could find nearby. He went away in the end laden with goodies. And these were the Jocks whose comrades had been shot in the back a few hours before, and who had just seen their murderers, fellow-villagers of the old man, identified and taken away. Jocks are good forgivers. Ewen Maclean's farewell words at that church-service at Barry-Buddon had not fallen wide of the mark.

We buried Milton and Hutchison that afternoon in the war cemetery at Ramleh, where there were other Black Watch graves from the fighting in 1917 and 1918 – the first of many funerals that I was to attend there. There was a strong detachment from their company, a firing party, and pipers to play *Lochaber No More* and *The Flowers of the Forest*. I never find it easy to keep back the tears when I hear those tunes; and the killing of the two young soldiers seemed so wanton and irrelevant. They had walked out of barracks proudly in their uniforms to see the sights of Jerusalem, and the quarrel in which they had been killed was none of theirs. I was to be involved in many more such incidents during my service, but with this first experience I grew up overnight.

During the months that followed I criss-crossed my area, sedulously compiling my track reports and village reports, and making friends with the Police in their remote posts. There were British District Commissioners in Jerusalem, Jaffa-Tel Aviv and Gaza, who I found tended to be rather patronising. I was small fry, very amateur and from their point of view a bird of passage. The Superintendent of Police in each of these places was rather more forthcoming, and I think they were amusedly aware that I had fallen into a state of romantic love with their Force. There were two Police posts with whom I became especially friendly: that at Hebron, and the little one at Artuf in the foothills north of Beit Jibrin, where there were six mounted British constables under command of the senior one, Stacey Barham. Theirs was a lonely life with no amenities. After I got home, I sent them a hamper of luxuries from Fortnum and Mason, as a thank-you for all their kindness to me.

A few miles south of them, at Tel Duweir, was an archaeological "dig," where the ancient city and fort of Lachish was being excavated by a team under Professor Starkey. It was he who had discovered the "Lachish Letters," a series of despatches written around 700 B.C., when the last Jewish forts were crumbling before the onslaught of Sennacherib. I was a little frightened of Starkey, who was no glad sufferer of fools; he made no effort to conceal his contempt when he heard that I was the new I.O. Southern Palestine, and was only now struggling with my first lessons in Arabic. "What the hell use do you think *you're* going to be?" But he took pity on me one day, when I arrived at Tel Duweir soaked to the skin from a shower of rain; he dosed me with whisky, lent me a change of clothes, and – the rain having stopped – shewed me all over his "dig," including the Temple of Mithras which he was in the process of uncovering.

After this unpromising beginning, I took to dropping in on Starkey. He spoke excellent Arabic, and was on good terms with his workmen. I asked him to keep his ears open on my behalf, to which he said: "If you think I'm going to start spying for you, you've got another think coming." But I did one day tell him that we were having trouble from a so-called Arab nationalist leader who was on the run with a gang in the hills around Tarqumiya, which lay between Beit Jibrin and Hebron, and who was really no better than a bandit. "What's his name?" asked Starkey, and I told him: Issa el-Haj Suleiman Battat, and gave him a copy of a photograph of Issa which I had had reproduced. He wrote down the name on the back, and said he would let me know next time I was around if he heard anything. Alas, a few days later when he was on his way to Jerusalem to buy stores, his car was stopped on the road by Issa and his gang, who shot him out of hand. We heard later that Issa had expressed his regret, because Starkey was well-liked by the Arabs: the fact that he wore a beard, unlike most Europeans, had caused Issa to think him a Jew, and therefore fair game. I failed in several attempts to round up Issa, but he was ambushed and killed some months after I left, and I think John Benson had some hand in that. I still have his "WANTED FOR MURDER" photograph in my scrap-book.

One of my few sorties outside my area was to Nablus, which has been a trouble-spot for centuries to every successive Power occupying Palestine. Nablus lies in a deep cleft between the two mountains sacred to the Samaritans, Ebal and Gerizim. Its Mayor was a lively, talented and attractive man of good family called Suleiman Tuqan, whose hostility to the British in those days was salted by a sense of humour. In later years I got to know him well. During the brief and ill-fated fusion between the Kingdoms of Jordan and Iraq, Suleiman became Minister of Defence in the joint Government, only to be assassinated in that tragic blood-bath in Baghdad of July, 1958, when the King of Iraq, Nuri-es-Said the Prime Minister (the most impressive Arab, apart from King Abdullah, that I ever met) and others were slaughtered in a single night by men of the puniest stature in comparison. Suleiman's half-brother Jamal, also extremely able, was one of Sir Arthur Wauchope's three Private Secretaries; he was later to be Mayor of Jerusalem and Foreign Minister of Jordan, and remains a friend of mine to this day.

Nablus at this time, a small city which has always pulsated with politics, contained two remarkable men: Suleiman himself, and Hugh Foot the District Commissioner, who was supposed to have the distinction of being the most shot-at man in Palestine. He was only thirty, but he was spoken of with affection and respect, as brilliant as he was brave. The Arabs admired him as being a man both of justice and of iron, but this did not deter them from shooting at him, day in, day out. He afforded no mean target; he was big and burly for a start, and he went about his unruly District as though no blood-curdling threat had ever been made against him. He had always refused hitherto to live anywhere but in his house, but had just complied resentfully with an order that he must shift his quarters into the Fort to reduce, though not by much, his risk of assassination.

There was at large in his District a likeable and entirely genuine Arab nationalist leader called Sheikh Farhan, leading a war-party which, unlike Issa Battat's, bore some resemblance to a miniature "liberation army." Farhan (which means "Cheerful") had a religious as well as a nationalistic background: one might suggest as a remote parallel an English Suffragan Bishop forming a small resistance movement, and ravaging the Thames Valley from the Chilterns. He was no respecter of the boundary laid down by the Army between North and South Palestine, and he used to operate across the borders of both sectors: so it was arranged that I should go and meet Hugh Foot and my opposite number from Haifa, to co-ordinate future operations against Farhan. We were to lunch with Foot in the Nablus fort. When I got there, I found the Haifa I.O., who shewed me a note from Foot, saying that he would be a few minutes late for luncheon, and would we help ourselves to a drink. In due course we heard a few rounds being fired, and said to each other: "That'll be Foot coming back to luncheon!" and so it was. He came in none the worse and quite unruffled, and I found him as impressive as I had expected.

A few weeks later, Sheikh Farhan was caught with some of his followers; I wasn't involved in the operation, but I think he was betrayed, and found hiding in an empty cistern some-where near Tulkarm. He was tremendously flattered that Foot himself was in the party that caught him. He was actually carrying arms at the time, so the law took its inexorable course and he was hanged. It so happened that the B.B.C. was launch-ing a much-advertised new Arabic service; and far away in Jeddah, King Ibn Saud had been invited by the British Minister to listen in to its inaugural programme. With that intrepid objectivity on which the B.B.C. has always prided itself, a news item was included to the effect that Sheikh Farhan had been executed that day. He had been a personal friend of Ibn Saud; and the story we heard – which I confess I cannot vouch for – was that the King rose grimly to his feet and left the room.

I loved that life, though it had its harrowing and worrying moments. I thought it would last for at least two years, and I had developed a real interest in Palestine and its two so different peoples, though I had a particular affection for the high country, and had to discipline myself to make sure that I spent an equal amount of time on the plains. We knew that we had to be strictly impartial as between Jew and Arab, and any officer who allowed himself to let slip any expression of sympathy for one side or the other was rightly, properly and promptly taken to task. In pursuance of this we were discouraged from mixing socially with either side, which may or may not have been sensible, but was certainly a great deprivation. There were a few Jews and Arabs in Jerusalem who mingled in British social circles, and one met some of them: otherwise our contacts were limited.

I did, however, get to know the great Dr Chaim Weizmann, the real creator of the State of Israel. My eldest brother was married to Frances Dugdale, Arthur Balfour's great-niece; her mother Mrs Edgar Dugdale, known everywhere as "Baffy," had been not only Balfour's niece, but also his close confidant and biographer, and deeply concerned with Zionist aspirations since Balfour first became involved in them. Thus in the same brief-case which carried my letter of introduction from Colonel Newcombe to the Mufti was another from Mrs Dugdale to Dr Weizmann; and this, unlike the Mufti's, I was able to present. I was bidden to luncheon, tea and dinner one Sunday at his superb little house at Rehovoth, not far from Sarafand. It was an oasis of taste and civilisation in what still felt like a frontier settlement; next to his house was a research institute around which I was conducted during the afternoon to see the many experiments in progress. Most of them were too elaborate for me to understand; but among the humbler I remember seeing ash-trays and similar knick-knacks being produced from the waste-products of citrus-peel. The great chemist's mind which had discovered acetone during the war, and put it at the disposal of the British, had now bent itself to spread across the whole spectrum of research, modest as well as ambitious; but even these activities were secondary to those mightier endeavours when he focused his energy like a burning-glass on the growth of his nation.

The key phrase in the "Balfour Declaration" was "a Jewish National Home in Palestine." What did it mean? Protection? An Enclave? Sovereignty? I had to live for so many years of my life with this problem that I will not allow myself to be drawn into discussing it now. Neither as a soldier nor, later, as a policeman, was I concerned with the rights and wrongs of the problem: only in the thankless task of holding the ring. If you argue the Jewish case, I will argue the Arab; if you argue the Arab I will argue the Jewish. The one thing I have never been able to puzzle out was what Balfour – whom I never met – had in mind. Is it an unworthy thought that he may have congratulated himself on finding a formula to meet the needs of the moment, without taking into account all its implications for the future?

I sat in Dr Weizmann's drawing-room that evening enthralled by all I had seen and heard. He and his wife had given me an excellent dinner, accompanied by wines from their own vineyards. He had a sonorous voice, reinforced by the prophetic fire of his convictions, and made tender by his affection for Mrs Dugdale, whose support for him had never wavered even in his darkest moments. But what sticks most in my mind is the combination of Dr Weizmann himself and Oswald Birley's portrait of him hanging just above his head. The two were in the same attitude: it was as though I were seeing double: the two heads, the two noses, the two mouths, the two bearded chins. Even the two chairs and the background were the same, for Weizmann was sitting where Birley had painted him; Birley's portrait seemed to be speaking with Weizmann in duet. I drove home to Sarafand through the sable darkness conscious that I had been in the presence of a great man.

A few days later, Vera Weizmann's brother was assassinated by an Arab. Dr Weizmann drove straight to the radio, and broadcast to his fellow-Jews a fervent appeal that there should be no reprisals. There were none.

3

ONE evening I returned to Sarafand from a long sortie to be told that there was a signal for me from the War Office. It offered me an appointment as an instructor at Sandhurst, and asked if I were willing to accept. At any other time I would have jumped at it. When we left Sandhurst, Lyon Corbett-Winder and I had agreed that there was nothing in the world that we would like more than to go back one day as teachers. To be asked to go as a subaltern was a rare honour, but I didn't want such an offer now, when I was just beginning to master the most fascinating job conceivable: so I refused. I was therefore appalled three days later to get another signal which read roughly: "No other officer currently available to teach French. Relief for Lieutenant Fergusson will be found as soon as possible. He will report for duty at Sandhurst on 1st February." To teach French? I loved France, and the French, and Sandhurst; but to be the French teacher was far from glamorous, and in any case my French wasn't nearly good enough. I fought hard, but even a remonstration by Wavell failed to get me off the hook, and I had to reconcile myself to going.

The first thing to do was to brush up my French. It was arranged that John Benson should relieve me as Brigade I.O. until my relief arrived, and that I should be given two weeks' leave in Syria, with a spurious Intelligence mission to justify it and fifty pounds to finance it. I exacted some letters of introduction from Pierre de la Chauvellais, the French liaison officer in Jerusalem, to various officers in the French Army across the frontier. De la Chauvellais and his wife were delightful people who, despite the tension in that part of the world between

French and British, were very well liked by us all, and had made many friends among The Black Watch officers and their wives. I said good-bye all round, exchanged presents with my interpreter Mansour, caught a train to Haifa, and booked a place among a taxi-load of Lebanese bound for Beirut.

This was the first time I had been so far north, and seen the glories of the coast beyond Haifa. After Acre the hills pressed closely on to the sea. The frontier was at Ras-en-Naqura, also known as the Ladder of Tyre, where the cliff dropped sheer into clear waters dotted with the sails of local boats. My francophile heart leapt to see the smart French uniforms at the frontier post; I brandished with my passport a written talisman furnished by de la Chauvellais and we drove on past Tyre and Sidon to Beirut, where I booked in at the Saint-Georges Hotel. It looked expensive; but the Lebanon and Syria were in those days among the cheapest countries in the world for the tourist; and had I not fifty pounds of the kindly taxpayers' money?

Francophiles were not common in Palestine in those days, nor Anglophiles in Syria or the Lebanon: relations between French and British in the Levant had never been more prickly. Suspicion lingered from the conflicting secret pacts made during the First War: the Sykes-Picot agreement, the McMahon-Hussein understandings. Each side suspected the other of poaching in troubled waters across the march fence. It was only six years since the Druze Revolt had flared up suddenly, taken the French by surprise, and surged into the suburbs of Beirut itself before being repulsed. The Druzes, whose main stronghold was in the Jebel Druze sixty miles south-east of Damascus, had many outlying colonies as well, some of them in Palestine. They disliked being governed by the French as much as they would have disliked being governed by the British; but because that happened to be the way things were, they were not above making overtures to us. I had met one of their leaders, Hamza Darwish, in Jerusalem, and sized him up as a pleasant rascal; but our meeting had been purely social, we had plotted no plots, I had been told by my masters not to get embroiled with him, and it was not an acquaintance about which I proposed to brag to the French. So far as I know, there were not the slightest grounds for French suspicions that we had connived in any way at the Druze Revolt: it would have been wholly out of keeping with our policy: we had quite enough on our plate in Palestine, and it was in our interest to maintain the *status quo* throughout the Levant.

Nevertheless, the French were sensitive. The two indefatigable publicist brothers, Jean and Jacques Tharaud, who were as prolific with their alarmist books as Edgar Wallace with his thrillers, had just produced one called *Alerte en Syrie*: which was being read everywhere, and which saw a bogy under every *burnous*; I was reading it avidly myself. The British were sensitive too. We were pretty sure that wounded Arab rebels were being treated in French hospitals, and that the dashing guerrilla leader Fawzi Kauokji was nipping in and out of French territory at will. It was known throughout the world that the Mufti was living sumptuously in Juneh; indeed, he was holding press conferences there. I went out one day to have a look at his villa. Several cars were parked in front of it, and others came and went, during the half-hour I spent there before people began to eye me suspiciously and I thought it time to move on.

Before going to my preparatory school I had had a French governess. I had spent two summer holidays from Eton in a French family at Tours. With three other Under Officers from Sandhurst, including Lyon Corbett-Winder, I had attended the *Triomphe*, or Passing-Out Parade, at St Cyr in 1931. In 1932, as a Second-Lieutenant, I had done a three months' attachment to the 32nd Regiment of Infantry, also at Tours. My spoken French was therefore at least voluble and fluent; and as on my first morning in Beirut I walked along rather nervously to the Grand Serail – a fine old Turkish building round a quadrangle, where the Army Headquarters was – I reminded myself of the details of French military etiquette. Thanks to another of de la Chauvellais's letters, I was well received, particularly by a captain called Boisseau, whose path and mine were to cross several times in future years. An emissary was despatched to find out whether the Commander-in-Chief would receive me, and in due course I was ushered into his office.

My interview with General Huntziger lasted no more than a couple of minutes. He was rather forbidding, with eyes of a startling blue. Half Alsatian and half Breton, he was reputed to be dead honest, but ruthless, ambitious and on the make. If it be true that he aspired to the highest of positions, his wish was granted in the most cruel fashion. It fell to him to lead the French delegation to sue for peace on the 21st June 1940 at the hands of Field-Marshal Keitel, in the Forest of Compiègne, in the same *wagon-lit* and on the very spot where Foch had exacted the same humiliation from the Germans in November 1918. He became Chief of Staff to Vichy under Pétain, and was killed in an air crash within France in 1941. I have always felt sorry for him, but my feelings would have been warmer if he had been a trifle more welcoming to the shy young Scotch sub-altern who came to pay him a formal call.

Early one misty morning, I went to the race-course to see the horses in training, and was button-holed by a stout Saudi Arabian princeling, with some wild ideas about enlisting British interest in a *coup d'état* to topple Ibn Saud from his throne and replace him with this fellow's brother. I was also tackled by the startlingly handsome son of the French High Commissioner, who wanted to take me round the night-spots of Beirut. I was tempted by neither of these projects; but the Saint-Georges Hotel soon became untenable for me, since the telephone began to ring for me every hour, and it was either the Saudi Arabian prince or Peter de Martel trying to seduce me into the one activity or the other. I decided that the time had come to move on to Damascus, and booked my seat in a taxi with three Syrians for the modest sum of 12s. 6d. in Syrian pounds.

Beirut had not then begun to straggle up the mountain, or to cover all its slopes to the sky-line as it has since done; it still lay in a modest half-moon round St George's Bay. Half-way up the hill were such fashionable outlying villages as Aley and Brumana, with their smart villas to which the more prosperous escaped from the summer heat. There were plenty of rich

Lebanese, but rich Sheikhs from the Persian Gulf had not yet begun to build their palaces with their astronomical royalties from oil. Apart from the harbour with its caiques there was nothing very alluring about Beirut; whereas it seemed to my romantic soul that to be bound for Damascus was really something.

As it twisted and turned up the hill, with the ratchet railway scrambling up in parallel, the road afforded glorious views of the Bay of St George, and the sea that Flecker, who was Vice-Consul here for two years before the First War, described so often and so well. I had fallen in love with his verse at Eton, and knew much of it by heart: –

> The dragon-green, the luminous, the dark,
>   the serpent-haunted sea,
> The snow-besprinkled wine of earth,
>   the white-and-blue-flower foaming sea.

At the top was the Pass of Baidar, guarded by the old Turkish gendarmerie post, still looking sinister, with the lock-up alongside. The taxi-driver decided that he wanted a drink of tea in the café opposite, and this was to my entire satisfaction: I was able to walk about on this col on the watershed of Mount Lebanon before descending into the Beka'a: I could savour the atmosphere. When we had driven down the hill, it was the passengers' turn to decide that we would like a glass of wine in the tiny, French-kept, trellis-girt hotel which was all that Chtoura boasted in those days, a white wine surprisingly dry for its yellow colour. I looked up the valley towards where I knew the ruins of Baalbek to be, and down it towards where I knew the important French military airfield of Rayak to be, hoping to be able to visit both during the next few days. The first wish was to be gratified; the second, for security reasons, not.

We were soon through the perfunctory Customs post between Lebanon and Syria, and climbing to the pass, much lower than Baidar, which leads through the Anti-Lebanon to Damascus. This is the least dramatic way to approach it. The Prophet

Mohammed described Damascus as "a pearl set in an emerald", a reference to its white towers shining in the Ghouta, the green oasis which enshrines it; but to see it thus you must come in from the East from Palmyra, or from the South from Deraa. If you come as I did that first time by the serpentine road through the Anti-Lebanon, you find yourself stealing into it sideways; and before you know where you are, the turbulent stream which has cheered you down the hill with its rollicking antics has sobered up to become the Barada – the "Abana" of the Bible – and is escorting you demurely along the main street between balustrades and shady trees.

The taxi dropped my travelling companions – we all shook hands with each other – somewhere near the Ommayed, and took me on across the river and up a small hill, of the same width and gradient but half the length of St James's Street, to the Orient Palace Hotel, where I booked in, my panama hat on my head and my camera dangling about me, tourist *au bout des ongles*. My bedroom looked across the road at the Hejaz railway station, the terminus of the railway line which the Germans had begun to build before the First War, which was designed to penetrate as far as Mecca, and which had been blown up at innumerable places by Lawrence; it was still linked with the Turkish system but, from Damascus, it ran narrow-gauge far down into Trans-Jordan, with its ratchet-spur to Beirut and another to the coast at Haifa in Palestine. Opposite the front door of the hotel was the entrance to the *Suq* or street market, which had been greatly tidied up by the French, and which boasted an efficient system of sanitation and a corrugated iron roof. In summer this roof rendered the place intolerably hot; but when, as soon as I had signed into the hotel, I went to explore the *Suq*, in my panama hat and all, I found it all too cold in this December weather.

Rationalised and regulated though it had been by the French, the Damascus *Suq* was still one of the great *entrepôts* of the Middle East. There were still plenty of tourist-traps, and it was in full knowledge that Asfar's was one of these that I went to it that evening, and bought some lengths of brocade at what was then the stupendous price of two pounds a yard. I did not agree on the final bargain for several days: I knew that one was expected to haggle, and I was able to beat the Asfar brothers down to a sum which satisfied my own *amour propre*, and which I am sure was more than satisfactory to them. But apart from tourists, of which there were not many at that season, this was a genuine Eastern bazaar, in which traders from as far afield as Trebizond and Tashkent and Trivandrum were doing business; and the brocades that I bought from Asfar were to decorate my mother for more than twenty years, and decorate my wife still. For the rest, the curled beards, the parrots on the shoulders, the clash of colours, the babel of tongues, the shouting, the haggling, the gripping and shaking of shoulders as bargains were made or not made, were ample reward for my first couple of hours in the Damascus *Suq*, and the too many cups of bitter Turkish coffee that I was obliged to have with the Asfar brothers. On my way back to the Orient Palace, I poked my nose into the Turkish bath just outside the gateway to the *Suq*; but I decided that such extremes of nudity were not for me, and pursued my modest way to the hotel, and a good French dinner.

Next morning I went to call on the British Consul, the first and least eventful of three visits that I was to pay to that office in the course of the next ten years. It was a pleasant house two or three hundred yards from the hotel, in the street that eventually becomes the road to Deraa and Trans-Jordan. Gilbert MacKereth the Consul was an imposing man in his middle forties who had been four years in Damascus. He was expecting me, and was pleased to see me only because it enabled him to blow off steam at the lunacy of sending a young whippersnapper like me to make enquiries within his parish. It was some time before I could persuade him that it was only a pretext to get me fifty quid and enable me to polish up my French. This mollified him, though he continued to rumble a bit. Having exacted a promise not to queer his pitch by going round asking silly questions, or committing other indiscretions, he invited me to dinner that evening.

I went back to the hotel, and asked for my key. I noticed

several Arabs hanging about the lobby looking at me, and I asked the clerk who they were.

"They want to see *you*, Sir," he said.

"Me?" I asked. "Why me?"

"They want to join the British Secret Service," he said.

I have dined out on this story for so many years that I am beginning to believe it myself.

Once again my letters from Jerusalem came in handy. I was made a member of the Officers' Club, a delightful place where there was a tiled garden with shrubs and fountains and small tables to which you could carry your apéritif. Here I made friends with officers of my own age, both from the Foreign Legion and the Tirailleurs Marocains. These last asked whether by any chance I knew Pat Tweedie in the Cameron Highlanders, who had just completed a long attachment to them: I was able to say that he was one of my closest friends, with whom among other things I had done a lot of sailing: upon which, for he had been very popular with them, they took me to their hearts. On the last night before I left, ten days later, I was the guest of six of them at the Club.

The vaunted affinity between the Scotch and the French is not wholly without foundation. Some of the old Scotch words of French origin – tass, justicor, groset – are no longer in use, though others, such as gigot and ashet, certainly are. As I write, I can see from my window the tower of Ardstinchar Castle, a mile away down the hill in Ballantrae, built by Sir Hew Kennedy who hailed from this valley: who won his knighthood from the King of France fighting for Joan of Arc against the English. Over the years I have met several French officers with Scotch names: Munro, Carmichael, Crawford-Knox; and there is a general serving at this moment called John James Fergusson: not, be it noted, Jean-Jacques. I have spent six months of my life serving with French troops, and two years and a half at S.H.A.P.E. as a colleague of French staff officers. My life would have been much the poorer without my friendships within the French Army.

Furthermore, I have shared with French brother-officers two

great disruptive experiences in twenty-five years: the split between Vichy and de Gaulle, and the tragic business of Algeria.
Not only was I personally and physically involved in both:
each time I had close friends on either side. Only a great nation
could have survived such catastrophe twice in a quarter of a
century. British officers have cause to thank their stars that
they have never been faced with any such decision: not, at least,
since 1689, though its shadow loomed for a few days over those
who were serving in Ireland in the spring of 1914.

I cannot claim that the arrival of the new French instructor
at Sandhurst caused much stir. Even after I arrived, I did my
best to get out of the appointment. Pat Tweedie was on leave
from abroad; he was willing to take my place, and his French
was infinitely better than mine. I lured him down from the
flesh-pots of London to be interviewed by the Chief Instructor.
I even offered to pay (having saved some money) whatever cost
might fall on the War Office to effect the exchange, and persuaded the Chief Instructor to back me up, but the War Office
was unmoved. There was nothing for it but to acquiesce, and
in the event I thoroughly enjoyed myself, though I had some
trouble with those of my pupils who knew more French than I
did. However, I had the ultimate sanction of the guard-room
behind me; and having explained to them that they were present
to discover what I knew rather than to uncover what I didn't,
I never had to invoke it.

One morning at Sandhurst in August 1938, at the height of
the Munich crisis, I happened by mischance to be the Orderly
Officer. I was sent for urgently by Eddie Goulburn the Adjutant
and found him in his office looking grim. Spread out on his
desk was a professional-looking sketch-map, of obviously sapper origin, newly unrolled and with its corners held down by
books and ash-trays. On it were marked the slit trenches and
air raid shelters to be dug in the event of war, tactically dis-
tributed all round both Buildings. Orders had come through
for the plan to be "implemented," as the Army calls it; and in
my capacity as Orderly Officer, I was to be in charge of "im-
plementing" it.

A posse of staff-serjeants, sappers, Under Officers and so forth was assembled to tape out the sites of the shelters and trenches. When that was done, normal work was suspended, and Gentlemen Cadets of all four companies were made available as navvies. They obviously found it a welcome diversion from their studies as they poured forth from their company blocks, tore off their shirts, spat on their hands, and set to work with pick and shovel. The turf was carefully removed from each site and piled up alongside the excavations, in case the scare died down and the holes could be filled in again. Within three days we had completed a magnificent system; within three weeks it had filled with water, and been christened "Fergusson's Folly."

Six months later, in the following March, Eddie Goulburn sent for me again, and said: "Remember all those holes you dug last August? Well, fill 'em in again, and don't forget to put the turf back." It did occur to me to point out that I wasn't Orderly Officer that day, but the expression on Eddie's face deterred me. Nor did I dare protest when six months later, in September 1939, Eddie sent for me yet again and said: "Remember those trenches of yours? Well, di g 'em out again."

When the war broke out, most of the Sandhurst instructors were sent in batches all over the country to start up new Officer Cadet Training Units. The training of the cadets who had already done some time at Sandhurst was speeded up, and they were commissioned within six weeks. Gentlemen Cadets of the new entry, who had arrived only a week before the outbreak of war and who were to be the last people to receive Regular commissions until it was over, were formed into two companies; I was given command of one and Jock Goodwin in The Welch Regiment – afterwards killed – the other. Jock and I were given no syllabus: we were merely told to do as good a job as we could in three and a half months, as the cadets would be commissioned on New Year's Day. Rarely in my life have I enjoyed myself more. I had good officers, three of them reservists, and a free hand; while the boys themselves were as keen as they could be. We contrived to mix hard work and frivolity in just about the right proportions.

I had been ordered to report to the Staff College the first week in January; I had qualified in the examination and been nominated to a vacancy earlier in the year, and it had been decreed that all such would report just as though there were no war on, only for a course shortened from a year to four months. Between Christmas and the New Year I stole four days' leave at Kilkerran, and returned to Sandhurst in time to witness the break-up of the Company before travelling a mile down the road to the Staff College. It was snowing heavily as we had our rather riotous farewell dinner. Next morning, as the Sandhurst servant who was calling me drew my curtains, he said: "Gorblimey, Sir, 'ave a look out of yer window!" I did; and there on the Square, tramped out by feet in the snow in letters three yards high, were the words: GOOD-BYE BERNARD! I confess I was touched.

Much of our study at Camberley turned out within six months to be irrelevant to the war as it was to be fought. There was little to be gleaned from the half-hearted patrol activity in the Saar, which was all that was going on. Various commanders and senior staff officers were brought back from the B.E.F. to lecture to us, but they had little illuminating to say. There was one especially gloomy, and very secret, talk on "The Advance," which confirmed our suspicions that there was a plan for the B.E.F. to move forward into Belgium in certain circumstances. The speaker told us that careful analysis had demonstrated the necessity for an Anti-Aircraft Regiment every x miles; there were only y A.A. Regiments with the B.E.F.; the projected advance was for z miles: *ergo*, the operation would be suicidal. I was to hear a similar exposition – or "presentation," as the Americans call it – at Dehra Dun in India four years later, concerning the recapture of Burma. It was equally wide of the mark.

At last our four months were over, and I found myself posted as Brigade Major to the 46th Infantry Brigade. This was a Territorial Brigade consisting of three battalions of Highland

Light Infantry, and belonging to the 15th Scottish Division, which had made a great name for itself in the First War. The Brigade was commanded by Harry Clark of the Argylls, who was known and loved throughout all the Highland Regiments: smallish, dapper, always smiling, quick with a pat on the back but a very demon for getting work out of people. The Division was supposed to be going to France in July; but by the time I caught up with it, having initially been directed to an out-of-date location in Scotland, the front in France was already crumbling, and the Division was being re-deployed to defend most of East Anglia. Our share of it amounted to fully half of Essex, from the mouth of the Blackwater River back to Epping, and thence down to Dagenham on the Thames, with vulnerable oil installations, highly inflammable, and docks. We were also responsible for three fighter airfields, North Weald, Hornchurch and Rochford. An extra battalion, of Royal Scots, was allotted to us, but even so we were desperately thin on the ground. Our battalions had no mortars and fewer than a quarter of their establishment of Bren guns; our Field Regiment had only eight obsolete 18-pounders; our Anti-Tank Regiment not only had no guns, they had no rifles either. In July we were reinforced by one of the newly-raised Commandos, which came to train in our area but was to come under command in the event of invasion. It was commanded by Bob Laycock in The Blues, with whom I had been at Camberley. Their officers were a high-spirited and unconventional lot, like something out of Evelyn Waugh: indeed, Evelyn Waugh was one of them, and Randolph Churchill another.

Harry Clark once gave me an evening off to dine with them in the modest house at Southend which they had taken over as a mess. Towards the end of dinner, the floor seemed to heave up, the ceiling to swoop down, and the atmosphere to become suddenly compressed. A parachute mine, then a new phenomenon, had gone off nearby. I was sitting next to Bob and opposite Evelyn. Instinct inspired me to get under the table with my glass of claret; and there I met Evelyn, whom instinct had inspired to bring the bottle with him. The damage in the neighbourhood was immense, but by the grace of God nobody was seriously hurt.

I never worked so hard in my life as I did during that hot, exciting summer. I was too inexperienced to know how to delegate, and I didn't make half enough use of the splendid Intelligence Officer, Stewart Gillies: then, in private life, Financial Editor of the *Daily Express*, and now for the last twenty years my devoted and inspired stockbroker. At least he kept me sane, bless him, pulling my leg whenever I took myself too seriously. I never got to bed before midnight, I stood to with the troops at dawn, and I spent too much time in the office: since Harry Clark always and rightly wanted to be visiting the widely scattered troops and both of us (thought I in my pomposity) must not be away at once. Still, it was a marvellous job, and we had an unrivalled view of the daily clashes between the R.A.F. and the Luftwaffe, with their vapour trails twining in and out of each other high up in the blue. We took over eighty prisoners from among the German aircrew who came swaying down on their parachutes. A surprising number made peremptory demands to be taken immediately to the nearest German troops, and refused to believe that none had landed.

Another factor that helped preserve my sanity was the return of Peter Dorans. Called up as a reservist on the outbreak of war, he had been posted to the 1st Battalion. The 1st Battalion, with most of the rest of the Highland Division, had been forced to surrender at Saint-Valéry, its ammunition exhausted. (There but for the grace of God went I: General Victor Fortune, its commander, had asked for me to go as Brigade Major of one of his brigades while I was at Camberley; the War Office had insisted on my finishing my course; and the officer who, to my chagrin, got the job instead spent the rest of the war in jail.) One officer and eighteen men had managed to escape, and Peter Dorans was one of them. Ordered to report to the Depot at Perth, he reported instead to my father at Kilkerran; and my father, with equal impropriety, gave him a week's leave and then ordered him to report to me. With me he remained, except for two short interruptions, until August 1944.

Just when invasion seemed most imminent, a signal arrived ordering me to report to the War Office "forthwith" as a G.S.O. 2. Harry Clark was out, as usual; I rang up the Divisional Commander, and he was out too. So I made a signal off my own bat: "Regret Major Fergusson not available," and never heard any more about it. These things are easier in wartime.

I have almost always been fortunate in my superiors, but I never had a better than Harry Clark. Even when his elder son, also in the Argylls, was reported "Wounded and Missing" – that ominous phrase – during the chaotic days of the fall of France, he never faltered, and kept up a brave front even before Stewart Gillies and me, who shared his office. We all knew that the evacuation had been completed days before. We were working late one evening when the telephone rang: the call was for Harry, and I passed him the receiver. He was looking drawn and tired; but suddenly his face lit up as he said: "Douglas!" It was his son, wounded several days earlier and evacuated to a hospital in Surrey. To begin with he had been in no fit state to ring up, and then, in the conditions of secrecy obtaining, had been unable to find out where to ring. That was a happy evening for us all.

Yet even during that time of anxiety Harry had radiated cheerfulness. I had been struggling to get out an Operation Order, and was wondering what on earth to put in the "Information about the Enemy" paragraph that the recipients wouldn't know already: their sources were as good, or as bad, as ours. I mentioned my difficulty to Harry, who at once suggested what eventually went out: "The Enemy is far too near."

The threat of immediate invasion passed, though not without some hilarious alarms. The ringing of church bells had been designated as the signal that German parachutists had landed; and one very still evening when a heavy summer mist lay thick over the Blackwater Estuary some tremulous voice rang up on the telephone to report that the bells of Stansgate Abbey were ringing. The map shewed Stansgate Abbey to be on the southern bank of the Blackwater River, and we despatched our so-called "mobile reserve," which consisted of a single company in 32-seater buses under a burly Regular H.L.I. officer called Bobby Sinclair-Scott. We ourselves didn't attach much credence to a single report, but I felt in duty bound to tell Division, who told Corps, who told Army. A mounting degree of interest was generated, and my telephone became so jammed with appeals for the latest news that I had to beg them to leave it clear for Bobby's report. At last it came.

"This is Major Sinclair-Scott speaking, concerning the report of bells ringing at Stansgate Abbey. My report is in three parts. One: No bells were ringing at Stansgate Abbey. Two: There *are* no bells at Stansgate Abbey. Three: Stansgate Abbey was pulled down by Henry the Eighth."

I had great pleasure in passing the report upwards *verbatim*. There were several ships, most of them prizes, one of them none other than the famous barque *Pamir*, lying at anchor in the Blackwater River; and we suspected that some nervous person had heard, on that especially quiet evening, a ship's bell, or several ship's bells, marking the passage of time. We got the practice stopped.

That and many other excitements were well behind us when in September I got another posting order, and this time I was ready for a change of scene. The new appointment sounded at least imposing: Military Assistant to the Chief of the General Staff, G.H.Q. Home Forces. So off I went to London, complete with Peter Dorans, though sad to leave the team with which I had spent such an historic summer: with nothing between us and the enemy, as Harry Clark used to say, but the North Sea.

I had assumed that my new appointment was a step up in the world. My *amour-propre* therefore suffered a set-back when I found that Rodney Moore in the Grenadiers, a Camberley contemporary, whom I was replacing, was in a champagne mood because he was going off to become a Brigade Major, such as I had just been. G.H.Q. was in Hammersmith, in the hideous buildings of St Paul's School. It was a forbidding place, and my new master, Major-General Bernard Paget, a startling contrast to Harry Clark. He was a Cromwellian and unbending soldier, and not then so mellow as he afterwards became. When he took the passing-out parade at Sandhurst the previous year, his valedictory remarks to the seniors about to be commissioned were a denunciation of the decadent practice of men calling each other by their Christian names instead of their surnames. I was required to work at a table in his own room; it would be inaccurate to describe it as a centre of jollity and fun. Earlier that year he had commanded the British forces in the later stages of the Norway operations, with skill and tenacity in daunting circumstances, and he was rightly bitter about the pickle into which they had been put. He was still working at intervals on his report. I like and admired him, but he was, at any rate to begin with, a chilly sort of chief.

I bracket Sir Bernard Paget with another full general, Sir Andrew Thorne, as having been thoroughly unlucky. Both were superb trainers of troops; both had a short run in those early stages of the war when the dice were against them, and proved themselves to be of the top calibre; both were given important and responsible commands in Britain; both had every reason to expect high command in the field; both were by-passed in the course of the war. Everybody expected Paget to command the British contingent in the invasion of Europe; he had been C.-in-C. Home Forces for eighteen months, and then, for six, C.-in-C. 21st Army Group, as the Headquarters formed for the invasion had been named. He had been in charge of all their training. But in December 1943 Montgomery was brought home from his triumphs in Africa and Italy and given the appointment, while Paget was fobbed off with the embers, now scarcely glowing, of the once glorious Middle East Command. All Thorne got was the bloodless liberation of Norway.

The only time I ever saw the great Montgomery during the war was in Paget's office, a few days after I joined him. He had lately been appointed to the newly-formed South-Eastern Command. He was planning some exercise, and having got wind of the secret fact that a parachutist unit had been formed he wanted it to take part. Paget was adamant that it shouldn't, partly on the grounds that there was only a handful of them, but chiefly for security reasons. Monty wheedled and cajoled, and indeed was extremely funny, but he got no change out of my master beyond a wintry smile or two. I had never clapped eyes on Monty before, though I had heard Wavell tell appreciative stories about him: notably how he had got into trouble with the War Office by leasing part of the training area at Portsmouth while commanding a brigade there to a travelling circus, to raise money for some project which the War Office had refused to finance. When at last he left the office, Paget unbent for a moment, looked at me, and shaking his head said: "Extraordinary chap, that!" I confess that in that short quarter of an hour I failed to spot the seeds of greatness.

The air raids over London were hotting up and the nights were noisy; but not for me: since I doubled my role as M.A. to Paget during the day with being Permanent Night Duty Officer in the emergency headquarters at night. Deep down under St James's Park by Storey's Gate had been burrowed out a rabbit warren of offices to which we were to repair if the invasion happened. They were highly secret: even the entrance, which was through one of the Whitehall offices, was known only to few and was non-committal in its appearance. The system was several storeys deep and air-conditioned; each door resembled those one sees in the bulkhead of a ship, with a brace of massive handles; the rooms, except for the Operations Room where I had to bring the maps up to date if anything were reported during the night, were small but adequate. There were a few "sleeping-cabins" there, including one, seldom used, for the Prime Minister and another (for some reason) for Lord Beaverbrook; my naval and air force colleagues and I each had one. There was also a small ante-room, where you could get a drink, and the whole was staffed and guarded by Royal Marines. My routine was to dine early at the United Service Club, stroll across the Park, and relieve the day-time duty officer, whose identity varied, over a glass of something at about 8.30 p.m. I was rarely disturbed at night; but once I was going to bed rather later than usual when to my astonishment the Prime Minister and General Ismay came into the bar. The Prime

Minister said: "There's a splendid air-raid going on upstairs: you ought to go and see it." I thought to myself that a wink from him was as good as a nod, and made as if to go; but when he suggested a glass of brandy instead I thought this a better offer, and accepted. Indeed, I accepted a second, and therefore cannot claim to have actually witnessed an air-raid in the distinguished company of Churchill.

Down in the depths one could hear nothing of the air-raids, and I used to feel rather ashamed when I emerged into the world, still dark, next morning at 7.30 or so, and saw the fires or felt my feet crunching broken glass. The car that brought my relief used to waft me back to a small room I had in Latimer Court, a block of flats which had been taken over near St Paul's School, to bath and shave, and to share General Paget's office for another day. My work was not dull, in that I had access to secrets, but it did not feel very soldierly, though from time to time I got a whiff of the world beyond.

One morning Paget said to me: "I have an odd-sounding chap coming to see me. Size him up, and tell me what you make of him." In due course there arrived somebody whose functions I was vague about, though I knew them to be ultra-secret, bringing with him a tubby little man with short legs, in his fifties and wearing thick spectacles. He had been an officer in the First War; but finding peace-time soldiering dull had sent in his papers and gone to America, where he had joined the Federal Bureau of Investigation, or F.B.I. There, according to his story, which was well authenticated, he had become one of their expert pistol-shots; and among other exploits credited to him was the shooting of Jack Dillinger, "Public Enemy Number One," in the foyer of a cinema in St Louis. He had come back to his native land to offer his sword – or, more precisely, his pistols and tommy-gun – to his country. The question was whether he was as good as he claimed, or whether he was a wind-bag.

I know now that he wasn't a wind-bag, because in the course of the next few years I ran across him several times, and know at first-hand of two of his subsequent performances. One involved going into neutral territory where his head would have been forfeit if he had been caught, and the other into No-Man's-Land between the British and the Japanese. On the first occasion he killed a spy, on the second a traitor. Furthermore, his proficiency with his weapons was such that in 1944, when my Brigade was recuperating between campaigns at Bangalore in South India, I got him down for four days to pass on his techniques to some of my officers and N.C.O.s: his skills were fantastic. At different times in his career, he also instructed the Palestine Police and David Stirling's Special Air Service; but I couldn't swear that he killed Dillinger, or to the truth of the story that follows, which was the sequel of his interview with Paget that morning in my presence.

Four German air force squadron-leaders were known to frequent an *estaminet* near Wimereux every Friday evening, to relax in congenial surroundings and to compare notes on their respective week's performance. A British submarine was to put "Tac-Tac" (so called from his frequent imitation of the sound his weapons made) ashore, accompanied by two men. One of the men he rejected at the last moment, because he had a cough; the other accompanied him to the beach in the submarine's dinghy, and returned with him twenty-two minutes later. Tac-Tac left him to guard the door of the room while he went in; six shots rang out within an equal number of seconds; another half-minute passed; and Tac-Tac emerged with the contents of the squadron-leaders' pockets, having killed them plus two French girls who were keeping them company. Do we know for certain that the girls were French? Do we know that Tac-Tac's companion wasn't a friend of his, willing to testify to anything? Did I see the alleged contents of the German officers' pockets? The answer to all these questions is "No." But I think he probably did what he claimed to have done.

Here is another story about "Tac-Tac," four years out of chronological order. When he came to me at Bangalore, I had one battalion which had had heavy casualties, and whose morale was at rock bottom. I thought that a bloodthirsty-cum-rousing-cum-funny lecture from Tac-Tac might cheer them up, and I told him why. He asked for an hour to make his preparations; I arranged the lecture for 11 a.m., and introduced him from in front of the curtain in the Garrison Cinema, pitching his past pretty strong. They had all heard of the killing of Jack Dillinger in the foyer of the cinema in St Louis, and awaited his appearance with respectful awe.

His stage management was perfect: there was a short burst of tommy-gun fire from beyond the curtain, which then went up, revealing Tac-Tac with his smoking gun pointing at some dummies in the corner of the stage which he had obviously just riddled. With the curtain up and still glaring at the dummies, he gave them another accurate burst, and then waddled on his little legs to the front of the stage.

He fixed us with a prolonged glare, and then barked out: –
"It's your duty to die for your country!"

There was a long pause. Shuffling and murmuring began. This wasn't at all the pep talk I had indented for, and the acting Commanding Officer of the Battalion – the real one was in hospital, wounded – began to wriggle too. But Tac-Tac's timing was planned, and before things got out of hand he roared: –

"That's what you're often told, but it's NOT TRUE! It's your duty to LIVE for your country, and make the other Blanker DIE for HIS!"

There was laughter, and he had them in the palm of his hand. He called individuals to the stage, gave them two or three goes at the dummies in front of their chums, shot off darts of his ferocious philosophy and after an hour walked into the wings saying: "I want a drink, and I think your Brigade Commander owes me one." Their cheers for him followed us up the road.

My feeling for Tac-Tac was a mixture of admiration and revulsion. I admired his mastery of his craft, and he taught me a great deal, including how to approach a houseful of thugs, and how to burst into a room with a gunman in it, which stood me in stead when a few years later I was training recruits in the Palestine Police. But his philosophy repelled me: it was his

72

boast that he was a "killer," and his definition of a killer was "a man who can kill without fear, without pity, and without remorse."

I was by now completely restored, both mentally and physically, from my exhaustion of the summer, and feeling *embusqué* and homesick for the 2nd Battalion in the Middle East. They had had one sharp little action in Somaliland in which they had done well, and my old company commander A. K. Hamilton was now commanding them. All my friends were there, and that was where I felt I should be. If I could only work my passage to the Middle East theatre, I thought, the rest should be easy. On the 28th October, Mussolini presented the Greeks with the ultimatum demanding that their country should be opened up to Italian troops, and invaded them simultaneously, encountering a ferocious resistance. A few weeks later, it was decided to send a British Military Mission to Greece, under Major-General C. P. Heywood, a fact which came to my knowledge in my capacity as Paget's M.A. Without any intrigue on my part, I happened to meet Heywood in the street, and he invited me to go with him.

I rushed back to the office and told General Paget of this wonderful offer. It never crossed my mind that he would refuse to let me go; but he did. For once I choked back my nervousness of him, which had diminished little during my two months in his room, and poured out my heart, ending up with the phrase: "Honestly, Sir, a chap with one leg could do this job I'm doing now." I took a look at him, and he was actually smiling: not only smiling, but saying: "Find me a suitable chap with one leg, and I might consider it."

Nobody ever believes the sequel to that conversation, but it is true. I went out into the passage, and coming towards me was a major I had never seen before, with First War medal-ribbons, including a Military Cross, and trailing a leg. I tackled him at once with the question: "Forgive me asking you, but how many legs have you got?" "Only one," he said, looking rather surprised. "Would you like to be Military Assistant to the Chief of the General Staff, Home Forces?" He looked even more surprised, but said: "Well, yes, I suppose so, if I were offered it." "May I ask your name?" "Miller," he said. "Follow me!" I said. Within two minutes of my leaving it I was back in General Paget's office with Miller in tow. I left them to it, and paced the corridor until I was summoned back in. For the first time in the two months of our association, Paget was laughing, addressing me as "Bernard," and wishing me luck in Greece.

But I never went to Greece. Another Military Mission was forming under General Marshall-Cornwall, although for sensitive political reasons it had to be called a "Liaison Staff." Marshall-Cornwall was a remarkable linguist, a qualified interpreter in more than a dozen languages, who – between several Buchan-esque adventures – had been an Intelligence officer on my father's staff, and whom I had got to know well while with Wavell in Aldershot. In these closing months of 1940 there was considerable doubt about the intentions of the Turks: Would they come in with us? Would they knuckle under to German threats? Would they stay neutral? To them, the phrase "Military Mission" was too reminiscent of the German General Liman von Sanders in the First War; but delicate persuasion had resulted in their agreeing to accept a "Liaison Staff," to keep them informed of our situation in the Middle East theatre. Marshall-Cornwall had spent two years of his varied career as the British member of the Thracian Boundary Commission just after the First War, and Turkish was among his many tongues; his Number Two was to be Air-Vice-Marshal Tommy Elmhirst, who had been Air Attaché in Ankara before the war; and somehow Marshall-Cornwall pinched me off Heywood's staff before I had even joined it, to be his staff officer. The only loss to me was the money I had spent on a Greek phrase-book: at least the Turkish one which I now purchased was easier to read, though I didn't get very far with it. The first phrase, I recall, was *güzelim*, meaning "I am beautiful."

After a week's leave at Kilkerran, Peter Dorans and I boarded *Northern Prince* at Liverpool in conditions of great secrecy. I knew there was no possible chance of getting Peter either a passage, or authorisation for him to join The British Liaison Staff to Turkey; and it seemed and proved simplest just to hang him with suitcases and cause him to walk up the gangplank behind me. It worked, and in fact turned out to be by far the most normal feature of a highly *mouvementé* journey to the Middle East. Marshall-Cornwall and Elmhirst had already gone on by air by the devious route which was then the only one practicable, via Lagos and other exotic places. They had abandoned their newly-appointed but devoted staff officer to the hazards of the sea.

Exactly as though on a peace-time cruise, we fellow-passengers soon took stock of each other. I found myself sharing a cabin with Peter Smith-Dorrien, whom I had never met before: he was going out to fill the slot on Heywood's staff which I had inadvertently left vacant. Far more *piquant*, his father had been my father's Corps Commander from August of 1914, throughout Mons, Le Cateau and the Aisne, until he had suddenly sacked him one day in November. Then in February of 1915, French decided to sack Smith-Dorrien, and deputed the future C.I.G.S., "Wullie" Robertson, who rose from Trooper to Field-Marshal, to break the news gently. This Robertson did, so legend still maintains, with the words: "'Orace, you're for 'Ome." It was my father who came out to relieve Smith-Dorrien in the command of the Corps, and there was never any rancour between them thereafter. Peter and I were relieved to find, piecing it together like a jigsaw tactfully bit by bit, that we both knew the full story, and were able to laugh at it. When Jewish terrorists blew up the King David Hotel in Jerusalem in July 1946, I lost several friends, but there were two whom I mourned especially: Roddy Musgrave, formerly of the Palestine Police, and Peter Smith-Dorrien, who used to describe himself as "The Original City Slicker."

Most of the other officer passengers belonged to the Fleet Air Arm, and were excellent company, not least on Christmas Eve, when the fun grew high and hectic. We were a week out of Liverpool, and had become accustomed to the orderly progression of our convoy: thirty merchantmen in three lines, with *Northern Prince* leading the middle line of ten, and *Berwick* and *Bonaventure* our escorting cruisers ever watchful and often changing stations. The word had at last been released that we, the faster ships, were not to go round the Cape but to make a dramatic dash through the Mediterranean, and our spirits were uplifted thereby. Possibly we celebrated Christmas Eve unduly: when I decided to go to bed Captain "Tramp" Tidd, the senior naval officer, bet me a fiver that I wouldn't meet him on the bridge at 8 a.m. I trysted to do so; but I admit that I awoke Peter Dorans, and promised him the fiver if he ensured that I made the tryst.

I did, and Tramp Tidd didn't. I was on the bridge when eight bells struck. It was a grey morning somewhere off the Azores, since our convoy had for safety reasons taken a long sweep out into the Atlantic. I was just leaving the bridge to claim my bet, when there was a whistling noise overhead, and a couple of what looked like white fountains sprang up out of the sea to port, just beyond the leading ship in the left-hand column. I looked to starboard, and there was *Berwick* wheeling in her track like a show-jumper and increasing speed. Far away I saw two orange flashes, like the sun glinting on a pair of binoculars. Again the whistle and again the two white fountains, this time between us and the left-hand column. Not till then did it dawn on me that we were being shelled, and I rushed below to Tramp Tidd's cabin, shook him by the shoulder and told him so. "Go away, you bastard: you're still drunk!" he said sleepily and untruthfully; but at that moment the third salvo came over all too audibly, and he was out of his bunk and pyjamas and into his clothes in thirty seconds dead, just as the signal for Boat Stations was sounded on the ship's siren.

We stood shivering by our boats. I was patting the pockets of my great-coat to make sure that I had all my essentials, including a flask of brandy my father had given me for just such an occasion. Within three minutes of the first alarm, heavy mist had come down on us. We had just been able to see smoke rising from one of our ships which had evidently been hit.* We could hear our cruisers banging away at the attacker. Visibility was down to two cables; and there was wireless silence so that no ships could communicate with each other. The convoy was scattering, and ships looming out of the fog and sheering away again: it was miraculous that there were no collisions. After a couple of hours we were stood down, and two or three days later *Northern Prince* arrived at Gibraltar, and anchored inside the Mole. On our second night there, it blew a full gale, we dragged our anchors, and fetched up hard aground, wrecking our rudder and steering-gear to such an extent that they had eventually to be replaced from the United Kingdom.

Partly there and then, and partly after the war, we were able to piece together what had happened on Christmas Morning. We wouldn't have been half so jolly on Christmas Eve if we had known that the German pocket battleship *Admiral Hipper* was stalking us. According to Churchill's account, our escort of three cruisers – I only remember two – was a surprise for her. She and *Berwick* each registered a hit on the other before the mist screened them both.

Northern Prince being well and truly stuck, Peter Smith-Dorrien and I sought other means of getting on to Egypt urgently. The Navy couldn't help, but we heard at high level that a flying-boat was coming through, and managed to wangle our way aboard. Tramp Tidd had arranged to transfer to another ship, and he agreed to adopt Peter Dorans and our heavy luggage. The flying-boat was carrying out to the Middle East a secret American emissary, Colonel "Wild Bill" Donovan, whose task was to take stock of the will to resist among the Balkan governments; he was later to become head of the Office of Strategic Services, the American equivalent of S.O.E. He was a charming man, and friendly to Peter and me. We took off before dawn and arrived over Califrana, the flying-boat base in Malta, at 4 p.m., to find that an air-raid was in progress;

*The *Empire Trooper*, according to Churchill: *The Second World War* Vol. II, p. 528.

so we bore away and steamed around the sky until we had no more fuel and were obliged to put down on the Califrana waters. The raiders had luckily exhausted their fuel at the same moment as we, and broken off the action; but they had managed before doing so to damage every other flying-boat in the place as she rode to her moorings. Colonel Donovan's priority was high, and next morning he was given an aircraft to take him on to Egypt, while our flying-boat was commandeered for local use until the others could be repaired; but there was no room with Donovan for Peter and me, and we were stranded once again.

Those first few days of January 1941 were an interesting time to be in Malta; nobody could blame us for not getting on with the journey, and we might just as well enjoy ourselves. Although the garrison had been beleaguered for six months or so, they were not yet feeling the pinch: there was still ample gin in the Union Club, for instance. What they were chiefly missing was strange faces and gossip from home, so that Peter and I were made much of as guests by everybody from the Governor (General Dobbie, Orde Wingate's uncle) down. We witnessed the first German air-raids on the place, two or three a day, and cheered with the others when one of the A.A. batteries scored a dramatic right-and-left. One evening we were just finishing dinner in the Club when an officer came in mysteriously and told us to follow him outside. An hour later we were steaming out of the Grand Harbour in an empty tanker whose name escapes me.

Our convoy was small. It consisted of a few ships which had gone into Malta laden, at great risk, and were now proceeding back to Alexandria empty, escorted by a single cruiser, H.M.S. *York*. We suffered bombing attacks on each of the first two days. Who would be a sailor? I was frankly terrified as we zigzagged this way and that, to avoid those bombs dropping visibly down at us, looking as though they were the size of grand pianos. From the third day on we were left alone. It was a relief to be steaming at last into that familiar grey discoloration, which spreads like the shadow of a giant sting-ray far into the blue of the Mediterranean, to betray the muddy waters flowing out of the Nile Delta.

Peter Dorans fetched up in Cairo only a couple of days after us, complete with our luggage and with exciting tales of the heavily-attacked *Illustrious* convoy, in which he had got himself involved on his voyage. As for the unhappy *Northern Prince*, after a month's delay in Gib, and a further delay with engine trouble in Durban – she had missed her convoy through the Mediterranean, and been sent round the Cape after all – she arrived off the Piraeus with her cargo of war-like stores for the Greeks, only to be sunk by a bomb while at anchor before she was able to off-load a single item.

4

MARSHALL-CORNWALL and Elmhirst and the A.D.C. Clive Burt (now a Q.C. and a Metropolitan Magistrate) were already on their first visit to Ankara; they were due back in ten days or so, and had left orders for me not to try to follow them up. So I was free to travel down to Nairobi with Wavell, seeing Khartoum for the first time, and hearing Wavell's discussions with Generals Cunningham and Platt, both in the middle of their successful campaigns. I didn't come back with Wavell because something went wrong with the aircraft at Nairobi, and there was no room for me in the substitute; so I had three bonus days of leave there, joining an Imperial Airways flying-boat at Kisumu and flying back down the Nile. It was a gracious way of travelling, and as we flew both low and slow we could see all there was to be seen: the Murchison Falls, the matted jungle of Equatoria, the vast stretch of marshland known as the Sudd, and finally the placid course of the River through the desert. I am rather a snob about rivers, and proud to have actually travelled on the Nile, the Brahmaputra and the Irrawaddy, and to have crossed in one type of craft or another the Mississippi, the Ganges, the Niger and the Salween.

I got back to Cairo a day before the Turkey party, in time to prepare our office in G.H.Q. I also recruited a G.S.O. 3, John Fanshawe in the Argylls, whom I had known as a J.U.O. at Sandhurst two years before. I found him in hospital at Helmieh recovering from a wound in his buttock sustained at the Battle of Sidi Barrani, where his regiment had distinguished itself two months before. He had so many splinters in him that if you had shaken him he would have rattled, and it was clear that he would be fit for nothing but light duty for a long time to come.

The situation of the Turks at this time was unenviable. So far the Greeks had only the Italians to contend with, and were running rings round them in the Epirus; but the Germans might intervene at any moment, and the Balkan capitals other than Athens were looking at Berlin as a rabbit would look at a stoat. For reasons I have never been able to fathom, it was British policy to induce the Turks to declare for the Allies. If they had done so, it would be only a matter of time before the Germans attacked; Turkish Thrace – Turkey-in-Europe – would have been untenable, and although the hostile and desolate uplands of Anatolia with their bad roads would have been awkward country to get through, and the Turks would undoubtedly fight desperately, there would be no real obstacle between them and Syria. Up till the collapse of France Wavell in Cairo and Weygand in Beirut had been in close touch. Guido Salisbury-Jones in The Coldstream, with Pat Tweedie as his Number Two, had been Wavell's liaison officer with Weygand, and their opposite number in Cairo had been Major des Essars, a Breton. When France fell, her forces and her civil administration in Syria adhered to Vichy. Salisbury-Jones and Tweedie were recalled; des Essars declared for Britain, and Wavell commissioned him off his own bat as a major in The Black Watch. He held that rank for ten days, acquiring a Glengarry and other regimental accoutrements, until de Gaulle's organisation in London took shape and des Essars became a Free Frenchman. The Germans were now strongly represented in Syria, and there was not the slightest chance of any resistance being offered by the French, under General Dentz, in the event of their arriving through Turkey or from any other direction: though the French were proclaiming their determination to resist anybody who might attack them, whether the Allies or the Central Powers.

The Turkish Army was strong in manpower but in nothing else. Those sturdy, stocky Anatolian soldiers with their curiously ruddy complexions were superb fighting material, but

their weapons and equipment would have been looked at askance even by the British Home Guard. The Turks had a single
armoured brigade, the whole of which was stationed in Thrace
under General Shamsheddin. Each of its three component
regiments was equipped with different tanks: one with British
Christies, the other two with French and Russian types respectively. They had few spare parts and no reserves. Marshall-
Cornwall had to work warily, for the Turks, like other proud
peoples, were resentful of advice; and at that time, despite
Wavell's recent spectacular success in the Western Desert, they
were far from confident that we were going to win the war.
My General did venture to suggest that it might be prudent to
withdraw the armoured brigade across the Marmara, to avoid
the risk of its being lost in a German *blitzkrieg* into Thrace; but
the suggestion was received so icily that he never made it again.

Ankara was a dismal place in those days. There was only one
European-style hotel, the Ankara Palace, pretentious and bad,
stinking of drains, with plush Victorian furniture and a Casino
in the basement. There was one excellent restaurant kept by a
White Russian called Karpitch. He had a passion for British
pipe tobacco which was unobtainable in Turkey, and an unlimited supply of caviare which was unobtainable in Cairo: so
a profitable barter trade quickly sprang up between him and
me.

Ankara may have been dismal, but it was certainly not dull.
The *dramatis personae* were fascinating. The British Ambassador was Sir Hughe Knatchbull-Hugessen, whose wife's
parents were friends of my father and mother. The Hugessens
were kind to me, and I stayed or lunched or dined with them
several times. I must therefore have been valeted and waited on
by the famous Cicero, whose penetration of the unfortunate
Ambassador's security arrangements became a classic of es-
pionage: unfortunately, although I still vaguely remember
having had my trousers beautifully pressed and my shoes
beautifully polished, I have no recollection of Cicero at all. Of
the Service Attachés, the outstanding one was Bobby George
the airman, who was also accredited to Athens and was on

terms of close personal friendship with the King of Greece: it was believed at the time, and I have since confirmed it, that he did much to stiffen the King's resolution to defy the German ultimatum when it came. Bobby's last employment was as Governor of South Australia from 1953 to 1960; he had a sad and unnecessary death when he was knocked down and killed by a taxi in London in 1967. He was originally a Gordon Highlander, dapper and debonair; and he dominated that Embassy even more than the Ambassador. One odd British personage on the scene was Admiral Sir Howard Kelly, who was in Turkey on an ill-defined mission as the personal representative of Churchill. He was well into his seventies, served no evident purpose, was notoriously indiscreet in a hailing-the-maintop voice (he was deaf), and spent most of his time playing bridge with dubious acquaintances in the Ankara Palace Hotel.

Of the non-British and non-Turkish characters, the most prominent was the perennial Von Papen, who was German Ambassador. Until a short time before, he had still been punctiliously raising his old-fashioned Homburg hat to the ladies of the British Embassy as he passed them in the street; but now, an attempt having been made on his life, he no longer walked from his house to his Chancery. I saw him often, and he was a nice old boy just to look at. His rather plump daughter was often in the bar of the Ankara Palace.

On the 19th February, Eden (Secretary of State for War) and Dill (C.I.G.S.) arrived in Cairo from Britain, after a miserable flight in which everything had gone wrong, to review the whole Middle East situation and especially to decide the scale of the support to be given to Greece. They decided to go to Ankara to take the temperature of the Turks. Marshall Cornwall was *hors de combat*, suffering from some infection which had poisoned the whole of his face; but Arthur Smith (Wavell's Chief of Staff), Elmhirst and I were to accompany them. There were various others, including Ralph Stevenson and Pierson Dixon of the Foreign Office, who both treated me rather superciliously as if I were the baggage officer. We flew in two aircraft, lunching in Cyprus and catching a special train at Adana in the evening. We were due at Ankara at 9 a.m., but while we were all breakfasting in the dining-car with plenty of time in hand, as we thought, I looked out of the window and recognised the outskirts of Ankara. I gave the alarm, and there was a great flurry as everybody abandoned his half-eaten breakfast and hurriedly put on his belt and cap and great-coat. Exactly as in some Charlie Chaplin film, I think *The Great Dictator*, our carriage drew up a hundred yards beyond the red carpet where the rank and fashion awaited us; some of us were out and some of us were in, and the group of high officials was beginning to scurry towards us, when the train decided to move back to the red carpet. It was not a dignified arrival.

After the greetings, our party drove off to the Embassy. We had been there only a few minutes when one of our most distinguished members clapped his hands to his head in horror. He had been reading with his breakfast an immensely secret document about the situation in Malta, which revealed among other things the fact that we had only three fighter aircraft still serviceable there; and he had left it on the breakfast table. I remembered exactly where he had been sitting, one along from me and on the other side of the aisle; so with a member of the Embassy staff who spoke Turkish I dashed down in a car to the railway station, though with little hope of finding it. The train was no longer at the platform, but we were directed to where it had been parked in a siding; and there was the dining-car, deserted by the waiters and with the breakfast-things not yet cleared away. There too beside a congealed plateful of bacon-and-eggs was the Document, still folded over at the page which X had reached. I thrust it into my brief-case, and we drove back at full speed to the Embassy, to put X out of his agony. Some pessimist opined that there would have been time for an agent to photograph it, but it didn't look as if it had been touched or moved.

I was rather piqued at being excluded from the top-level talks; I had always been "in" with Marshall-Cornwall at his conversations with the Turkish Commander-in-Chief, who had the engaging name of Marshal Çakmak, pronounced Chuckmuck. He was not easy to deal with because he was deaf, though not quite so deaf as the President General Ismet Inönü: both had been close associates of Mustapha Kemal, or Ataturk. However, we all knew that the Turks were sensibly refusing to be bounced off the fence on which they were sitting. They merely confirmed that they would fight like hell whoever might choose to attack them, just like the French in Syria. Whenever they asked, as they constantly did, what help we could afford them if the Germans invaded, we could not in all honesty promise them much: neither in terms of troops or armour on the ground, nor aircraft in the air, nor the commodity in which they were chiefly interested, anti-aircraft artillery.

They gave us hospitality, in full measure. The first evening there was an enormous banquet at the Ankara Palace, which went on until the small hours of the morning, adjourning half way through to the Cabaret downstairs, where a Filipino band was playing and where there was a series of artistes of every sort of nation and colour to entertain us. Saraçoglu the Foreign Minister and Numan Menemençoglu the Permanent Secretary of Foreign Affairs led the revels, and Mr Eden, entering into the spirit of the thing, covered himself with glory by rising to his feet and reciting by heart long chunks of Persian poetry, which to the Turks is the height of academic polish. I had forgotten, if I had ever known, that he had studied Oriental languages at Oxford. There was no doubt that by this *tour de force* he had risen immensely in the esteem of our hosts. We had had a tiring journey, a long and busy day and an exhausting evening, with too much to eat (off gold plate, by the way) and drink in an atmosphere heavy with cigar smoke; and when the party broke up at 4 a.m. we were horrified when the word was passed round that we were all to be present at a conference to be held by Eden at 8 a.m.

Most of us were bleary-eyed, but not he. He looked as fresh as paint as he cleared the decks and our minds for the agenda of the day's meetings. There was to be a reception that evening at the British Embassy, for which the invitations had already gone out, and another banquet afterwards. My heart sank.

It was a bad day anyhow. It was the moment when the Yugo-
slavs were under the utmost pressure from the Germans. Three
weeks before, the Regent, Prince Paul, had obeyed a summons
to visit Hitler at Berchtesgaden, where he had been duly brain-
washed, and invited to follow the example set by Bulgaria on
the 1st March in joining the Tripartite Pact. On the 25th March,
two representative Ministers had signed it in Vienna. On the
27th there was a *coup d'état* led by General Simovic of the Air
Force, which sent the Regent out of the country (eventually to
exile in South Africa), put the 17-year-old King Peter officially
on to his precarious throne, and cocked a snook at the Germans, with the full support of a cheering and defiant nation.
This was happening while we were actually in Ankara, and the
news was reaching us in snippets throughout the day. It was
confusing for us all, but especially for the unfortunate Yugoslav
Ambassador, who had no means of telling from hour to hour
which side he was supposed to be on.

It had not taken long for Von Papen to learn that there was
to be a reception at the British Embassy, and he decided to give
one too, and at the same hour. He must have thought that this
was the golden opportunity to make the switherers in the
Ankara Diplomatic Corps shew their hands. The Turkish hierarchy was already committed to attending the Knatchbull-
Hugessens' party. After all, Eden and Dill were there at the
agreement of the Turkish Government, if not precisely at their
invitation, and were merely returning the hospitality of the
night before. Obviously the Norwegians, the Dutch, the Poles
and the representatives of the other countries which had been
overrun by the Germans would accept the British invitation;
so would the Americans and various other neutral countries
who had already shewn where their sympathies lay. Equally obviously the Italian, the Hungarian, the Bulgarian, the Spanish
Ambassador, would accept Von Papen's, and probably the
Russian. But what would the Japanese do, or the Rumanian?
And above all, the Yugoslav?

I cannot now remember what the Jap or the Rumanian did.
The poor Yugoslav tried to back both horses. He accepted Von

Papen's invitation, but explained that he would have to leave early; he accepted Knatchbull-Hugessen's, but explained that he would have to arrive late. I don't know what sort of send-off he got from Von Papen's, but I witnessed his arrival at Knatchbull-Hugessen's. Dixon and I had been told off to wait for him in the hall, and to divert him when he arrived to a waiting-room nearby. We were then to advise Eden and "Snatch," as the Ambassador was called behind his back. The unhappy man eventually came, very late and looking miserable; I fancy he had found it difficult to get away from the Germans. Dixon chaperoned him in the room, while I went off to warn our principals. They kept him waiting for a bit. Then they went in; Dixon came out; five minutes passed; they came out; one minute passed; Dixon and I went in. There was the poor devil sitting in a chair with his head in his hands. Heaven knows what they had said to him. We restored him with a drink, and finally coaxed him into the gilded throng next door, and gave him another. I was terribly sorry for him.

The talks ended next day, and it was decided that I should fly back to Cairo to bring Wavell up-to-date with what had gone on so far, while the rest of the party, reinforced by Bobby George, flew on to Athens. They had an unpleasant flight, skimming the Sea of Marmara at twenty feet or so above sea level, narrowly avoiding hitting some island or other, and spending an unscheduled night somewhere *en route* in discomfort. By the time I got back to Cairo, Wavell had been summoned to join them in Athens: so I might just as well have gone there too, as I had dearly wanted to do.

I don't remember how many times I travelled between Egypt and Turkey during the five months that the British Liaison Staff in Turkey (christened BLAST for short by Arthur Smith) lasted: perhaps six in all, usually with Marshall-Cornwall but twice at least on my own. I always enjoyed the journey, and particularly the sunset as the train climbed up through the Taurus Mountains, and the dawn advancing over the sombre Anatolian plateau, which reminded me of the bleak moorland between Muirkirk and Douglas on the road from

Kilkerran to Edinburgh. It used to recall the lines from a hymn: –

> On your far hills, long cold and gray,
> Has dawned the everlasting day.

And always, whether or not the General was of the party, our Turkish liaison officer, Captain Emin Dirvana, was there to help. He had never been to Britain in his life, but his English, learnt at Roberts College in Istanbul, was impeccable. Long afterwards he became the first Turkish Ambassador to Cyprus.

Once during an overnight stop at Nicosia in Cyprus, I went to a night-club, and was astonished to see among the Cabaret artists two performers, a man and a woman, whom I had last seen doing their act in the Ankara Palace Hotel. This seemed fishy to me, and I alerted the security authorities, who took the matter seriously and detained them. They turned out to be Hungarians, and being unable to establish their *bona fides* and having bogus papers were interned for the rest of the War.

It was interesting to see the famous and historic Chatalja Lines, on which the Turks had traditionally relied for the defence of Istanbul, and in which they still had confidence. They wouldn't have lasted two hours against an assault by modern armour. Between Chatalja and Istanbul, some twenty miles, there ran a single asphalt road; between Chatalja and the frontier at Edirne (formerly Adrianople), another sixty or seventy miles, the road was a series of potholes. There was also, of course, the railway, along which in peace-time ran the Orient Express, the reputed haunt of mysterious countesses who spent their time picking the pyjama pockets of King's Messengers; but for obvious reasons it no longer ran in 1941.

On that particular tour we saw much of Turkish Thrace, thanks to the persuasiveness of Marshall-Cornwall; the Turks were a little coy about it, but relented when they became aware of how well he knew it, from the days when he was helping to delineate the frontier. We went to Çorlu, Luleburgaz, Babaeski and Kirklareli, with its oddly Scotch-sounding name. At each we caught more and more fleas. But I recall especially our night at Edirne, when resistance in Greece was failing fast, since the Germans now had access through Bulgaria. The Intelligence staff in Cairo used to cite in their appreciations the Maritsa River, which constituted the frontier between Turkey and Greece, and which looked on the map to be a fair obstacle. That evening at Edirne, knowing that the Germans had burst into Greek Thrace and were getting near, I walked down in plain clothes – we wore no uniform in Turkey – to the river, where the Turkish guards were lounging, and looked across to the Greek customs-post on the other side, with its customs-officers and soldiers equally at their ease. Children were splashing about in the river, and I was horrified to see that the Maritsa, which had featured so largely as an obstacle in all the British appreciations, was no more than two feet deep at this point, and with a gravel bottom. After dinner we were entertained to an interminable film before going to bed. During the night I heard shooting. It didn't last more than ten minutes; but when I went down to the river again at first light, the uniforms on the other side were no longer Greek: they were German. I felt oddly invisible, standing there in my tweed jacket and grey flannel trousers, with only 200 yards between us. I went back to the billet, woke up the General, and told him what I had seen. At breakfast, as I pretended to enjoy my bowl of that filthy stuff *youghort* that had been set before me, I could sense that our hosts, still smiling, still friendly, were now exuding sympathetic tact. It was not only the Greek front which had crumbled during the night: so had the British in the Western Desert. They had heard it on the B.B.C.

Mercifully for us, the strain on our stiff upper lip did not have to be preserved for too long. Our tour was over, and our seats were booked on all the proper trains from Istanbul to Ankara, where we had to spend a day, and from Ankara to Adana, where we were to catch our aircraft. But it was humiliating to hear hour by hour from the B.B.C. how our troops were falling back, and then from the German radio that they had captured in a single day Generals O'Connor, Neame and Gambier-Parry. When at last we reached Adana, we were told that there would be a three hours' delay; and the local military commander, General Fakhri Belen, sat with us throughout those hours, alternately commiserating with us on our defeat, and intoning Persian poetry extolling the beauties of the spring. On this particular trip, General Dickie Creagh had been with us, giving talks on his successful Desert campaign six months earlier, and the Turks had listened admiringly: now all that was dust and ashes, and I for one was wishing that Creagh had never come. The only satisfactory memory I was taking away with me was of hearing my General interpreting on the platform of Haider Paşa railway station from Norwegian into Turkish and back into Norwegian, for a group of Norwegians who had somehow escaped through Russia and were hoping to make their way to Britain: they eventually did. Not many people could have brought off that linguistic feat.

Back in Cairo, Marshall-Cornwall was summoned at once by Wavell. After the disaster of the 7th of April, there was an acute shortage of generals, and Wavell needed him to assume the command of British Troops in Egypt. In that capacity, he did a great deal in spite of other people's apathy to prepare what was afterwards known as the Alamein Line, for which in Wavell's view and in my own worm's-eye one he never had due credit. Anyway, he was lost to BLAST. So also was Elmhirst: he was snatched away to become Marshall-Cornwall's opposite number as Air Officer Commanding Egypt. So BLAST shrivelled, and was reduced overnight to me (christened by General Arthur Smith "BLAST Major"), and John Fanshawe ("BLAST minor"); and was banished from our smart suite of offices close to Wavell's into a dreary little hole in a less fashionable building, where such few people as were interested in us could never find us. The glory had departed. I knew full well that the Turks were still, so to speak, Pasha-conscious, and would never pay heed to a mere major, however handsome or intelligent, and I submitted that our show ought now to be wound up; but I was ordered to go back to Turkey once more, with certain specific tasks to do. In retrospect, I am glad that I was, for in some ways this was the most interesting trip of the lot, and punctuated with some unexpected incidents.

The day before I was due to leave, one of the mystery men in G.H.Q. came to see me, with the request that I should hand over an envelope at midnight to somebody who would come and call on me in my sleeper in the Taurus Express. Primly I said "No." My visits to Turkey were wholly with Turkish conni-vance, and I had been strictly ordered not to get mixed up in any monkey business. The mystery man withdrew, but I was summoned an hour later to a high quarter, one with which I had neither the right nor the desire to argue; I was told that I had been quite right, and a good boy; but that nevertheless I was to comply. So I accepted the envelope, which I was told to hand over to an Englishman who would report to me in my sleeper at midnight precisely on whatever day it was. This was a purely incidental task. I was also to do various routine jobs in Ankara and Istanbul, and to go to Smyrna (Izmir) to see what progress was being made with the two airfields being built there for the Turks under the supervision of British Royal Engineer officers and serjeants in plain clothes.

My routine of travelling to Turkey never varied, except on the Anthony Eden occasion, when R.A.F. aircraft had been put at our disposal. I used to take the weekly flight by Misr, the Egyptian state air-line, which flew from Cairo to Lydda in Palestine, where it refuelled; on to Adana via Nicosia; back to Nicosia that afternoon; and so next day *via* Lydda back to Cairo. I would peer out of the windows fascinated at the Pales-tine scene that I had once known so well, and resent it bitterly when the aircraft turned away to seaward. I used to arrive at Adana in time to spend an hour or two with the British Vice-Consul, Shaw, and then catch the Taurus Express at about 6 p.m. Dinner in the dining-car was good, the sleepers were comfortable, and the only rule was that the porters must put your luggage in through the window, and not come on to the train, for fear of their introducing fleas. This precaution, though sensible, was not effective.

On this particular flight we stopped as usual at Lydda to

refuel, arriving at about 8 a.m.: for some reason we always started at crack of dawn. I was having a second breakfast in the familiar airport restaurant when the R.A.F. Station Commander, whom I knew slightly, came in and said: "You speak French, don't you? Would you mind coming to interpret? There's a French Potez overhead that looks as though it's going to land: it's probably another deserter from Syria; we've had three or four these last few months."

Delighted at the prospect of airing my French in such a good cause, I hurried out with him; and there indeed was a Potez, but behaving in a very odd manner. It made several approaches to the runway, but kept on over-shooting and deciding to "go round again." At last it came in low and unsteadily over the control tower, touched down later, and shot through the boundary fence until it pulled up in the long grass somewhere near Wilhelma village. The Station Commander, cursing, jumped into a car and took me with him. By using various tracks we found the plane, which had been only slightly damaged. Beside it was standing an exceptionally good-looking young Frenchman of not more than nineteen, grinning from ear to ear. He was dressed in a flying suit, and no badges of rank were visible.

"I'm afraid I can't congratulate you on your landing," I said in French, and in a friendly manner.

"Please don't be too hard on me," he replied: "it's the first I've ever done!" He turned out to be a radio operator, with plenty of experience as a passenger, but none as a pilot, who had got himself posted to Syria determined to join the Free French. He had carefully watched how pilots flew Potez's; had checked up the evening before that this particular aircraft had plenty of fuel in its tanks; had sneaked down to the hangar at Rayak before dawn; had slid the doors open, started her up, taxied out, taken off, and followed the coastline down to Lydda. I wish I had taken a note of his name, so that I could have checked on his subsequent career; but I didn't, and I have no notion whether he is alive or dead.

Next evening in the Taurus Express I had my usual leisurely

dinner, drinking red Turkish wine from Brusa and washing down bitter Turkish coffee with even more bitter Turkish brandy. At midnight I was sitting in my sleeper pretending to read a book, but feeling in reality terribly Secret Service. It was at midnight, plus or minus, that an appropriately surreptitious knock came on my door; I opened it, and a perfectly ordinary Englishman came in, resembling in no sort of way the kind of secret agent that Compton Mackenzie has described in his various books about Intelligence in the Levant. He seemed mildly on edge, but not unduly. He said: "I believe you've got an envelope for me;" and I gave it him without further ado. I said in my turn: "I believe I've got something else for you:" and poured him a tot of whisky (and also one for myself) out of my father's flask, into one of the sleeper's ultra-thick glass mugs. He grinned and relaxed, saying: "It's several weeks since I had a taste of this." I don't quite know how to convey his personality. I had never met him before, but I met him several times thereafter, at intervals; and I once asked him: – "Do you consider yourself what people call a 'Levantine'?" His considered answer was: – "Well, it's always considered rather a pejorative word, but I suppose that's exactly what I am." He spoke both Greek and Turkish well enough to pass himself off as a Greek in Turkey, and as a Turk in Greece. His English was that of a London drawing-room, and his French of a Paris *salon*. We had a second dram together and he withdrew.

After a couple of days in Ankara, I went down to Smyrna by the overnight train, to see how the British sappers in plain clothes were getting on with the two military airfields which they were secretly helping the Turks to build. It was my thirtieth birthday, and I was wondering how to celebrate it; but the decision was taken out of my hands: I spent it under arrest. A Turkish officer challenged my credentials, and was unimpressed by them. He drove me back into the town at pistol-point, while my taxi-driver followed bleating for his fare, and marched me in front of his General, who happened to be Marshal Çakmak's son-in-law. The General spoke fair English; he was civil and even friendly; but he would not let me go until he had checked with Ankara on the telephone. It took him eight hours to get through, and to establish that my visit had been approved: somebody had forgotten to tell Smyrna. From 10 a.m. till 6 p.m. I sat all alone in a small room with nothing to read, consuming the innumerable cups of coffee sent through to me and the midday meal of bitter bread, good sour cheese like crowdie, and a handful of olives.

I didn't see the General again. At six I was released by a junior officer, and was walking back to my hotel in the dusk when I was accosted by a ragged and unshaven man gabbling in French: "I have the impression that you are a British officer! I am an officer of the Royal Hellenic Army! I have just escaped from Greece! Hide me! Save me!" I am rather ashamed to say that I shook him off and hurried on, feeling that I simply couldn't afford to get embroiled in any more adventures that day.

I travelled on by train to Istanbul, a route I hadn't travelled before. It was late April or early May: the wild flowers were out; and towards the end of the journey we came down off the plateau and travelled along the shore of the Sea of Marmara. Here for forty or fifty miles there were not only wild flowers; all the blossom was out, and I gazed entranced from the window at this blaze of colour and at the sea. As the train passed the naval base of Izmit there was one sombre contrast: the Turkish battleship *Yavouz* lying at the moorings she was reputed never to leave. Twenty-seven years before, in her previous incarnation as the *Goeben*, of the German Navy, her coming into these very waters with her consort the *Breslau* had been one of the odd assortment of factors which had brought Turkey into the First War against us. She was now a ship of prestige rather than of power; but she looked grim as she lay off that long coast-line so bright with the colours of spring, and the water breaking gently on the rocks.

I knew this would be my final visit to Turkey, and resolved to enjoy my last couple of days in Istanbul. I dined well with the Assistant Military Attaché, and went to bed; but soon there was a discreet knocking on my door. It was my friend of the

Taurus Express of a couple of weeks before, still calm, but slightly less debonair. He had done whatever he had to do (I know now what it was) and needed badly to get out of Turkey. His liberty and possibly his life was at risk: could he somehow attach himself officially to me? Once again I felt a cad, as I had with the Greek officer in Smyrna. I was tempted to say "Yes"; but to do so would go far beyond what I had been told to agree to in Cairo, and would be a breach of the terms on which our British Liaison Staff had been allowed into Turkey. The temptation to get myself involved in a sort of Sandy Arbuthnot, secret service operation, just for the fun of it, was hard to resist; but I knew that I must keep my fingers out of any such thing. The most I could do was undertake to raise some money for him, first thing in the morning. This I did, and got it to him. Little did either of us think that some years after he would be doing me much the same service in reverse.

Two nights later I left Ankara station for the last time. As I boarded the train, I noticed that there were even more Germans among my fellow-passengers than usual, presumably bound for Syria. When I went along to the restaurant car for dinner, everybody but me seemed to be German. I found a table to myself, at which I was shortly joined by a drunken Norwegian. He quickly spotted my nationality, and to my embarrassment began telling me in a loud voice in English the details of his escape from Norway. I was about to warn him, when he electrified me by saying: "If I could see a German now, I vould *kill him!*" The prospect of seeing him trying to kill a whole restaurant-car load of Germans, with its certainly deleterious effect on the service of dinner, made me hold my tongue and put up with his monologue.

"I know I am dronk. So vould you be dronk if you had chost escaped from Norvay and those Germans. I used to be an officer on my Oncle's tonker, and my Oncle vould have no dronkenness on board his tonker, but my Oncle vould have been dronk if he had escaped from Norvay and those Germans; and if I could see a German now I vould *kill him!*"

I was aware that the Germans all around us had begun by

being annoyed, but by now were highly amused, and it was all I could do to avoid catching their eye and sharing the joke with them. Eventually the Norwegian voice died away into a mumble; he put his elbows on the table and his head in his hands, and went to sleep. I restricted my dinner to a single course, and made my way to my sleeper.

5

THE first thing I did after getting back to Cairo was to write and submit to General Arthur Smith an eloquent little paper entitled: "Case for the abolition of BLAST." He duly pronounced a funeral oration over us at his next bi-weekly conference. John Fanshawe was transferred to G.H.Q. proper, and I to a newly created appointment on Wavell's personal staff.

The reason for this new job was simple enough. It was then mid-May of 1941, and the Middle East theatre was bubbling wherever you looked. In the West, the enemy, to use Harry Clark's phrase, was "far too near," and Wavell was being urged to attack Rommel in strength (which he hadn't got) before Rommel could launch an offensive himself. To the North, the evacuation of what could be got out of Greece had been completed by the end of April. (I had been waiting in Arthur Smith's ante-room when General Jumbo Wilson arrived back, and I asked him how he was. He replied, with his usual cold-in-the-nose intonation: "Well, codsideringk I've beed kicked all the way frob the Yugoslav frodtier out through the bub edd of the Pelopoddese, I'b dot too bloody awful, thangk you!") An attack on Crete was obviously pending, and might happen any day. To the East, Rashid Ali Gailani the Prime Minister of Iraq, after months of dissembling, had thrown off the mask and attacked the British garrisons. Only in the South, where Generals Platt and Cunningham were rolling up the former Italian East African empire like an out-of-date map, were things going well.

Wavell was finding it hard to keep in personal touch with his commanders and at the same time to cope with the bombardment of signals from Britain, mostly (except for those from Dill) unhelpful and wanting in understanding of his difficulties. These were reaching him three times a day. The idea was that I should become an extra Military Assistant to him, taking off his shoulders whatever could be delegated to so junior an officer. From my long association with him, I was well known to his subordinate commanders, and he thought I should be of use as a confidential liaison officer whenever he was tied to his office or visiting one of the other fronts.

It didn't in fact work out that way. The Prime Minister was still sour over the *débâcle* of the first week of April, when the Western Desert front had folded up like a concertina. This was a classic case of crying over spilt milk, and it was far from helpful in this moment of crisis everywhere to insist, as Churchill did, on an enquiry being held. My first task in my new capacity was to be put in charge of it, a one-man band installed in a special office, and empowered to summon anybody not actually fighting at that moment who might be able to throw light on the elusive story. The generals most nearly concerned were prisoners and unavailable. Some of the other senior officers were resentful at being asked to account for their actions by so junior an officer as I was. I did my best, but with most of the key witnesses missing it was possible to establish only approximately what had actually happened.

Then on the 20th of May the invasion of Crete began. All of us in G.H.Q. had a horrible feeling of helplessness, intensified in my case by the knowledge that my old Battalion was in the thick of it at Heraklion. The commander was Bernard Freyberg the New Zealander, and the greatest optimist of all time: so our hearts sank when we got a signal from him which included the words: "It would be wrong of me to be optimistic." The battle went on for ten days, but the end was inevitable. There were and are plenty of wiseacres to say that the place need never have been lost if enough men and materials had been put into it in the first instance; but nobody has yet made a reasonable suggestion about where they could have come from, or at the expense of which other campaign.

During part of the Crete battle, the officer who normally took the minutes at the meetings of the Commanders-in-Chief was sick, and I stood in for him. All three were quietly dogged and determined. The man present whose anxiety shewed most openly was Peter Fraser, the Prime Minister of New Zealand. The flower of New Zealand's manhood was in the Middle East; they had already lost heavily in Greece. We couldn't believe that after the heavy losses to ships and men on the first day of the evacuation the Royal Navy would have another go; but they did. Of the two cruisers and four destroyers that went into Heraklion, both cruisers were damaged and two destroyers were lost. Fewer than thirty Jocks of the Regiment were killed on the island, but over 200 at sea; out of 240 who embarked in the cruiser *Dido*, 103 were killed.

The survivors were sent to Qassassein in the Canal Zone, where Wavell sent me to greet them on his behalf, explaining how sorry he was to be too busy to come in person. I found their tails well up: indeed, they were resentful at having been evacuated, since at Heraklion they had had the best of the fighting, and still did not realise how badly things had gone elsewhere. At Qassassein they were on ground familiar to the Regiment: you could actually see from the camp the lump of Tel-el-Kebir ("the big hill") where the Highland Brigade, including our 1st Battalion, had led the assault in 1882. Just over a year before, while I was still at the Staff College, I had lunched with the old Duke of Connaught in his house at Bagshot Park. He was only a few weeks short of his 90th birthday, but his memory of the details of the battle, in which he commanded the 1st Guards Brigade, was complete: he fought it for me all over again, using knives and forks, pepper pots and mustard-pots, to illustrate the movements. He was no mean link with the past, for the great Duke of Wellington was his god-father, and he was the only man I ever met who had clear recollections of my grandmother: she died in 1871 when my father was only six, and the Duke twenty-one. The rest of his talk was mostly about how much he had loathed his attachment as a young officer to some crack regiment of the German Army: "my brother-officers considered themselves tremendous gentlemen, but *I* thought they were a lot of pigs."

The last two days of May witnessed both the final evacuation of Crete and the ignominious flight across the frontier into Persia of Rashid Ali, with his tail of disconsolate cronies, including Haj Amin el Husseini who still called himself the Mufti of Jerusalem. While all this had been going on, de Gaulle had been demanding an instant invasion of Syria, and in this he had strong support from Churchill. There had unquestionably been German aircraft on Syrian airfields on and after the 12th May, and there was a risk that German troops might be flown in. On the 18th, General Catroux, de Gaulle's representative in Cairo, said he had reliable information that the Vichy French were withdrawing all their troops into the Lebanon so as to hand over Syria proper to the Germans. He went back on this three days later, but not before it had affected London thinking. He claimed also to have incontrovertible evidence that feeling among the French troops in Syria had swung over largely to de Gaulle, and that if the Free French, supported by British, went in they would not be strongly opposed. This information also cut more ice in London than it did in Cairo, and proved to be equally false.

The pressure on Wavell to invade, whatever his judgment, can be gauged from a signal which reached him from Churchill while the battle for Crete was at its height. It included the words: "Should you find yourself unwilling to give effect to the decision, arrangements will be made to meet any wish you may express to be relieved of your command." It took time to collect even the tiny force which was all that was possible, but in the early morning of the 8th June the frontier was crossed at three places: one Australian brigade on the coast (Pat Tweedie was with it); another at Merjayun in the centre; and on the right, opposite Deraa which lay five miles north of the Trans-Jordan frontier, the so-called "Free French Division," under command of General Legentilhomme, plus the 5th Indian Infantry Brigade under Wilfred Lloyd. The Free French consisted of two brigades, each with one white and two black

battalions. In one brigade, the white battalion belonged to the
Foreign Legion: they were perfectly prepared to fight, but not
against the Foreign Legion battalion on the Vichy side. The
whole advance was coordinated by the Australian General
Laverack, with his headquarters at Nazareth; and over him was
Jumbo Wilson in Jerusalem.

I had spent the day of the 12th in G.H.Q. We knew that,
contrary to Catroux's forecast, the Vichys (as we called them
for convenience) had reacted strongly and were fighting
bitterly; the Australians were held up, and there was little news
from the Free French. Wavell had gone up to Jerusalem to see
Wilson. I had dined in my flat with two Black Watch friends
who had been in Crete, when the telephone rang. It was the
duty officer in G.H.Q., saying that I had been ordered to report
to General Wilson for duty as soon as possible.

Thirty-six hours later, having failed to get an aircraft and
travelled across the Sinai desert by the night train, I was in
General Wilson's office in Jerusalem. Before getting down to
business, he shewed me a letter he had just had from Glubb
Pasha, the commander of the Arab Legion, begging for some
extra officers. His specification included the following sentence:
"They must have seen some fighting, they must be gentlemen,
and they must speak Arabic." With a chuckle and in his familiar
nasal voice, Wilson said: "*Doe* gedtlebad speaks Arabic!" He
then told me what I was wanted for. Wilfred Lloyd had sent an
S.O.S. for a trained staff officer who could speak French, and
Wilson had asked Wavell if he could borrow me. Wavell, re-
calling that I had also some knowledge of Damascus and its
environs, had agreed: hence the signal to G.H.Q. I was to get
up to the Deraa front at once. Legentilhomme had apparently
been wounded, and Lloyd himself was commanding for the
moment; communications were bad, and there was no recent
knowledge of the situation, but apparently they had got some
way up the Damascus road against opposition before being
finally held up. Their R.A.F. liaison officer was in the building,
and would travel with me. I was to consider myself as having
direct access to General Wilson if I needed it.

I found the airman: he had no vehicle. Want of transport was one of the factors which had bulked biggest in the signals between Cairo and London concerning the difficulties of mounting the campaign. We managed in the end to persuade Allan Michie, an American war correspondent representing *Life*, to lend us the taxi he had on permanent hire, promising that we would send it straight back. As we moved up the lines of communication, I saw what a thoroughly job lot of vehicles had been pressed into service: ramshackle buses with precarious roofs, old citrus trucks still slippery with orange-peel. Peter Dorans sat in front with the Jewish driver, while in the back the R.A.F. officer told me how the battle had gone so far. It had begun, he said, with Hugh Foot and a Free French officer called André Brunel driving to within hailing distance of the garrison of Deraa, alighting, and displaying a flag of truce. The garrison had opened up with what sounded like an anti-tank gun, and removed, clean as a whistle, the engine of the car. Foot, I was told, had raised his hat, as politely as ever Von Papen had done in the streets of Ankara, bowed in the direction of Deraa, and walked slowly and with dignity away.

It was a most confused campaign. After it was all over, I tried to describe it to a group of senior officers in G.H.Q. on large sheets of foolscap and with the help of coloured chalks. There had been so many moments when formations of either side had been surrounding each other in concentric circles that my attempts at sketches looked like archery targets. At one time the remains of an Indian battalion was surrounded in a house in Mezze, with our own relief force round two sides of their besiegers; our own lines of communication were cut at Sheikh Miskin; and our British battalion was surrounded in Quneitra by the Vichy with another relief force from our own side trying to extricate them. The cutting of the road at Sheikh Miskin was done by a Colonel Bouvier, commanding a detachment in the Jebel Druze, who at one time was expected to change his allegiance (*permuter* was their word) to the Free French; he was accompanied by a large posse of Druzes under my old acquaintance Hamza Darwish, and part of his booty,

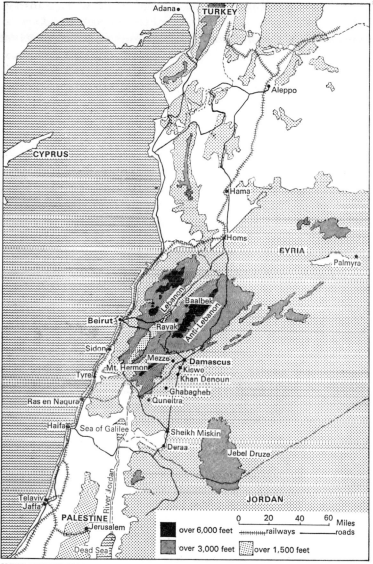

SYRIA AND LEBANON, 1941

or Hamza's, was half a case of whisky on its way up to me.

I found the Free French Divisional Headquarters established in the *mairie* of the small village of Ghabagheb, which they had rechristened "Rhubarb" to avoid the tricky Arab gutturals. There were only four small rooms, all over-crowded, with people sleeping even in the hall. It was already dark, and the only lighting came from a few hurricane lamps, whose reek and heat added to the general air of confusion. We picked our way over prostrate bodies into the tiny room in use as an Ops Room, where people were poring over maps and scribbling on bits of paper. One of them detached himself and greeted me as an old friend: it was Boisseau, whom I had met four years before in the headquarters at Beirut in 1937. He was now G.S.O. 2 of the Division, but he had had one hell of a time since I had last seen him. Suspected of having sympathies with the Free French, he had been arrested, but managed to escape and get away over the hills into Palestine. His wife and children were still in Beirut, and he had no knowledge of what had become of them.

He took me to the G.S.O. 1, a tall, thin-faced, fair-haired lieutenant-colonel with a beaky nose, who astounded me with his greeting: "*Aha, le bon Red'Ackle! Le Black Watch est arrivé! Nous sommes sauvés!*" He enjoyed my bafflement for a few minutes before revealing that he had been attached to our 2nd Battalion in Silesia shortly after the First War, when Arthur Wauchope was commanding and Archie Wavell a company commander. This was my first meeting with the future Général d'Armée Marie-Pierre Koenig, soon to be recognised as one of the most distinguished Frenchman of his generation, and honoured by all as such. He had come to Britain with the French contingent which had been in Norway, and joined de Gaulle there instead of returning to France. His name was soon to resound as the Free French commander at Bir Hakeim. His later appointments were to include the command of the Free French Forces of the Interior – in other words, all the Resistance throughout the invasion and the fighting that followed it; French High Commissioner in Germany; and Minister of Defence during the Presidency of de Gaulle. Of Alsatian stock and Norman upbringing, he had spent much of his time with the Foreign Legion, and he always had a few Legionnaires about him as personal orderlies: indeed, as High Commissioner in Germany he had a whole bodyguard of them. During that campaign in Syria, the pendulum of fortune swung almost as fast as the hand of a metronome, but nothing flustered Koenig. He has been one of my heroes ever since that first meeting in the smoky little room at Rhubarb; we have always kept in touch, and we foregather whenever I go to Paris.

Legentilhomme himself returned to Rhubarb two days after I got there, looking very pale and with his arm in a sling, but game as ever. An attack which Lloyd had staged and mounted was in full swing, and Legentilhomme made no effort to intervene, contenting himself with taking over the reins afterwards. He was a dapper little man in his late fifties, a Norman who had served mostly in the Colonial Infantry. When the war broke out he was C.-in-C. in Jibuti, and co-operated closely with Wavell in plans for the defence of Somaliland against the Italians; when France fell he declared for de Gaulle, but pressure within Jibuti was too strong for him, and he was obliged to escape to Aden by night at the beginning of August 1940. All his plans fell into Italian hands, which greatly helped their assault on Berbera. Since then he had successfully commanded the Free French Forces in their campaign in Eritrea. I liked him immensely, but he lacked the phlegm of Koenig, and was apt to get worked up when things went wrong. The last time I saw him was soon after the war, when he was Governor of Paris and had just married the British widow of an officer in the Royal Navy.

These were the principal *dramatis personae* on our side; on the other were the French Commander-in-Chief General Dentz, about whom I know little, and the Commander of the troops defending Damascus, General de Verdilhac. By all accounts de Verdilhac was a charming and dedicated man; and to illustrate the tragedy of this appalling war between Frenchmen, he was Legentilhomme's *camarade de promotion* both at St Cyr and at the Staff College; they were close friends, and Legentilhomme used to scratch his head and try to guess, from his long personal knowledge of de Verdilhac, what his next move might be, just like the two leading characters in General Swinton's *The Green Curve*.

The drama itself was too complicated to describe chronologically, but the setting deserves a word. Towering over us on the left, and parallel to our line of advance, were the tops of Hermon, snowy even in June. Along its foothills ran the other road to Damascus, emerging from northernmost Palestine and passing through Quneitra, which was held by the British battalion of the Indian Brigade. Quneitra from Rhubarb was only twenty-five miles as the crow flies, but sixty by road, since one had to travel right back to Sheikh Miskin: the country in between was strewn with rocks like lava, and uncrossable. The Quneitra road and our own converged gradually on Damascus, but there was no lateral to link them until you reached the range of low hills fifteen miles south of Damascus, that range being our next objective; and there the two roads were about ten miles apart. Immediately south of the range ran the biblical river "Pharpar." Beyond and above I could see the top of the familiar Jebel Qassioum which towers over the City; there would obviously be hard fighting ahead of us. The country was bare and without cover all the way south to Deraa, and this was one of the reasons why we suffered so heavily from air attack and were consequently so short of transport.

We were woefully short of artillery also: the French had one battery, the British the 1st Field Regiment R.A., plus one heavy and one light battery of A.A. We had also four, and only four, anti-tank guns, (not mentioned, these last, in the *Official History*). We shot down two aircraft in the course of the campaign, and one of them, alas, was British. It came over us suddenly, unexpectedly and low from behind a little hill; we were all cheering as we saw it hit and begin its somersault into the ground; and then we saw its R.A.F. roundels. It was a photo-reconnaissance plane, presumably trying to drop us some air-photographs; warning of its intended sortie had been sent us but, so shaky were our communications, had never reached us. There were no survivors.

There was one survivor, however, from a Vichy aircraft which we also shot down, and which fell a mile or so to the west of Rhubarb. The R.A.F. officer and Peter made their way across the lava to the wreck, which had not caught fire. They found in it the bodies of a captain and a lieutenant, and nearby a serjeant, injured but alive, who had been thrown clear on impact. I was present at his interrogation, which was gently done. When asked why none of the crew had tried to use their parachutes, he said that before taking off from Rayak they had been told that the Free French were shooting all prisoners, so it didn't seem worth it. One of my French comrades said: "That's the sort of thing we are fighting, then!" I tried to make him talk further after the others had left, but he turned on his face and began to weep.

I saw three of the six friends who had given me a farewell dinner in Damascus in January 1938. One, a Corsican called Cristofini, was with us; of another I saw the dead body; the third was a prisoner. He said to me: "I never thought to see you come into Syria like this. You would have been welcome as a guest." To Cristofini he would say not a word.

A successful but costly attack was mounted on the range that lay between us and Damascus. By sheer bad luck for the Vichys, it went in at a moment when a relief was being carried out. We heard afterwards that they were convinced there must have been treachery, and that we had had a tip-off, but it wasn't so: just luck. If we could have pushed on then, we might, in the confusion, have had a clear run into Damascus; but it was precisely now, while we were re-grouping and withstanding the inevitable counter-attack from my old comrades the Tirailleurs Marocains that we heard that our supply line had been cut at Sheikh Miskin, and that the British battalion at Quneitra was being heavily attacked, its outpost company having already been overrun. Sheikh Miskin was cleared fairly soon, though it cost the life of one of the Free French brigade commanders; but we had to draw heavily on our strength to find the troops to do it. The Quneitra situation was going from bad to worse. De Verdilhac had certainly made good use of his detachments, and timed his diversions brilliantly.

The liaison officer from the British battalion arrived, having driven all the way round by Sheikh Miskin, where he had been delayed by the fighting. He was an ex-Company-Serjeant-Major of that battalion, now a captain, and trying desperately to summon up his ultimate powers of persuasion. His battalion was in grievous trouble: surrounded, running short of ammunition and being attacked by tanks. (I didn't know it then, but I learned afterwards that attacking and surrounding Quneitra from the north with the help of tanks had been a stock peacetime French manoeuvre for years. It was reminiscent of Guderian's attack in France in May 1940, when he was able to lift his operation orders bodily from a "war game" held some months before, altering only the dates and times.) He begged me almost tearfully for some anti-tank guns, but I refused even to submit his request to Legentilhomme, and for strong reasons, apart from not wanting to embarrass the French with a British request. We would need our four anti-tank guns – all we had – to help blast our way into Damascus, and once we had got Damascus the problems of Quneitra, I thought, and its garrison, would be solved. (I was wrong.) Secondly, if we were to detach these precious four guns from the Damascus battle and send them lumbering round to Quneitra by way of Sheikh Miskin, they might well arrive too late to help the British battalion and would be lost to both flanks of the battle at the moment of its climax: an incident of war for which there is ample precedent in military history, including Waterloo and the Marne.

I hardened my heart, and in retrospect I am sure I was right; but I felt like a butcher. I had known that battalion all my service, and had many friends in it; I was casting myself in the role of "even mine old familiar friend whom I trusted . . ." The liaison officer looked at me as though I were Judas. He set off back on his long unhappy journey to Quneitra, and tried to insinuate his way through the Vichy French cordon; but it was impossible, even though an Australian battalion was now desperately trying to burst in. At 4 p.m., with not a round left to fire, the battalion surrendered. Satisfied with their triumph, the Vichys then withdrew with their prisoners. By this time, we, the main body, had extended to the west, and were astride the Quneitra-Damascus road. According to my calculations, we were now in a position to intercept the Vichy from Quneitra and liberate their prisoners. Unfortunately, with their local knowledge, they were aware, as we were not, of a track which led through the foothills of Hermon down on to the Damascus-Beirut road; and they gave us the slip, with their prisoners and all.

After the capture of the ridge, I was sent forward to find a new tactical headquarters, one which would be handier for the next phase. By this time, whatever my official position might be, I was *de facto*, and certainly through no desire of my own, G.S.O. 2 of the Free French Division and all attached troops. An honourable post it might be, but it was also most exhausting. Surprisingly few of the French spoke English and disgracefully few of the British spoke French, apart from the liaison officers who were seldom available at headquarters. I found myself involved not only in reducing orders to writing, but writing them out twice in both languages: in Camberley style for the British recipients (fresh in my memory), and in French style (desperately un-fresh) for the two French brigades. French orders are cast in a totally different sequence. Fortunately I had Boisseau's help for the French edition, but his English was not as good then as it was later, and the process was long. I used to go to bed in the small hours of the morning, whacked.

In my search for a new headquarters I was accompanied only by Peter Dorans. I settled on a Hobson's choice, which was luckily perfect for the purpose. It was Khan Denoun, a mile south of Kiswe village, well forward, but screened from enemy O.P.s by the hills; and I was the more encouraged to choose it because two Vichy 105mm. shells had struck the walls without penetrating. A *Khan* in this sense is what the poets call a caravanserai, dating from old trading days; a stone building, usually of two storeys, built round a square, in this case about a hundred yards each way. The lower storey was used for stabling and for storing the merchandise, the upper for sleeping accommodation. It made an admirable headquarters; and though it was shelled occasionally – it was such an obvious place for us to be in – its walls were so thick that we never had a casualty, and our vehicles were safe in the square, for reasons of trajectory. We were also bombed from the air once or twice, but without damage.

I went forward one day with a Free French officer to visit some Indian troops on the forward slopes of the range, from which they had a fine view first over the open ground, then of the green gardens of the Ghouta, and finally the minarets and towers of the City itself. It was terribly hot, the heat scorching up from the rocks in a sort of throbbing rhythm; several Indian soldiers died that day of heat stroke. Warned at their headquarters on the reverse slope that any movement on or over the sky-line would draw fire, my companion and I edged forward on our tummies, visited the two companies and returned over the crest. We had just stood erect again when there came to our ears the unexpected sound of trumpets. "Cavalry!" said the Frenchman incredulously. We went back to the top, not worrying this time about cover, and stood astonished at what we saw. It had indeed been a cavalry charge, by a squadron of Spahis, which without warning had broken out of the Ghouta and galloped across the open ground towards the lower slopes of the Jebel Madani, the hill on which we stood. By the time we reached our viewpoint the wave had spent itself, and the scene was like that of an old print, with riderless horses and running men making back for the shelter of the Ghouta, and others twitching and kicking on the plain, horses and men alike. There had been a cavalry charge by native mounted *askar* at Keren, led by a gallant Italian officer – killed – on a grey horse against a British battery, and everybody had assumed that that would be the last in history; but I had just seen, or just not seen, another one. It was a spirited performance, but they hadn't a hope of reaching their objective: even though the Indian troops, unable for a moment to believe their eyes, had withheld their fire for an appreciable time. I have never discovered who ordered it – if it was ordered – or who led it.

We were now held up all along the line of the range; but a plan was hatched for a new attack, with the French in the centre and the Indians, or some of them, thrusting on the left. They were to try to get along the last few miles of the Quneitra-Damascus road, and to cut at Mezze (where the airfield was, and still is) the road between Damascus and Beirut, a mile or so west of the City. It was a grim task, and we all knew it as Lloyd gave out his orders, glancing from time to time at his much-folded and dust-stained map. The colonel pondered them, looking at his own map, consulting his pencilled notes, and asking an occasional question. At last he looked direct at Lloyd and said: "I think you are condemning my men to death, Sir." Lloyd looked back at him, and said: "If you won't do it, I'll have to find somebody who will." There was a long pause; there was not a sound; my heart was bleeding for the colonel. At last he said: "In that case, of course I'll do it."

The attack went in that evening after dark. An hour later, one wounded British officer came back from the Indians, very pale and with five bullet-wounds through his upper arm, reporting that they had bumped into trouble on the road soon after beginning their advance, and were trying to by-pass the opposition by going round through the foothills on the west. We heard nothing more of them for thirty-six hours. Meanwhile the Free French, having made some progress, suffered heavily from artillery fire, and were compelled to fall back almost to their start line. The only cheerful news was that a British brigade, less one battalion, and two Australian battalions were on their way to reinforce us; the British brigadier, "Sunny" Lomax, had already arrived to study the form.

Early on the morning of the 20th, three exhausted officers stumbled into our lines, and were brought to our headquarters: André Brunel; a young sapper captain with the M.C. who had been with me in Essex in 1940; and an Indian Jemadar. The

Indians had successfully reached the Damascus-Beirut road by way of the hills by 5 a.m.; had cut it and blown the railway line; and had played havoc for a couple of hours, until the Vichy recovered from their surprise and set about them with machine-guns and medium tanks, against which they had no defence. By 9 a.m. all who had not been killed or captured had been driven into a house and garden overlooking the river, where they were attacked all day long by tanks and even by .75 guns. They had no food, many wounded and a number of prisoners. The house belonged to the local manager of the Iraq Petroleum Company: they had replaced the wine in the bottles in his well-stocked cellar with petrol from his equally well-stocked garage: with the resulting Molotov cocktails they had kept the tanks at bay all day, but with ever-mounting casualties. They had no wireless, for they had been unable to man-handle it through the hills, and therefore no means of communicating with us. These three officers had responded to a call for volunteers, and after dark had climbed the wall, got into the hills and brought us the news.

A small relief force was put together under a gunner major, Bourke. The first Australian battalion was just arriving, but they proved to be only 250 strong. It was decided to give them a few hours' rest before involving them. Later in the morning I was sent up to liaise with Pat Bourke, which I did in a 15 cwt. truck, driven by an Indian; Peter Dorans and a *Daily Mail* correspondent, a glutton for punishment, came with me. We were shelled all the way from a fort on the top of a hill on our left, and had an uncomfortable run. Later Bourke and I had a bad five minutes on the edge of Mezze aerodrome from a Vichy machine-gun, having to skulk in a ditch until it was stalked and put out of action by some of our people.

During the early hours of that morning I had been driven nearly mad at Khan Denoun by the badgering of war correspondents. They had their job to do, but so had I, and I was abysmally tired. They wanted to know the plans for the capture of Damascus. At last I finished writing the orders in both styles and languages, and agreed to see them; I warned them that the plans were terribly secret, and that if they leaked out, hundreds of lives would be forfeit: they promised they would reveal nothing. I told them everything, and went to bed. Suddenly I realised that half of them were Americans, and – America being still neutral – not bound to keep their mouths shut. Dog-tired as I was, I couldn't sleep a wink for worrying; but I need not have fashed myself: not one of them gave a thing away. I had learned a useful lesson about the Press.

For twenty-four hours, we had heard loud explosions from Damascus: they were blowing up dumps, a good sign; there were other indications also that they were preparing to pull out. Meanwhile Lloyd, picking up some of the Australians, had joined and reinforced Bourke, and was crashing his way into Mezze, with the guns firing over open sights. They reached the defenders' house at 6 p.m., to find that all was over. One side of the house had collapsed; within the walls were over a hundred bodies. Three burnt-out Vichy tanks lay just outside the garden. We found in a hospital afterwards an Indian medical officer who had been left behind with the surviving wounded, and he told us the rest of the story. The roof had fallen in shortly before 2 p.m., when there was practically no ammunition left. They had sent out a Vichy officer prisoner with a white flag to parley; but as soon as the gate was opened some Senegalese troops poured in, shot two Indian soldiers and were restrained only just in time from shooting the little group of surviving officers in the corner of the garden. They had not so much surrendered as been overwhelmed.

Next morning the defenders of Damascus had gone. Some had probably left already by the Beirut road; the remainder went north towards Homs and Hama. Unfortunately we had recovered none of the prisoners. The Vichy troops had fought with skill and courage, and our victory, if it could be so described, was rather hollow; but all the same Damascus was ours.

The honour of being first into Damascus went to two American war correspondents, friends and professional rivals of long standing. Although neutrals, they had to wear uniforms like all other war correspondents. They used to address each other as "General McClellan" and "General Burnside," on the grounds that those Civil War officers had been the two most incompetent wearers of uniform ever known – hitherto. When Damascus was obviously on the point of falling, they decided to trust to their neutral status to get them in with impunity, so that they could witness the triumphal entry from the receiving end. They therefore set out along the road; but having got a certain distance they were fired on by a Vichy armoured car. They dismounted from their own vehicle and took shelter in a culvert that ran under the road. Unfortunately it narrowed, so that while one of them was well in, the rump of the other was sticking out. Desmond Young, afterwards well known as the editor of the *Rommel Papers*, was present with the force as Public Relations officer, and had rashly decided to accompany these two. As there was no room for him in the culvert, he remained on the road with his hands up. He was therefore privileged to hear the following dialogue from the bowels of the earth: –

First Muffled Voice: "General McClellan, will you please get farther in? My ass is stickin' out."
Second and even more Muffled Voice: "Sorry, General Burnside, I cann't get my head any farther in."
First Muffled Voice: "But say, General McClellan, my ass is a more important militairy target than your head."

In the end they were both dragged out, and taken with Desmond as prisoners to Damascus. There they made such a fuss about their neutral and non-combatant status that they were taken to Beirut, the last thing they wanted, while Desmond was retained.

To anticipate a little, the bulk of the British and Indian prisoners taken at Quneitra and Mezze were recovered in the Lebanon after the Armistice, which was negotiated at Acre and signed on the 14th July – the Quatorze Juillet, the French national holiday; but the officer prisoners had already been removed overseas, and were in durance at Salonika. The Armistice terms, as insisted on by Wilson, included the return of these officers; and an equivalent number of Vichy French officers was to be retained until our own had come back. It still surprises me that the Germans did not veto what followed: the officers found themselves doing a Cook's tour through Europe, including Germany and Occupied France, to Marseilles, whence they were eventually returned to Beirut and released. But the party, when it arrived, was one short: an Indian Jemadar had been taken ill *en route* and was detained in hospital. Wilson released the Vichy officer prisoners who had been kept as hostages, all except one, whom he held pending the return of the Jemadar; and that one was General Dentz himself. The exchange duly took place, but I doubt if the bitterness engendered by the equation of the French Commander-in-Chief with so junior an officer was worth the candle.

The triumphal entry was at least more dignified than Desmond Young's, but not quite as dignified as we had hoped. It was planned for 4 p.m., and Legentilhomme was looking forward to it as a small boy to a treat. He despatched Colonel Collet (whom the French regarded in much the same light as we regarded Glubb Pasha) into the City to engage and send out for us some suitable cars, and superintended in person the polishing of his best boots. Representatives of the City Fathers had already driven out to call on us at 10 a.m. At 3 p.m. the cars arrived, and we were about to get into them when there was a clamour of noise from the south, and lorry after lorry of yelling Australians drove past, covering us all with dust. Legentilhomme, livid, made one attempt to stop them, but had to jump clear; I didn't have the guts to try. We brushed each other down, and got into the cars; Legentilhomme and Koenig in the first, Boisseau and I in the second.

A few hundred yards short of the Hejaz railway station, not far from the British Consulate where I had called on MacKereth, we were met by a mounted escort of Collet's Circassians. The cars changed into bottom gear, to keep pace, but not being royal Daimlers the result was unhappy: they hiccoughed, spluttered and stalled. What was more, nobody had thought to stop the trams running, and they halted at all their usual places to set down and pick up passengers in their accustomed manner: the streets being narrow, we were obliged to stop too. We went down the hill, across the Barada and up the other side to the Etat-Major, where the Syrian Cabinet was awaiting the General. In the crowd, cheering like mad and waving his hat, was an Australian lieutenant-colonel wearing most un-military pince-nez. I recognised him as the man who had been sitting beside the driver of the leading Australian lorry as it squealed past us at Khan Denoun. Presumably because I was the only British officer in the party, he shook my hand saying excitedly: "I was first!" I was wondering whether this might be one of the few occasions when one dared suggest to an Australian that he should have behaved otherwise, when my eye fell on his 1914-1918 medal ribbons. Ragged as they were, the first was indubitably the Victoria Cross, the first I had ever encountered unexpectedly; so I choked back whatever it was I had in mind to say. He turned out to be one Arthur Blackburn, in private life Coroner for the City of Adelaide: another good reason, perhaps, for keeping my mouth shut. He was afterwards made prisoner by the Japs while commanding the Australians in Java, but survived his captivity.

Just opposite the Etat-Major was the Officers' Club, which I immediately entered. Behind the bar was the same Syrian barman as of old, who recognised me at once; and as he gave me a drink he said: "I have a surprise for you!" He opened a door behind him, and there emerged Desmond Young, looking filthy and with a three-day growth of beard, hung with bits of spider's web. He and the officer prisoners from Mezze had been given a meal in the Club before being driven away up the Homs road; Desmond, with the connivance of the barman (who realised that the probable duration of the defence could be measured in hours) had hidden behind the bar: here he was. I was enjoying a drink with him, when the General's A.D.C. came in looking for me: I was wanted at once. I followed him across the street into the Etat-Major, and found Legentilhomme at a long polished table, with all the Syrian Cabinet Ministers, some in Arab but most in European dress. He made me sit beside him for a moment while he told them who I was. Then he turned to me.

"These gentlemen tell me," he said, "that there is only enough food in the town for to-morrow's needs, and after that – nothing. Please arrange for one hundred tons of wheat to reach Damascus daily until further notice. Thank you!"

"Certainly, *mon Général*," I said, and left the room accepting grateful handshakes from Cabinet Ministers as I passed along the table. But my heart sank. How did one do this? I had had fast balls bowled at me at Camberley, but never one of this type. Now was the time to use that direct access to Wilson which he had promised me. I made him a signal headed "General Wilson from Fergusson – Most Immediate," a prefix which I was not entitled to use, explaining the situation and hoping for the best. Then, telling the A.D.C. where I was to be found, I went and booked a room at my old stamping-ground, the Orient Palace Hotel, where again I found a welcome from members of the staff who remembered me, though unlike the trams it was scarcely running on "Business as Usual" lines.

So I decided to dine at the Officers' Club. Others had had the same idea, and there was quite a gathering of Free French officers and the two or three British liaison officers. Suddenly the door burst open, and in rushed Bob de Kersausson, an ebullient Breton major who had not only joined the Free French, but also, somehow, the 11th Hussars, and always wore their famous cherry-coloured trousers; he had already contrived to make himself a prominent figure in Middle East military society. He had invaded General Dentz's house, and found a pile of invitation cards for a cocktail party there that night; the names had not been filled in, and obviously they had been ordered before our crossing of the frontier. He thrust one on each of us, and I kept mine for ages.

It wasn't a very merry party, apart from that; the events of the past few days hung on us too heavily. As I left the Club, I passed a heavily-veiled woman in black, who looked at me and gave me a slight bow as she passed on. I went back to ask the barman who she was. It was Madame de la Chauvellais, the widow of Pierre who had given me my letters of introduction in Jerusalem in 1937: he had been killed fighting for Vichy at Kiswe a few days before.

Back in the hotel, I found in the *foyer*, just arrived from Jerusalem, Charlie Mott-Radclyffe in the Rifle Brigade, one of Jumbo Wilson's liaison officers; we had been at school together. He had come forward to get a clearer picture of our adventures and fortunes than it had been possible to piece together back at base. There was another bed in my room, so we doubled up. Early next morning I heard lorries driving past, and Charlie and I went out on to the verandah of the window in our pyjamas. It was a long convoy of trucks, and every one of them was carrying wheat. "Golly!" I said to myself; "that was quick work." Half an hour later I was told that I was wanted downstairs, and was met in the foyer by a couple of grateful Cabinet Ministers, who thanked me effusively. "*Mais c'était la moindre des choses,*" I said airily. I learned later, first, that Wilson never got my signal; secondly, that the wheat had been arranged for by John Gardener the former Consul-General, who was on his way back in uniform as Political Officer – he had foreseen the need; and thirdly, that when Gardener eventually arrived, expecting some modicum of thanks, all he got was an earful about this wonderful chap Fergusson, who had procured quantities of wheat overnight.

That was a memorable morning for another reason: we heard over the radio that Germany had attacked Russia. We were so concerned with our own affairs that this news seemed to belong to another world; I don't think we realised what a turning-point it was in the war: we just got on with tidying up the local mess. I had strict orders that for political reasons no British, Indian, or Australian troops were to enter Damascus; and these clashed with the wishes of the Free French, who wanted their own troops released to continue the pursuit. This was surprising: my orders stemmed from the anxiety of the British not to get involved in the Syrian desire to kick the French out; it was intended as a demonstration of our impartiality in the matter, whereas the French took it as another instance of our unwillingness to co-operate.

From this arose my first and only meeting with General de Gaulle. He arrived in Damascus on the 23rd June, and I hoped I might have a chance of being at least introduced to this paladin of a man. I was, but I didn't enjoy the experience as much as I was expecting to. He said to me coldly that he understood I was refusing to allow Imperial troops (as they were still called in those days) to enter Damascus to release French ones for other purposes. I explained that these were my orders from Wavell and Wilson, and that I had no option but to comply with them. He said: – *"Mais moi, de Gaulle, j'annule vos ordres!"* I trembled a bit, but stood my ground. After a few more exchanges, he said: – *"Quittez mon bureau!"* and I quit it, and to my regret have never met him since.

Meanwhile, I couldn't stir in the streets without mysterious Syrians sidling up to me with anti-French propositions. What with them, and with French officers at lower levels than de Gaulle and Legentilhomme pleading with me to ignore my orders, and do the opposite, and allow Imperial Troops into the City, it was a relief to open a Secret letter from Cairo, enclosed in several envelopes and heavy with sealing-wax, giving me a job to do which would take me out of Damascus.

This was from General Arthur Smith. One of the cloak-and-dagger organisations in Cairo – Aly Khan had something to do with it – had made startling claims concerning their achievements behind the Vichy Lines, both before and during the recent campaign. They had certainly paid out large sums of money to their agents. Bridges had been blown here, arms dumps there, sabotage committed at the other place, if their reports were true. G.H.Q. was sceptical: would I check, covering as much ground as possible and submitting a report in five days' time? A list of claims was enclosed. I commandeered a car with a Syrian driver, and set off with Peter Dorans down the familiar road past Khan Denoun to Sanamein, Sheikh Miskin and Deraa. I also visited Quneitra, cross-examining the local inhabitants about the fighting there. I made my way gradually to Beirut, still checking on these claims: only two, possibly three, out of a dozen had any substance. While I was in Beirut there was a major brawl in the streets between Australians and Free French soldiers. Colonels Monclar and Casaud, two Foreign Legion officers, witnessed it; and instead of sending for the Military Police had joined in, like true Legionnaires, getting bloody noses for their pains. I was deputed to offer them an apology, but they waved it aside. Monclar said: "Don't apologise: it was one of the best fights I've ever been in!"

I now got another message from General Arthur Smith: a signal this time, and one which had been chasing me all round Syria and the Lebanon. I was to report to Cairo at once.

6

ALL the way down from Beirut I wondered what was in the wind: whether I was being sent on some other special job, or merely returned to my desk. It was a bombshell when General Arthur Smith told me that Wavell was being relieved by Auchinleck, and was to go to India as Commander-in-Chief in his stead: close as I had been to Wavell, I had no idea of the degree to which his relations with the Prime Minister had deteriorated. The second shock was when Arthur Smith said that I was to accompany Wavell as his Private Secretary. I am ashamed that I at once said I didn't want to go: here was my chance to get back to the Battalion, which had been my whole object in getting myself posted to the Middle East. Arthur Smith said that if I let "the Chief" down now, after all that I owed him, I would never forgive myself as long as I lived; and at once I felt very small, and of course gave way. He bound me to secrecy, for no announcement had yet been made; but Auchinleck was already on his way, and Wavell and I would be leaving within two or three days, with one A.D.C. When the moment came, the little gathering of subordinates and staff officers who came to see the party off at the airfield could hardly believe what they were witnessing. Among them was Major des Essars, who got into trouble with de Gaulle for being present.

I have written at length elsewhere* of the six weeks I spent with Wavell in India. He had promised when we left Cairo that he would release me as soon as he could, and he was as good as his word. Within seven weeks I was back in Cairo, and in the same flat with the same stable-mates. I was still Wavell's

*Wavell: Portrait of a Soldier, pp. 63-66.

man, in that I was working on his final Middle East Despatch. This involved burrowing among mountains of signals, cables, appreciations, arguments, counter-arguments, which had accumulated over the seven or eight months before Wavell's final dismissal. The period covered Ethiopia, the Sudan, Greece, Crete, Iraq, Syria and several different campaigns in the Western Desert; and I was working against time, since Wavell expected to pass through Cairo shortly on a visit to Britain, and the draft had to be ready for him by then: checked to the minutest detail, polished as to its prose, and typed. After that, he had said, so far as he was concerned I could go back to the Regiment.

Arthur Smith laid on me a specific extra duty while working on the Despatch. He gave me access to a file which he had put together gradually over the last nine months or so, and told me to keep an eye open for similar material as I went through the mass of documentation. He was concerned that some day historians and others might be seeking to allocate praise or blame as between Churchill and Wavell; and he wanted every relevant scrap of signal or letter which had passed between the two to be not only preserved, but easily located when the time came. Some of them had hitherto been seen only by Wavell and himself. I did as he told me, adding some documents to the file and removing others which no longer seemed to have a direct bearing. I know that Arthur Smith intended only two copies of the ultimate file to exist: no doubt one was destined for "the record," and the other for Wavell himself. I do not know what happened to them, or whether they were available to the Official Historians or to John Connell, Wavell's biographer. Certainly the summing-up in the Official History* of the strained relations between those two great figures shewed understanding and sympathy for Wavell's position, and attracted much attention when the relevant volume appeared in 1956, eight years before Churchill's death and six after Wavell's.

By the time Wavell reached Cairo early in September I had a respectable draft ready for him. (I can still detect a few traces of my own hand in some of the duller passages.) For three solid

*The Mediterranean and Middle East, Vol. II, H.M.S.O. 1956, pp. 244-6.

days we worked on it until he was satisfied that it was ready for the press; I had already sent great chunks of it to him in India. Meanwhile, I had encountered trouble in arranging for his onward passage to Britain. A week before his arrival in Cairo, I had gone blithely along to fix it with R.A.F. Headquarters, which were in the same "Grey Pillars" building as G.H.Q., not expecting any bother. I found myself being fobbed off with every sort of obstruction. I asked to see Tedder, the A.O.C.-in-C. but he was away. I managed to see his Deputy, whose name there is no need to reveal; he said that Wavell was no longer of any importance to the Middle East theatre, and he could take his turn on the waiting list like anybody else. I reported to Arthur Smith, who signalled Tedder, and all was well; but I found it hard to forgive that churlish Deputy, even when he was killed some years later in an air crash.

Wavell went on to London, with his devoted A.D.C. Sandy Reid-Scott in the 11th Hussars, who had lost an eye in the Desert early on; Sandy, of whom Wavell was to write to his father that he was "one in a million"; Sandy, who was to die of cancer at the early age of forty-two in 1960. I was left lamenting like Lord Ullin; I could have done with a trip home; but I lamented even more when I discovered that I still hadn't succeeded in working my passage back to the Battalion. I found myself a G.S.O. 2 in the Operations Branch. I put in a typed plea to Arthur Smith, pointing out how long I had been away from regimental duty – ever since September 1937, four years exactly – and added in my own hand: "Surely this will melt the stoniest heart?" It came back, endorsed in *his* own hand, and in the green ink which only he in all G.H.Q. was allowed to use: "Heart half melted. Try again in three months, and see what's happened to the other half. A.F.S." I have it in my scrap-book, and I had the fun of shewing it to him when he was my guest in Scotland in 1968, twenty-seven years later.

This was a cruel disappointment. I had been virtually certain when I left India that I would be allowed back as soon as I had polished off the Despatch. By the end of October I was feeling even worse about it. The Australian garrison which had been

cooped up in Tobruk since the previous April was being relieved by the British 70th Division, which except for one
battalion consisted of Regular battalions which had been in the
Middle East on the outbreak of war. My own Battalion travelled
up there on the night of the 22nd October, in three destroyers
and a fast mine-layer; I felt I should be with it, but I was still in
G.H.Q. My only consolation was that if one had to be there
the Operations Branch was the most interesting. We were small
and select: counting the Brigadier at the top, there were only
ten of us altogether. Pat Tweedie was one of the others.

Though different in so many ways from Wavell, Auchinleck
also inspired deep affection and respect. I had met him first
when I was Wavell's A.D.C. There had been a Kipling-type
campaign against the Mohmands on the North-West Frontier
of India, when a situation with all the makings of a shambles
was redeemed by "The Auk's" intervention at the crucial
moment. This Nahakki Pass battle had caught the public
imagination, and for a short time, until it was diverted by other
things, he was a national hero. He had come to Aldershot to
witness some manoeuvres of Wavell's before returning to India
to be Deputy Chief of the General Staff. He had taken a prominent part in the Norwegian campaign, and then been made
Commander-in-Chief of Southern Command in England, an
appointment without precedent for an officer of the Indian
Army. Everybody liked and trusted him. It always seemed to
me that he still had the frank, open and uncomplicated look and
character of a Wellington prefect, which was exactly what he
had been. It was in keeping with that character that he was
sensitive to the anti-G.H.Q. gibes of the fighting troops, and
to such phrases as "Gaberdine Swine" and "Mena Household
Cavalry" – a reference to Mena House, a smart and expensive
hotel near the Pyramids.

In great secrecy, preparations for the winter offensive were
building up. Auchinleck was refusing to be hurried by Churchill, and was determined to take his time. The Desert Army
was commanded by Alan Cunningham, brother of the naval
Commander-in-Chief Andrew, who had been such a staunch

friend and ally of Wavell through all the ups and downs of the last year. General Cunningham's defeat of the Italians in East Africa had raised his reputation to a great height. That campaign had been a triumph of doggedness and improvisation over every sort of obstacle, especially those of terrain and climate. There could have been no more complete contrast to the swiftly-moving war of the Desert, and the mental adjustment required of Cunningham would have been difficult for anybody. It was tantamount to saying: "If you can drive a bulldozer, you can drive a racing-car." I remember when I was still at my desk in Cairo, during the early phases of the battle, anguished signals coming in from Sandy Galloway, Cunningham's Brigadier General Staff, saying that he was out of touch with his Commander. I fancy that during the slow-moving developments of East Africa and Ethiopia an absence of a few hours, or even a day or two, might not affect the issue of events, whereas in the Desert it could be, and nearly was, disastrous.

Although not concerned with the Desert myself, I was naturally *au fait* with what was going on, since John Ormiston, the staff officer directly concerned, worked in the same room. I knew that on the 21st November 14th Brigade of 70th Division – and my Battalion belonged to that Brigade – was to break out of the Tobruk Perimeter, and link up with the relieving troops. Obviously there was hard fighting ahead of them, but the auguries looked good. We heard in the afternoon that the link up had failed, and my heart sank: there were bound to have been heavy casualties, but no details had come in.

I was working late in my office. The others, including the weary John Ormiston, had gone home. My telephone rang, and on the other end of it was David Rose, in the Regiment. He had been wounded, and had won an immediate D.S.O., with the 2nd Battalion in Somaliland in August 1940; after a spell in hospital in India he had been put on the training staff of H.Q. British Troops in Egypt until he was fully fit again. He was virtually my contemporary: six months junior to me. I remember the conversation word for word.

"Are you coming back to your flat soon?"

"Well, I could come back now. Where are you speaking from?"

"Your flat. Have you seen the casualty list?"

"What casualty list?"

"The Battalion's. It's bad."

"I'll be back at once."

I found David in the flat, having a drink, with a slip of paper in his hand. It contained the names of all the officer casualties sustained during the break-out, and it included almost everybody we knew. Nine officers had been killed, and sixteen wounded; the figures for the other ranks ran into hundreds. David and I between us could think of only three officers not on the list, though obviously there would be others lately joined whom we wouldn't know of. But twenty-five officer casualties meant that at best they would be down to half a dozen. Obviously we were needed.

Next morning at 8 a.m. I waylaid Arthur Smith as he arrived at G.H.Q., and told him the form. He said: "Come up to my office." Once there, I shewed him David Rose's list. With a grim face, he wrote at his desk, and handed what he had written to me. He said: "Come back and see me before you go, and I'm sure The Chief will want to say Good-bye to you."

His chit read roughly as follows: –

1. Major B. E. Fergusson, The Black Watch, to be relieved of all duties with effect from this morning.
2. Major Fergusson is authorised to collect all officers and men of The Black Watch, whatever their duties, who are fit for active service, and to take them up with him to rejoin 2 B.W. in Tobruk.
3. Major Fergusson and his party will be given top priority for all transport necessary to get them to Tobruk as soon as possible.

A. F. Smith
Major-General.

I rang up David Rose, and we got together at once collecting people. It took a little time, but within three days we were on our way to Alexandria, six officers and sixty-four men: ex-staff, ex-leave, ex-hospital, including, of course, Peter Dorans. We were stuck for two nights in the transit camp at Amiriya; however much I might brandish General Smith's magic piece of paper, there just was not a ship ready to take us up at that moment. On the third day, at crack of dawn, we boarded the *Chakdina*, a British India ship which before the war had been on the run between Calcutta and Akyab. She was chock-a-block with troops and stores.

Beleaguered Tobruk was being sustained by two types of convoy. It was winter, and the nights were comparatively long, though not, of course, by British standards. The first type consisted of swift in-and-out trips by destroyers during the hours of darkness; the second of convoys which had to risk much of the passage by daylight, but still arrived, discharged and departed in the dark. *Chakdina* had not done the run before, but our convoy was to be, in theory, one of the second category. As the various ships – they were not numerous – assembled off Alexandria, a destroyer steamed close by us, and addressed us through her loud-hailer.

"What speed can you make?" she asked.

"Seven knots," came our answer.

"Christ!" said the destroyer; and paused before adding: "Well, in that case, good luck!"

We then saw the rest of the convoy, plus the escorting destroyers, creaming off to the westward with all speed, while we churned along breathlessly astern, with the gap between us widening every minute. Long before the afternoon was over, all other ships were out of sight, though we passed a few lighters on their way back, presumably, from Tobruk. Crowded though the ship was, we were able to prowl around a bit, and I found one or two old friends. It was a bright blue, chilly day, but nothing to the chill of the night when it came on; and we did not object to the orders that we should remain fully dressed with our greatcoats on, in case of trouble during the hours of darkness.

It came just about dawn. We had passed all the other ships in our convoy hastening back to Alexandria, having got rid of their passengers and cargo under cover of night. Our slow speed had condemned us to entering and discharging by day. The alarm suddenly went, and we all stood by our boats while a German aircraft, seeming to hover just above us, loosed an aerial torpedo at us – and missed. In the growing light we saw the white houses of Tobruk beyond the harbour. The entrance had been partly closed by a boom, so that it was only a cable wide. As we drew nearer, enemy guns opened up, and the narrow gap looked like a mass of water-spouts. We had been warned before sailing to bring with us only what we could carry; now the ship's loud-hailer told us to stand by to disembark with all speed as soon as we were alongside. We needed no encouragement. Between water-spouts we could see the masts and funnels of sunken ships sticking out of the sea all over the harbour.

It seemed incredible that we should get through unscathed; but we did, and berthed by a ship or a lighter which had been sunk alongside the jetty. Aboard her a bearded naval officer, despite the racket of the shelling, was calling out orders calmly through a megaphone. Gangways were out immediately, and we filed quickly across the sunken ship and ashore, where guides awaited us. They took us to rear headquarters for the day. There over innumerable cups of tea we heard details of that single bloody early-morning hour in which the Battalion had been reduced to a quarter of its strength.

Its task had been to pass through the perimeter at 6.30 a.m. and to advance two or three miles in a south-easterly direction, supported by tanks. The tanks had failed to report in time, and the advance had to start without them; when at last they arrived, they set off on a wrong bearing, so that the Battalion on the left had twice its allotment of tanks, and The Black Watch none. Even without the tanks, they carried almost the whole way to their objective. Rusk the Colonel, whom I had known ever since my boyhood, went off in a truck, having already had two vehicles shot from under him, collected the tanks and brought them back on to the objective, where the remnants of the Battalion joined them. Out of thirty-two officers and 600 men who crossed the start line, eight officers and 160 men were all that was left an hour later. Two of the companies had no officers at all; one had fewer than ten men, and was being commanded by its C.S.M., who had been a lance-corporal in my original platoon ten years earlier. "Big Jim" Ewan, one of my corporals in those days, now a captain and a company commander, was one of the unwounded: his company and a handful of sappers took over the left flank; my first cousin Richard Boyle and the remnants of the other three rifle companies the right; H.Q. Company under Gerald Barry (a former Coldstreamer with a Military Cross from the First War who had joined us from Rhodesia) the centre. Roy the Pipe-Major, my former platoon piper, had played the Battalion into action, continuing to play despite three wounds. He had already been wounded and taken prisoner in Crete, but had escaped from Greece through Turkey and rejoined, refusing an offer to be repatriated to Britain. For the rest of his life, until one day he dropped down dead in Edinburgh Castle, he was known throughout Scotland as "The Piper of Tobruk." His younger brother Neil, also a piper, was to be killed with the 1st Battalion in Korea in 1952.

After dark, we climbed into trucks, and were driven by Gordon Nicholson the Transport Officer and his men as far forward as was safe. We were then led stumbling through the night to the position, and a warm welcome from a weary "Ruskie." We had already heard what a wonderful battle he had fought: he had taken more risks than anybody, and nobody could think how he had come through: he had also been one of the few survivors of the Battle of Loos in 1915. He had been warned of our arrival, and had already re-organised the Battalion accordingly in his mind's eye. David Rose was to be Adjutant (Mungo Stirling had been fatally wounded, though he was still fighting for his life in hospital), and I to take over D Company. It was therefore in D Company's position that I stood to at dawn, with two officers who had come up in the *Chakdina* with me; and I was glad to find that I knew two of the N.C.O.s from of old. Among the killed was a Kilkerran man, Serjeant Andrew Scobie, whom I had enlisted in 1932.

Except for occasional shelling, things were pretty quiet. The slightest movement by day would bring on ten minutes' punishment, so it was strictly forbidden. I was astonished to learn at first hand what I had so often been told: what a tremendous amount of shelling you can withstand without incurring casualties if you are well dug in with plenty of head-cover. Early on, I witnessed fifteen minutes' hard on Battalion Headquarters, and began composing obituary notices for Ruskie and David, since I was sure they must have been obliterated; but it didn't even break the telephone cable. I rang up as soon as it stopped, and heard David's voice reassuring me that they were "Dirty, but otherwise fine." My own company got a pasting the following day, but the only damage was one broken arm and the loss of a dixie of tea.

While in Cairo, I had suffered like Marshall-Cornwall from a skin complaint, and had been recommended to a Jewish-Austrian specialist. His advice was to forego all salt, and anything out of a tin. I was following this régime religiously, and getting steadily worse, when I went up to Tobruk. There everything came out of a tin, and all the water was brackish: within a week I was right as rain. Probably the real cause of my trouble was Ali's rich *cuisine*. We were on half-rations in Tobruk. The only thing that seemed to be plentiful was tea, but there was only enough water where we were for three or four mugs a day. The weather was desperately cold, with a biting north wind, and we were wearing everything we possessed, so that one could hardly raise one's arm to the salute; but the worst feature was the fleas. We were occupying former Italian positions and using Italian blankets *faute de mieux*.

The relief force, which the sortie had been intended to help, had been bogged down south-east of Tobruk, taking part in hard fighting at Sidi Resegh and elsewhere. The enemy had detached enough forces to prevent any further attempt by the Tobruk garrison to intervene, but was otherwise content to leave us alone. We could hear the guns thundering away, and at times see the dust of tanks manoeuvring round each other on the high ground about El Adem and Ed Duda. At no time were we attacked, but we took all precautions, with patrols and listening posts thrust out by night. These last would take out telephones with them, unreeling the cable behind them.

Ruskie was holding a conference one evening after dark when we heard some shots away out in front of my company position. A few minutes later the N.C.O. in charge of my listening post came back with all his men, saying that he had been driven in by a stronger enemy patrol. He was rattled; he confessed that all the shots had been fired by his own people; everything had been quiet for the last two nights; and the most likely explanation was that they had panicked. He had abandoned his telephone and failed to reel in the cable. It was arranged that I should take out a fighting patrol to investigate; and I told Richard Boyle that I would go out from my front, and come in through his. I put on a pair of white tennis shoes so that my feet would be visible to those immediately behind me; and off we went, with the signal cable running through my hand as a quick guide to our destination. As we expected, there was no sign of any enemy; and I sent three men back the way we had come, with the telephone and reeling in the line, while with the rest of the party I did a cautious chukka round before making my way on a compass bearing towards Richard's company front. We approached it with caution, and I was hoping that my navigation would prove accurate, when I heard a loud voice shout: "Fire!" and a lot of small arms fire broke out, including at least one Bren.

We dropped to the ground, and I called out in rude and unmistakable English rude and unmistakable reproaches. A voice called: "Cease fire! Who the bloody hell are you?"

"Major Fergusson and his patrol. Is that Major Boyle's company? If so, get him."

There was a pause, while we continued to lie on the ground. Mercifully nobody had been hit. Then came Richard Boyle's voice, with its familiar stammer: –

"Is that you, B-Bernard?"

"Yes, it is!" I roared; "and I'm going to write to Uncle Jack about this!"

Apparently the conference had continued after I left it; he had only just got back, and hadn't had time to warn his people that I would be coming through. Assured of a safe conduct, we entered his position, and I met for the first time Duncan Menzies, the officer who had legitimately opened fire on us. He was a magnificent South Australian Rhodes Scholar of Highland descent, who had first enlisted and then been commissioned into the Regiment from Balliol as soon as the war broke out. He was pretty abashed at this moment, though it wasn't his fault. He was one of the only two rifle company subalterns who had come unscathed through the holocaust of the 21st November.

Our chief source of news in Tobruk was Gerald Barry's wireless set, which he had brought up with him from Egypt. It was from this that we heard of the Japanese attack on Pearl Harbour, and of the devastating loss three days later of the *Prince of Wales* and *Repulse*. For all that these events were happening so far away, for all that we realised that America was now in the war on our side, for all that our own immediate battle was over, our morale slumped to a low level. The snakes in this war game seemed so much more numerous just then than the ladders.

The tide of battle eventually passed us by, the German withdrawal sweeping westward away to the south of us. For the one small mopping-up operation in which the Battalion was engaged, my company was somehow overlooked; and I didn't know that anything was happening until I found that Battalion Headquarters and everybody else had left their locations. Then the relief was complete, and we were withdrawn inside the perimeter to lick our wounds. I was walking down a road when a car drew up with a squeal of brakes, and out got Neil Ritchie of the Regiment, dressed as a lieutenant-general. I goggled a bit; I had seen him less than two weeks before, as a major-general and D.C.G.S. in G.H.Q. The news had not percolated through to us – perhaps it had not then been announced – that Alan Cunningham had been superseded, and Neil Ritchie appointed in his room.

It was not until we came out of the line that we had confirmation of the rumours about *Chakdina*, the ship that had brought up my party of reinforcements. There were so many casualties in the Tobruk hospital that the staff could not cope with them, and some poor unknown devil has or had on his conscience the decision to send them back to Egypt on board a non-hospital ship. Since the war I have met several Germans who know about the sinking of the *Chakdina*, and who have maintained with vehemence, even though I was not contradicting them, that she was not a recognised hospital ship. I can only suppose that they knew about the episode because one of their most distinguished generals happened to be aboard her.

Genuine hospital ships and their passage are known and notified. I remember how, when travelling from Malta to Port Said in that tanker with Peter Smith-Dorrien, an Italian hospital ship had crossed our bows, on a south-to-north course: her lights blazing, her Red Cross brilliantly lit up. A cynical ship's officer from Scotland had said: "That settles oor hash; Red Cross or nae Red Cross, she'll report us: I'm tellin' ye!" We couldn't believe him: she looked so pacific, almost reproachful. But *Chakdina* was not a hospital ship, neither marked nor registered nor illumined as such; and consequently fair game for the aerial torpedo that sank her, four hours after clearing Tobruk, and fifteen after she had put my detachment ashore there.

She sank in three and a half minutes. Of the twenty-three Black Watch wounded on board, only seven were rescued, including Neville Blair and John Benson. The German General Von Ravenstein, the commander of the 21st Panzer Division, captured by the New Zealanders a few days before, had been locked in his cabin by the British officer escorting him. When the ship was hit, he wriggled through his porthole, and so was among the rescued; his escorting officer went below to look for him, and was among the lost. Seven years later, when I was commanding our 1st Battalion at Duisburg in the Ruhr as part of the army of occupation, I found Von Ravenstein, stripped of his estates in East Prussia, working humbly as Assistant

Town Clerk, and living in a two-roomed flat with his wife, the German-born cousin of a Scotch Duke. I contrived a meeting between him and Wavell, but somehow it wasn't a success: Von Ravenstein was at his most loquacious, Wavell at his most taciturn.

We had only been two or three days out of the line when I was suddenly told to take over the prisoner of war cage, which I did in the middle of a dust-storm when I couldn't see anything. When the dust had died down, I found myself in the following situation. Within a barbed wire rectangle 1,200 yards long and 350 broad were 6,000 Italian prisoners, 300 German prisoners, and a captured joint German-Italian hospital. At one end, by the main gate, were a few tents, which housed the aforesaid hospital, my own office, the guard-room, and the stores. There was no other accommodation except for holes in the ground. There were no facilities for ablution. There were no latrines. My staff consisted of two officers and sixty-five Jocks of the 2nd Battalion The Black Watch, and one Greek officer from Alexandria who spoke both German and Italian, loathed both Germans and Italians, and was powerfully built and free with his fists. Once again, I was confronted with something outwith the Camberley syllabus.

I grappled with this by tightening my mental as well as my physical belt. The whole garrison was by this time desperately short of food. I had no other resources than those I have just mentioned, except for some vast cooking coppers and extra dixies. My own men were going hungry; the prisoners were ravenous, and only sentries with fixed bayonets and demonstrably ball ammunition could keep them from rushing our meagre stores. I called for, and got, volunteer cooks from among the Italian prisoners; but even they had to be sifted by the Greek interpreter, since almost every man-jack out of the 6,000 claimed to be a cook when I was first so foolish as to proclaim my need for people to deal with food. After less than an hour of trying to run the place with a velvet glove, I realised that an iron fist would be the only way.

It took at least two days to get a routine established, and

during that period when milling, hungry men were trying to rush our embryo system, considerations about the Geneva Convention had to walk the plank. I am not in the least ashamed to confess that early on we used our rifle butts quite a lot. The first time I walked into the place, brazen and confident, against all advice, I only got a few yards before I had to turn back: so many prisoners were clawing at me. The Germans, who were in a small compound of their own, gave no trouble: they were dignified, aloof and contemptuous, under a Warrant Officer whom in retrospect I still greatly admire. He saw to it that all his men shaved every day, though their ration of water for that purpose would not have overflowed a thimble. I equate that Warrant Officer with our own Serjeant-Major Lord of the Grenadiers, captured at Arnhem, who won fame by exacting the same kind of discipline in similar case.

I sought among the Italians responsible people to help us to help them: we were so thin on the ground that we could not hope to do it unaided. I found them, and I gratefully recall the five of them: the Padre, the doctor, the two Warrant Officers and Conrad, the multi-linguist who in peace-time had been the receptionist in a hotel at Bolzano. These five, plus a few others, helped us with the distribution of food. They at least realised how terribly short of it we were ourselves, how hard-worked my own small team was, and how we were trying to be fair. My own cooks, supplemented by the carefully-chosen Italian volunteers, were working in shifts all round the clock. We had at last managed to arrange that the Italian prisoners would form themselves up in queues, three to a rank, consisting of 150 each: shoved into line by *ad hoc* military policemen organised by the Italian Warrant Officers, to whom we gave strips of camouflage scrim to put round their upper arms as their sign of authority. These were checked by Jocks moving from queue to queue, saying in impeccable Italian with Fife or Angus accents: "*Cento Cinquante Completo*, Eh? O.K., Antonio!" And then the Italian orderlies would serve them with their entitlement.

Heaven forgive us, it was scanty; but it was little less that we had ourselves. They got two biscuits and a cup of coffee first thing in the morning, bully stew at midday, and more coffee and biscuits in the evening, with some soup when we could manage it. Even so, the cooks and the cook-house were at work all the twenty-four hours. The only respect in which we were better off than they were was that we got a bit more meat and usually a ration of potatoes and tinned vegetables. About 2,000 a day went out on working parties, under guards who came to fetch them; the making up of these parties took a lot of organising too.

At last the camp was run down to a mere 250, who were being retained for fatigue duties. The war by now had rolled away to the westward, and 70th Division was to return to the Delta. I handed over my prisoners to an Indian company, newly arrived from Egypt, and the Battalion concentrated on Hogmanay Night at El Adem airfield. Bitterly cold it was, too. Next morning two companies of us, with me in command, clambered on to the lorries of the Supply Company of the Royal New Zealand Army Service Corps, and bowled joyously across the Desert with those cheerful Kiwi drivers, the fastest brewers-up of tea I ever encountered. We passed through the frontier wire at Sheferzen, and arrived at rail-head shortly after noon. There was nothing to be seen there except a few tents, which I was told was a sub-area headquarters and – joy of joys! – an empty train with an engine on its eastern end pointing towards Egypt and the flesh-pots, with steam up. It looked too good to be true, and it was.

The Jocks were decanted from the trucks, and I left them under Richard Boyle and Hewie Dalrymple while I went to the tents. There I found a surly major in a tent marked "D.A.Q. M.G.," and told him who we were, and how many. I said I presumed we could take that train.

"Then you presume wrong," he said. "Your train comes to-morrow."

"But that train's empty!" I said.

"That's got nothing to do with it."

"Where do we sleep?"

"Anywhere you damn well like."

"What about food?"

"There's no food for you here. If you didn't bring any with you, that's your look-out."

"I want to see the Sub-Area Commander."

"You can't. He's having lunch."

"Then I'll wait till he's finished."

"You can please yourself."

At that moment a car flying a flag drove past the tent and away. In it was the obvious Sub-Area Commander. When I taxed this dreadful creature with having lied to me, he was quite unrepentant, saying: –

"I wasn't going to have you bothering him."

At that moment the train whistled and started off down the line. How I kept my hands off the blighter I don't know. I contented myself with telling him that if it was the last thing I did I would get him sacked, at which he laughed. But I did it all right. Next time I saw him, he was a captain in Cairo – which was probably exactly where he wanted to be. When I pursued my vendetta against him at G.H.Q. and suggested that he ought to be given a taste of the front line, everybody cordially agreed: they were out for his blood as much as I was. Unfortunately when we looked at his documents he turned out to be of low medical category. I'm afraid he had the last laugh. I trained my guns also on the Sub-Area Commander, who never came near us as we shivered half-starving on the sand and without shelter from the north wind; but I don't know whether I managed to get him unstuck or not. In my general experience people on the staff are all out to help people in the field, and exceptions like these are rare.

Our train arrived next morning, steel trucks with no seats but with straw on the floor; they were roofed, but the doors were missing, and there was one hell of a draught. I had the daft idea of making a fire with the straw, and nearly choked us all before we could kick it out. I did manage – no thanks to that D.A.Q.M.G. – to get a message down the railway telephone asking for some food to be got to us at Mersa Matruh;

and somebody did us proud, producing vast dixies of fresh meat stew – no bully – fresh vegetables and fresh bread, the like of which the Jocks hadn't seen for three months. We arrived at last at Qassassein, the traditional ending-place of a campaign; and right glad we were to see it.

From Qassassein we all got leave. Since 1937 my brother Simon had been serving with the Equatorial Corps of the Sudan Defence Force. By crafty string-pulling I managed to fly down and stay with him in his remote post, eighty miles east of the Nile and 3,000 feet up. The mixture of jungle and savannah around Torit afforded the perfect contrast to my various environments of the past year, and those ten days were idyllic. I got back in time to accompany the Battalion to Syria, to a small village in the hills just west of Damascus, to help prepare a redoubt: the perennial scare of a German invasion through Turkey had flared up again. We spent our days digging and blasting and roofing; I spent most of my evenings with Pat Tweedie, who was installed in comfort in Damascus, and engaged in mysterious doings with some congenial colleagues. Late one night we were told to pack up quickly, and found ourselves heading south by train. The news from the Desert, where Rommel had counter-attacked, was bad, and we all assumed that we were going to join the party; but at Ismailia the train appeared to take a wrong turning, and we found ourselves boarding the *Mauretania* at Suez, bound for Rangoon.

Three days out, we heard that Rangoon had fallen, and we were decanted at Bombay. A train was waiting for us, into which we docilely got. I was awakened early in the morning by a scream from one of my brother-officers of: "POONA!" and looking out of the window there indeed was that legendary name on the platform of the station at which we had stopped. A few hours later we detrained at Ahmednagar, and marched to a not uncomfortable camp. Here we were bidden to begin immediately the study of jungle warfare. Diligent reconnaissance revealed one small clump of trees eight miles away.

As usual, a few Jocks had been absent without leave when we left Damascus. One morning, when we had been at Ahmednagar about a week, my C.S.M. reported to me that the two missing from D Company had turned up. They had been spotted washing with the others in the ablution hut an hour before, mingling unobtrusively in the hope that they had never been missed. They were marched before me at Company office, wearing nervous but disarming smiles.

"Why did you go absent?"

A long pause; and then one of them said: – "We couldnae thole thon diggin', Sir."

"Where did you go, and what did you do?"

A broad smile this time, and the spokesman said: – "We got a cushy wee job as caretakers o' yin o' thae kirks in the Auld City o' Jerusalem, Sir."

Not for nothing had these two been in the Middle East for more than four years: they knew their way about it. But the moral of this story is that they had deserted when they were bored, and not because a battle was looming. As soon as they heard on the Jerusalem grapevine that we were on the move again, they trailed us; discovered that we had sailed from Suez for the Jap war; had found the Bedfordshire and Hertfordshire Regiment, which had been brigaded with us in Crete and Tobruk and were awaiting their own ship; spun them a yarn about having missed the boat; and caught up with us after a week's glorious hospitality from another Regiment. I had no need to urge Ruskie to let them off as lightly as possible: he was as proud of them as I was.

After three weeks, we were ordered to Ranchi in Bihar, 200 miles west of Calcutta, where there really was some jungle to train in, and a reasonable camp to do it from. Just as we were getting set to go, a signal came posting me to the Joint Planning Staff in G.H.Q. New Delhi. It was only three and a half months since I had won back to the Regiment after more than four years away from it. I was so sure of being able to persuade General Wavell to cancel the posting that I told Ruskie blithely that I would be rejoining him at Ranchi within the week. I saw the Battalion off from Ahmednagar station early in the morning, went for a swim with Peter Dorans, and caught with him the later train to Delhi, with a suitcase, having sent on all my heavier stuff with the Battalion, so confident was I. I entered Wavell's office with a light heart and came out with a leaden one. He had said: – "There is such a thing as duty, and your duty is here. In fact, you are here on my orders." He gave me a pat on the back; said "Bad luck," and offered me a bed for the next two or three nights until I could find somewhere to live.

I was six months in Delhi on the Joint Planning Staff, and it was not a happy time. It was not a happy time for anybody, so small were our resources, so low our place among the priorities; but it could have been less unhappy. From my point of view, the most dismal feature was the high level at which the right to take a decision was frozen. In G.H.Q. Cairo, we G. 2s were expected to know and to adhere to the policy, and were able to take decisions and to despatch signals on our own authority within it. In G.H.Q. Delhi, not even a G. 1., let alone a G. 2., had the authority to send out a signal without the "dhobi-mark" of at least the D.C.G.S. or his equivalent, and delays were inevitable. Furthermore, the battle-front being more remote than it had been in Cairo, there was less sense of urgency among most of the staff. There wasn't the equivalent of an anxious Sandy Galloway, whom you could picture with his bush-shirt caked and stiff with desert dust, speaking in riddles on the radio from the battlefield.

Obviously at that time our principal concern was with Burma. Not one of us in the J.P.S. had ever been to Burma, or even seen it from the air. I arranged for myself a flight over those parts of it with which we were most concerned, in an R.A.F. bomber. The night before I was due to go, the C.G.S. cancelled it on the grounds that it would be "unprofitable joy-riding." One of the plans drawn up on paper against a possible Japanese drive into India relied on a stand on the Son River, which joins the Ganges between Benares and Patna: I flew over it once on the way between Delhi and Calcutta, and saw that it was dry from bank to bank. (Shades of the Maritsa on the Turkish frontier!) An appreciation of the situation about an offensive into Burma in 1943, by the general who would have to mount it, was suppressed. I ought to have had the guts to exploit my long association with Wavell by going to talk to him *via* the back door. Half my instinct told me I should, the other half that I shouldn't. In the event I didn't. It would probably have made no difference either way.

On the whole, I do not think that Wavell was well served in India by his senior staff officers, although Heaven knows they had a difficult task. There were exceptions, and I would make one for his Intelligence staff, which was headed by Walter Cawthorn and seconded by a one-armed Gurkha colonel, Bobby O'Brien. These two were undeniably good, and I remember them with admiration as well as affection; but even they were drawing in through the remoter tentacles of their tortuous organisation some fairly bogus stuff which it was hard for them to sift or assess. I recall how angry I got in Burma in 1944, when they dared to tell me what was happening, and what they alleged I was failing to see. It concerned the traffic on a road sixty miles behind the Japanese lines, astride which my own people were sitting, while Walter and Bobby were doing their sums in Delhi.

I claim to hold the record for escaping from G.H.Q. India. I did barely six months there. Orde Wingate was planning his "deep penetration" raid into Burma, and this was the only "plan" which looked like having any immediate future. When he asked me to join him, the only person who gave me any encouragement was Wavell himself. Owing to the ridiculous rules of the Indian establishment, I had not been allowed to retain Peter Dorans in any capacity during my time at G.H.Q., and had had to attach him instead to the Parachute Brigade. I now disentangled myself from G.H.Q. with Wavell's full blessing, claimed Peter Dorans back, and set off to join Wingate in his lair in the Central Provinces, where he was training his Special Force.

7

I JOINED Wingate early in October 1942. So began two years of my life which were utterly different from anything that came before or after. The first expedition of the two was incomparably the harder; and for me personally it was a sort of spiritual watershed.

I found the Brigade lying in the depths of a vast stretch of forest, which, though it resembled in few respects the type of jungle we were to find in Burma, was good enough for learning the techniques Wingate sought to teach us. The constituent Columns were dotted about within easy reach of Brigade – too easy, I quickly decided, and marched mine twenty miles away to an Arcadian spot by a river, where we wouldn't always be under Orde Wingate's eye. I found that I was physically as soft as butter after six months in Delhi, but I quickly hardened up and was soon fitter than I had ever been since Sandhurst. We practised all the arts of concealment, ambushes, river-crossing, dispersal and re-grouping, getting into and out of bivouac by night, animal-management – each column had sixty mules and a dozen ponies – and the rest. I had sixteen officers from every conceivable background. I imported as Adjutant from my own Regiment Duncan Menzies; he was first-class in every way, and might have been bred for the job. As my second-in-command I appointed John Fraser of The Burma Rifles. He had already been captured by the Japs earlier that year, but had escaped, travelling from Burma to India by a high, remote pass, which had only been traversed twice by Europeans and never before in the monsoon. This also turned out an ideal choice, and the three of us became almost telepathic.

What we would have done without the Burma Rifles I hate to think. When the Army was struggling out of Burma early in 1942, somebody at a high level in Delhi had given the idiotic order that all Burman soldiers should be paid off at Imphal and told to make their way home. We on the Planning Staff heard this too late to countermand it. Obviously every Burman soldier would be of the greatest value when we re-invaded; and Wavell had already and characteristically given orders, long before the evacuation was complete, that studies for the re-invasion should be put in hand at once. Denis O'Callaghan, who commanded the 2nd Burma Rifles, had the sense and the guts to ignore the order. Thanks to him and him alone, we had this one precious and excellent battalion in India; and it was allotted to Wingate, along with one Gurkha battalion and one British. The Gurkha one was newly raised and scarcely trained, the British one had an average age far above the normal; it had been raised and sent out to India for garrison duties only. The Gurkhas were organised in four columns; the British, owing to wastage on training, into three; and the Burma Rifles were split into seven strong reconnaissance platoons, one to each Column. They were our eyes and our ears, and our foragers too. My particular lot were Karens. I have often paid tribute to them before, and it is a privilege to do so once again.

Wingate's original plan was linked to a proposed offensive into Burma by IV Corps, whose Headquarters were at Imphal. Imphal was the capital of the semi-independent state of Manipur, lying on an unexpected oval plain in the tangle of mountains between India and Burma. Along the eastern foot of these ran the River Chindwin: the unacknowledged boundary, across which both sides were playing Tom Tiddler's Ground, between the British and the Japanese. Wingate's Brigade was to infiltrate across the Chindwin and play havoc with the Japanese communications up to a hundred miles or more beyond the Chindwin while the British offensive was developing. By the time we were poised to go in, and already concentrated at Imphal, it had become all too clear that the British offensive would have to be postponed for a year for logistic reasons. There was therefore a strong case for postponing our operation too; but against this there were several factors. We ourselves were all keyed-up, and not even Wingate could have maintained our morale for another sterile year. A venture now would prove or disprove Wingate's theories about what he called "Long Range Penetration," and the efficacy of supply by air. We were bound, assuming that we got through the Japanese outposts, to learn a lot about their dispositions, preparations and reactions. And finally, the British were in need of a diversion. Wavell took the decision, and across the Chindwin we went.

We had reached Imphal partly by train across India, partly on flat barges towed by tugs up the Brahmaputra, and partly – the last 120 miles – on our own flat feet: marching by night so as to avoid interrupting the work on the road by day, and also for reasons of secrecy. We had had ten days' rest in bivouac near Imphal, while the decision about whether or not we were to go "in" was still being thrashed out. I was a proud man when I shewed Wavell round my Column, and Peter Dorans equally proud when he was greeted by name as he stood in the ranks. From now on we were off the leash; we marched by daylight, and "everyone suddenly burst out singing." One day short of the Chindwin we met the ultimate battalion, which had patrols like tentacles out to the River: the 1st Seaforth Highlanders, among whom I met several friends. Of these, the most unexpected was a Second-Lieutenant whom I had known as a schoolboy, when he used to come and stay with his uncle John Ferguson, the head keeper at Kilkerran. It was a nostalgic talk indeed that he and I had that night, more about grouse and pheasants than about Japanese. He volunteered to come with us. I tried it on his Colonel, but got blown out of the ring.

Two of the Gurkha Columns crossed the River twenty miles south of us; they were heading for different objectives from ours. Brigade Headquarters and the other five crossed close together without interference from the enemy, and had a clear run for several days without a brush, though we heard several times of Japanese patrols nearby who must have got wind of us. We had our first supply drop from the air a mere eight miles on the enemy side of the River: it seemed to me a brazen thing to do, but we got away with it except for one unfortunate particular. One bag containing mail was dropped in the wrong place, where it was almost certain that the enemy would collect it. He did; and by this single stroke of bad luck early on he learned that we comprised a Brigade Headquarters and at least seven Columns. From the names and the addresses he was probably also able to deduce with fair accuracy the number of men in each Column. He still didn't know where we were bound, or what our object was; but within a few days of our crossing the Chindwin, he knew our approximate strength.

After a week, two more of the Columns were peeled off from the main body. Mike Calvert's Gurkha Column, No. 3, was sent to attack the main railway line from Mandalay to Myitkyina at a place called Namkhan. Mike was a stocky, cheerful Regular sapper, an Army champion at both boxing and swimming, brimming with ideas, and brave beyond belief. I rate him as the best fighting man I ever saw. He spoke not a word of Gurkhali, except for a few conventional greetings which I am told he always got wrong; but his Gurkhas adored him, grinned whenever they saw him, and fought like wildcats under his leadership.

The other Column to be detached was mine: No. 5, all British except for the Burma Riflemen and the muleteers, who were Gurkhas. My task also was to sabotage the railway line by blocking it where it ran through a gorge; but my sapper officer pointed out that this could be quickly cleared, and that it would be much more rewarding to blow the bridge at Bonchaung railway station three miles farther north. I decided to do both. By this time, from talking with the locals, we knew where the enemy posts were and the habits of their patrols. At dusk on the evening of the 5th March, after two very long marches, we settled for the night into a cosy little bivouac 300 yards off a motorable road – not shewn on the map and with all the appearance of being newly made – three miles short of Bonchaung. After our evening meal of rice we tuned in to the B.B.C. and heard to our horror our exploit of the morrow being reported as a *fait accompli*; it even said "near Indaw," which was a junction a mere ten miles north of us. I was badly shaken, but Duncan said sleepily: "Oh, never mind. It'll be all right. 'And gentlemen in England now abed shall think themselves accursed they were not here'." We rolled up in our blankets and went to sleep, our cooking-fires all out, and no sound except for the familiar bivouac noises: somebody clearing his throat, the calling of a night-bird, the shuffling of the hooves of the mules among the leaves.

At first light I split the Column into four pre-arranged detachments. I despatched John Fraser and his Burma Riflemen towards the Irrawaddy, thirty miles east of us, to spy out the land. Tommy Roberts, with two other officers and forty men, I sent down the road to the southward, to create a diversion, if they could find a suitable target, while the demolition parties were doing their stuff. The third lot, with a platoon to protect it, was the party to blow up the Gorge, under Jim Harman. The main body, under myself, would go to Bonchaung with David Whitehead and the other demolition party. John Fraser and Tommy Roberts had been gone about ten minutes and the rest of us were just moving off, when the sound of shooting broke out from the south, quite close at hand, light automatics as well as rifles.

I told Jim Harman to get to the Gorge as quick as he could, and Duncan Menzies to take command of the main body and move at once to Bonchaung, where I would join them later. Both were to get on with the demolitions. Then Peter Dorans and I ran out on to the main road as fast as we could with our heavy packs, and down it towards the shooting. In a few hundred yards we came to cultivation on our left, which indicated that we were nearing a village; then to a solitary private soldier, who said: "Captain Roberts and Mr Kerr are just ahead, but be careful!" and then to a point where a track took off from the road and ran fifty yards down a little slope into a village. At the fork, lying in the road, were two apparently dead Japs, John Kerr and three of his N.C.O.s, John with one of his legs in a bloody mess, one of the N.C.O.s dead and the other two wounded. I tried to give John a shot of morphia, but he said: "Let me tell you what happened first in case it muddles me."

Apparently they had bumped into a lorry-load of Japanese who were just jumping down over its tailboard, presumably with a view to searching the village; both parties were equally surprised, though Tommy's was naturally the more on the alert. The driver had reversed the lorry quickly, and driven off southwards down the road. Meanwhile a fire-fight had developed on the ground, and Tommy and John had reckoned that all the Japs who had managed to dismount had been accounted for. To give the Gurkhas a bit of a break from leading mules, which they hated, I had replaced a few of them that morning with temporary British reliefs, and attached them to Tommy's party. One of them had gone in with the *kukri*, and killed five Japs with it: John told me of this, indicated where I would find them, and I saw the gruesome evidence. Thinking that all the enemy had been disposed of – he had counted sixteen dead – but that the lorry-driver would soon come back with reinforcements, Tommy had decided to push on and lay an ambush with a roadblock on the road, telling John to collect his men and follow. John had summoned his platoon serjeant and his three section commanders for some rapid orders; and while he was giving them out a light machine-gun which they had not spotted opened up and made casualties of four of them.

While he was speaking, I nearly jumped out of my skin. Peter Dorans, standing beside me, had suddenly fired his rifle twice. I spun round, to see one of the "dead" Japanese writhing in the road. He had flung himself up on his elbows and pointed his rifle at me. Peter had not been hanging on John's words, as I was, but keeping alert: a lucky break for me.

The enemy machine-gun now opened up again from a new position. We stalked and killed the two men manning it. We were now facing in reality the problem that we had decided long before hypothetically: the abandonment of our wounded. In a speech to every column before we ever left base, Wingate had made it clear that there was no question of evacuation. If a wounded man could walk, he could take his chance, but the pace of the march would not be slowed down for him. If he could not walk, he must be left. Anybody who could not face this problem might withdraw now, and no obloquy would attach to him. Not one man chose this option.

Altogether there were two dead men, two dying and six wounded, of whom only one, a subaltern with a hole in his shoulder, could walk. The other five we carried down into the village, from which the inhabitants had run away, and laid them in the shade under one of the houses: houses in Burma are built on stilts. We put earthenware jugs of water beside them, and some bunches of bananas off the trees. John Kerr said: "Don't you worry about us, Sir, we'll be all right." Corporal Dale said: "See and make a good job of that bridge!" Not one of them made it harder to leave them than it already was. Before we left, I had a look at the dying; but they were already dead.

I hoped the villagers would succour my wounded when they came back, but the hope was vain. After the war, John Kerr, the only survivor of the five, told me that one of the men, a stout-hearted chap I well remember, said he reckoned he had a chance of being able to walk if he could lie up in hiding for a few days, and then perhaps make his way back to the Chindwin. John gave him permission to try, and wished him luck. He punted his way painfully with a stick out of the village and into the trees, but he was hardly out of sight when there were sounds of a scuffle, and the man's voice cried out: "Mr Kerr, Mr Kerr, they're murdering me!" When the Japs arrived in force later on, John told them what had happened; they went to look, and found the man with his head battered in by the villagers. They then turned on John and treated him to a brutal interrogation, running a stick of bamboo to and fro through the hole in his leg to make him answer, but he managed to hold his tongue until it mattered no longer.

We blew the Bonchaung Bridge without interruption at nine o'clock that night, a most stimulating performance. David Whitehead warned us when it was about to happen, and I passed the word to the muleteers to get a good grip of their

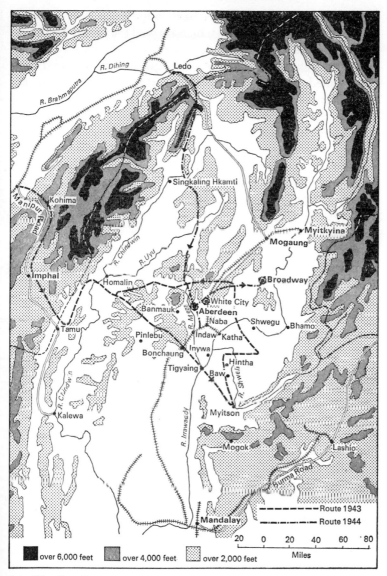

General Map: Upper Burma

beasts. There was a glorious bang which echoed round the hills, and a tremendous flash which shewed the jungle a dazzling green, and the plunging mules chocolate smudges against it. David Whitehead inspected the damage and pronounced himself satisfied. A little later we heard the explosions from the Gorge, as we marched on towards where I had planned to bivouac. We had done what we had come so far to do, but John Kerr and his men hung heavily on my mind.

Our next problem was the crossing of the Irrawaddy. It was no mean river, and the best part of a mile wide. It had seemed to me that the obvious thing was to occupy a steamer-station complete, where we could be sure of finding plenty of boats; and Tigyaing was the obvious place. It was for this reason that I had sent John Fraser on ahead; and talking to him in riddles on the radio I learned that he had sent men in plain clothes to reconnoitre the place, who reported it clear of Japs. So four days after blowing the Bonchaung, with all of us reunited at a pre-arranged rendezvous, we marched boldly into Tigyaing in threes and in step, with our rifles at the slope. All we lacked was a band, or preferably some Pipes and Drums. There was a little elderly man on a balcony who kept calling out: "God Save the King! Long Live the King!" as we marched past. Nothing would induce him to stop his loyal cries, even though we warned him that we were only raiders and that he might be informed against. Two years later I was able to tell this story to the King; and seventeen years later, in 1960, I traced the man himself to Mandalay, now very old and totally blind.

At the request of the Chief of Police, a friendly Karen, we threw his rifles in the River and locked him in his office, in order to keep him sweet with the Japanese. We then began our four-hour regatta, with boats flitting to and fro across the River like water-beetles. None of them were engined; they all had to be rowed or paddled, and the mules to be towed astern. If it had not been for the more recalcitrant animals we would have been across in a third of the time; but we needed them for our heavy loads: the mortars, the machine-guns, the wireless sets, and the many impedimenta that each of these entailed.

The mules that had been carrying our explosives were spare for the moment, but we hoped to get more dropped soon, as I had nefarious designs on a certain suspension bridge that carried the important road link between Lashio and Myitkyina across the Shweli River. We knew that the Japanese had a garrison at Tawma, eight miles away, and that they were bound to know pretty soon about our aquatics since there was no lack of tale-bearers – we had already captured one with an incriminating written message on him the day before; but I hoped we would complete our crossing before they could arrive.

In the event, its completion and their arrival were simultaneous. Just as the light was failing, the boatmen suddenly disappeared as one man, and we knew that this must mean that they had word of the imminence of the Japs. We pulled our guns on the crews of the last two boats returning from the far bank, and induced them to remain in our service for one more trip. We were luckily down to the two final boat-loads, and darkness was falling with the merciful swiftness of the tropics. Our embarkation point was on the edge of a sandbank 500 yards out from the village. In the dusk we could see the flashes of the enemy's rifles as they began firing wildly into the dark, and a few mortar bombs fell on the sand, but none of them near us. We last thirty or so clambered on board, loading the boats right down to the gunwales so that there were only a few inches of freeboard. I waded more than waist deep pushing out the last boat, and owing to the weight of my pack had to be lugged on board unceremoniously by the pack itself and the seat of my pants. Every time I tried to shift so that I could sit the boat rolled frighteningly and everybody hissed at me to keep still, so I remained on hands and knees with my stern sticking out towards the enemy. Hence my favourite boast, of being the only British officer ever to have crossed the Irrawaddy on all fours.

From this triumphant moment onwards our fortunes began to decline. First we missed a supply drop through being held up in jungle so thick that we were a day late at the pre-arranged place. Then, bound south as we were in accordance with orders received from Wingate, we found ourselves in country so waterless that we were obliged to dig for it in dried-up rivers; the Burma Riflemen showed us where to seek it, on the outside of curves: but it was a long process, the sides of the "dig" had to be shored up and finally one had to wait for the water to clear itself of mud. After a few days we at last reached a river with water in it. By this time we were all dead beat, and I resolved on two days' rest and a supply drop. This one again went wrong: we were showered with new boots and shirts and trousers, and even money and rum; but the aircraft carrying the food crashed on take-off, so we got no rations. We had last stocked up with food in Tigyaing, but not methodically, since we had been expecting a supply drop. We had now missed two, we had been on short commons for a week, and many of the men had not eaten since two days before.

My Medical Officer and John Fraser came to see me now with long faces. The former warned me that I could expect to start losing men from weakness in the course of the next day or two, and that a supply drop was imperative. I was short with him: I had to be. Meanwhile some Burma Rifle scouts of mine were caught by the enemy, while others brought back the news that the Japanese were bringing up strong reinforcements from Maymyo, were patrolling the motor road just south of us, and were in the small town of Myitson, four miles away, to the strength of several hundred. I called up Wingate on the wireless to report this, and a few hours later we saw British bombers going over and heard the thud of bombs as they fell on that unfortunate town.

My orders from a few days back had been to join up with Mike Calvert and to march on the Gangtok Viaduct eighty miles away with a view to blowing it up; I was sorry to forego my suspension bridge, but the Gangtok Viaduct was bigger game. These were suddenly countermanded by orders to retrace my steps, and to join Wingate and the two Columns still with him at a place called Baw. (One Column had been mauled and broken up fifty miles short of the Irrawaddy: many of its men got back to the Chindwin in small parties, but we were not to know this till afterwards.) I begged Wingate for a supply drop, but all he said was: "Hurry north and we will arrange supplies for you here." It was a painful and hungry march. There were no villages in which to forage, and I ought to have deduced from the absence of villages on the map that the rivers in that area ran dry in the months before the monsoon. I had the sense to plot our northward march farther to the east and nearer to the Shweli River, which ran parallel to our route, since dry tributaries usually retain some water as they near the main river. This calculation was justified, and although we went hungry we did not this time go thirsty.

We drew so close to Baw that from a clearing on the top of a hill through which our jungle path was leading us we actually saw, from four or five miles away, the supply-dropping planes coming over and beginning their drop; and then with leaden hearts we heard a battle break out, with mortars, machine-guns and small arms all going hammer-and-tongs. The aircraft circled a few times more, but ceased dropping, and then headed back towards India. I had told Brigade that I expected to join up with them by half-past six that evening; but the going had not been as good as I hoped, the extreme weakness and weariness of the men had slowed us down, and I decided to let the Column bivouac while I pushed on with a small escort of Burma Rifles. I reached the rendezvous with Brigade only to find no sign of them: the interruption to the supply drop had evidently altered their plans. I told the escort to get some sleep and to move on in the morning to a new rendezvous, which I gave them, and set out myself with a single Rifleman to rejoin the main body.

We were short of maps, and I was without one; I thought that five minutes' intensive study of Duncan's had imprinted the whole neighbourhood on my mind: but in the failing light everything looked different from an hour before. Very soon I realised that I was lost, and I could find neither the main body nor my former escort.

The night that followed was the loneliest of my life. Desperately hungry and tired, I quartered that area of jungle throughout the night, yanking or even kicking to his feet the wretched Burma Rifleman, who kept sinking to the ground. Next morning, knowing that both my parties would have moved on, I set off vaguely north; and at seven o'clock we heard the sound of troops brushing along a track. We hid behind the undergrowth to see whether they were friend or foe, till my companion called out joyfully: "It is the Adjutant! It is our Column!" And within a minute the escort party I had left fourteen miserable hours before also came up behind us on a converging track.

Like Good King Wenceslas' page, I could go no longer. I halted the reunited Column, moved it off the track, mounted sentries and went to sleep. I woke up a few hours later, and cursed Duncan for not having roused me before. He soothed me by saying that a patrol had made contact with Brigade Headquarters and we now had a new rendezvous. We were soon reunited with Wingate and the other two British Columns, the first time we had seen them for almost a month. We also got some food, but alas! only one day's worth.

Wingate with his two Columns had crossed the Irrawaddy at Inywa a week after us, but unfortunately we had got ourselves into a bag, and we were now in serious trouble. Round three sides of us were the Shweli and Irrawaddy Rivers, and closing the bag at the bottom was the east and west motor-road near which I had bivouacked a few days before. I never really established what induced Wingate to follow us across after so long a pause, and into such a pocket. The Japs were already confiscating all the boats on our side of the two Rivers, and were patrolling the far banks. Wingate had now resolved that we must turn back, and had made up his mind to attempt the reverse crossing at Inywa, on the grounds that the Japs would not expect him to use the same place again. If this failed, Columns were to break up into small parties and make their own way back. I argued that, with three more or less intact Columns, plus his own Headquarters and that of the Burma Rifles, he had a concentration of fully 1,000 men, which would more than outnumber any concentration of Japs, who had to watch a wide area. I reckoned we could seize and hold a bridgehead on the far side for long enough, if we were quick, to get clean away. But he preferred the concept that out of many small parties some at least would get through, and that if the first attempt at Inywa failed, that must be the plan. In retrospect he was proved right. Meanwhile, we were to jettison the animals, except for those carrying wireless sets, and all the heavy weapons.

For the march north and then west to Inywa, my Column was designated the rear guard. We were now in bad physical shape, worse than the others, who had fared better in the matter of supply drops. I let the main body get ahead, and we were distributing a slaughtered mule for meat in a dry stream-bed, when a Burma Rifleman who had left the bivouac area to relieve nature was fired on. This was our first warning that we were being followed up closely. I announced, as was our custom, a rendezvous to make for if we had to disperse into our constituent groups, and we moved off again. We marched by moonlight, and at three or four in the morning we came to the village of Hintha, which straddled a cross-roads of four major tracks. As usual when using tracks, I was leading the Column, and I halted it as a precaution while I went on with a Burma Rifles serjeant, as interpreter if I needed one, to check that the village was clear. As a further precaution I had a grenade in my hand with the pin out.

We reached the cross-roads without incident, and from there I saw a fire on the track thirty yards to my left, with four men sitting round it. Still without misgiving, I approached them and asked a question in Burmese. They looked round startled, and the Karen serjeant said: "They're Japs!" at the same moment as I realised it myself. I dropped the grenade – indeed, I was so close that I almost placed it – on the fire between them, and ran. They were so surprised that they made no move. It was a four-second grenade, and when it went off I looked round. All four men had fallen outwards from the fire, and only one shewed any sign of life. There was a platoon, Phil

Stibbe's, not far behind me, and I shouted for it to come up. I was aware of Peter Dorans beside me. A man ran past me from the direction of the fire. I shot him in the side with my revolver at three yards' range, and he fell on his face; but as I took my eye off him he got up and ran on. I guessed he had gone to rouse troops quartered in that end of the village. There were some spare men standing just behind me, and I put them under Peter's command and told him to get out along that track and block it.

Phil's platoon arrived, and I told him to clear the left end of the village. They had just begun to advance when a light machine-gun opened up from beyond the fire. I shouted to him to get in with the bayonet, but he called back: "I'm afraid it's pretty hot; I've been hit myself." I too was hit about now on the hip-bone by a piece of a grenade which went off in front of me. There were the sounds of a grenade fight also up the track to my right. Peter Dorans had sent back all his men, having first taken off each of them the two grenades every man carried; he was lying in the ditch by the track-side pulling out the pins one by one, and rolling them among the Japs as they came cautiously along. I don't know how many he killed, but I could see a number of heaped bodies in the moonlight.

Dawn was just beginning to shew, and I wanted to by-pass the village rather than capture it, and get on towards Inywa. I sent two officers, Alec Macdonald and Jim Harman, and two men up a small track I had noticed coming in which looked as though it might skirt Hintha; but there was a light machine-gun covering it, and Alec and one of the men were killed, and Jim shot through wrist and shoulder. Still farther back Duncan had found several alternative tracks, all going in the right direction; and having got back such of the wounded as could walk, I ordered the "Dispersal" to be blown on the bugle. Soon each "Dispersal Group" was on its separate way, and for some reason the Japs made no attempt to follow up.

The attempt to cross at Inywa failed. A handful of men under David Hastings – son of Sir Patrick Hastings the famous King's Counsel – managed to get across, and were seen walking up to the bank towards the jungle when shooting broke out, and David and others were seen to fall. A few of them actually managed to reach India, but it was obvious that there was no prospect of a crossing, and orders reached the Columns to break up into small parties. I was miserably unhappy, as some of my dispersal groups were missing: and it wasn't until after the war that I was able to piece together anything like the full story. My Burma Riflemen, having become separated from their officers, decided – and who shall blame them? – that they had had enough, and agreed to slip into plain clothes and go home. Another group, including my excellent serjeant-major, missed my rendezvous but met another Column: the Column that decided to withdraw into China, and whose survivors were eventually flown to India some time in June. The doctor, Bill Aird from Glasgow, a superb man, found himself with some sick and sorry and wounded. I have never discovered how, for most of them died in Rangoon Jail; but somehow he got them back across the Irrawaddy and all the way to the Chindwin, on the very bank of which they were captured. They were taken to Mandalay *en route* to Rangoon, and in Mandalay Bill died. As for Phil Stibbe, his men got him on to a pony, but he found he was delaying them, slipped off it and insisted on being left. A Karen Rifleman, Maung Kyan, volunteered to stay with him, nurse him back to health and eventually escort him to India. Maung Kyan was betrayed to the Japs by a Burmese from whom he was trying to buy food. The Japs said: "We know you are hiding a British officer: where is he?" Maung Kyan refused to answer, and eventually, after much suffering, died. Phil survived his imprisonment; and in his book *Return Via Rangoon* he wrote: "As long as I live, I shall feel that my life is not my own." That applies to more of us than care to acknowledge it.

The strength of my Column was now greatly reduced. The mule carrying my wireless set had been shot during the withdrawal from Hintha, and had fallen into a gully from which neither it nor the set could be recovered. I was therefore unable to call for a supply drop, and as almost every village now had a

Jap garrison foraging had become nearly impossible. I decided not to try to cross the Irrawaddy, but to turn northward or eastward and cross the Shweli instead: we could then get into the Kachin Hills, where we could count on food, rest and sanctuary. I did not succeed in crossing the Shweli until my third attempt. On the first, I could find no boats; on the second, the Japs in the village opposite came out of their houses, and we looked at each other through binoculars. The third, and if you can call it so, successful attempt still haunts me. It involved crossing the Shweli between two villages on the far bank, both of which were occupied by Japanese. All we had been able to come by were two dug-out canoes, both manned by boatmen under duress whom we didn't dare release, and capable of carrying only two men at a time. We waited until nightfall, and then they began ferrying us across to a sandbank in mid-stream. From there to the far bank one had to wade in darkness and in swift-flowing water well up to my chest, and I am six foot two inches tall. By daylight or even by moonlight it would have been less intimidating; but the moon that had lit up our skirmish at Hintha was no longer with us, our physical condition was far below even what it had been then, and it took courage to launch forth when one could not even see the farther side.

Several men were swirled away drowning in those black waters, and we could do nothing to help them. More than thirty – I shall never know the exact numbers – lost their nerve and remained on the sand-bank. John Fraser, who had already made the crossing once and who, by the way, could hardly swim at all, went back to the sand-bank to urge them to steel themselves for a try. Only a handful did; and on the way back John Fraser himself lost his footing and was swept away. Somebody hauled him out several hundred yards downstream, in bad shape, spewing water and furious because he had lost his spectacles. For myself, I had lost my eye-glass, and both of us completed our return march to India in a blur. But that was a grim night. It was my decision, right or wrong, to leave those men on the sand-bank and to march on with those who had faced and survived the hazard. Once again dawn was breaking, and calling for a decision quickly. I made it, and we struggled on. We were now down to a little over seventy, and none of us had eaten for several days except for the odd scrap. Duncan and I between us had one battered tin of cheese which we had husbanded for weeks: two inches across and an inch deep: one good mouthful each.

We broached it the following evening, sharing it with John Fraser. The following day we reached our first Kachin village, and were being stocked up with food when the Japanese arrived. We were in no fit state to fight, and got out at once. The following day Duncan went in cautiously on patrol, was caught, tied to a tree and later bayoneted. The Headquarters of the Burma Rifles arrived in the same village the following day, the Japs' main body having left. Duncan was still just alive; the Japanese had kept him a prisoner for a full day before his execution. L. G. Wheeler, the Commanding Officer of the Burma Rifles, had become a great friend of Duncan's, and Duncan entrusted to him his watch, and then asked for a lethal dose of morphia. Wheeler had just given it to him, when a shot rang out from a concealed Japanese sniper and killed Wheeler. The two were buried together, in graves now forgotten. Even the village no longer exists.

Before being chased out of that ill-omened place, we had collected enough food to give each man a few mouthfuls of rice and a lump of pork about the size of a golf ball, the first food we had had for four days and only our second meal in eight. Two days later we had the good luck to come on three water-buffaloes; I sent Peter to stalk and shoot them, and he made no mistake with his three rounds. This was in a little clearing by a stream, and although I could not stop the men from eating their first mouthfuls raw I persuaded them in the end to cook it properly. We all had our shirts off for the first time since leaving the river where we had the foodless supply-drop, and I was appalled to see how wasted we all were: our ribs were sticking out, and below our ribs were mere cavities. Already several men had been unable to rise up after a halt, and had had to be left; and now, despite all our efforts, some men overate and were forced to drop out on the next stage.

We now emerged from the jungle on to paddy-lands, where we felt horribly conspicuous. We found a village which was willing to sell us rice, and also some stuff called chantaga, a rich, sweet fudge which did us all good. One of our symptoms during the last few days had been difficulty in enunciating, but the chantaga seemed to cure us of this. We were fairly near the Irrawaddy and I hoped well upstream of the area where the Japs had been collecting boats; but although two different lots of men agreed to ferry us over, neither kept the rendezvous. My officers urged on me to adopt the plan of splitting up into smaller parties, just as Wingate had ordered. I was hesitant to do so, as it seemed to be running out on my responsibilities towards my surviving men; but in the end I agreed. I made up three parties of something over twenty each, putting one under Tommy Roberts, one under Denny Sharp the R.A.F. officer, a New Zealander, and the third under myself, with John Fraser, Jim Harman and one other officer.

My own party got across that hateful River at the next attempt and in two flights, thanks to a couple of boys of thirteen or fourteen who thought the whole thing a great lark: I suspect they had borrowed the boat unknown to its owner. We had a few scares, and I thought I was going to lose two men from sickness; but we managed to dodge all patrols, and fifteen days after crossing the Irrawaddy we got clear across the Chindwin. Denny's party reached the British outposts on the same day as we did, having had one brush, which cost them two men. Five of Tommy's party caught up with us while we were passing through the Kachin Hills: they reported that Tommy had got hold of a small boat, and these five were the first flight, but firing had broken out on Tommy's side of the river and no more had come across. I heard from Tommy after the war that he had had to withdraw, but had finally managed to cross two weeks later and about fifty miles farther upstream, after a long march well away from the river. They had got four days' good marching behind them when they bumped a body of Japs which

far outnumbered them. With two men killed and five wounded
out of the eight which was all that now remained to him, they
exchanged shots for four hours until Tommy's men ran out of
ammunition, when he stood up and surrendered them. They
had watched seven of the Japs being buried. Tommy was the
only member of the expedition to receive the dubious honour
of being flown to Singapore for interrogation.

In cold statistics, my Column went into Burma 318 strong,
and ninety-five got out. This includes those who went to
China, and three small parties, one led by Bill Smyly, who
marched the 300 miles to Fort Hertz in the far north, the one
toe-hold still held by the British, from which they were flown
to India. Twenty-eight more including men left on the sand-
bank were found as prisoners after the war, but many others
had died in jail. In other words, I lost almost two-thirds, dead,
of the men whom I commanded. This is a fact I have had to
learn to live with. It was especially grievous to leave behind
the wounded and the weakened. The death of Duncan Menzies,
to whom I had grown very close, remains a bereavement. The
decision to abandon those men on the sand-bank haunts me
still, even though I now know that the Japanese arrived within
half an hour of my leaving: had I waited longer I would have
lost still more of my men. My memories of those crowded,
weary, hungry, anxious months are not all happy, but they are
all precious.

Wingate's Second Expedition of 1944 was on a vastly bigger
scale. His "Special Force" now consisted of six brigades, of
which Mike Calvert commanded the 77th, part British and part
Gurkha, and I the 16th. I had known 16th Brigade in the
Middle East, and two of its four battalions, one of Queen's and
one of Leicesters, were still the same. The other two had to be
converted into infantry during the three months of the training
period: one was the 45th Reconnaissance Regiment, the other a
composite one made up of two Gunner batteries which had
become separated from their original units by the fortunes of
war. Both these latter regiments were first-class material and
converted admirably. I was very sorry for the existing Briga-

dier whom I was displacing; but Wingate had laid down that he would have nobody in the Force aged more than forty, and this unfortunate officer was well over that, whereas I was a whipper-snapper of thirty-two.

Thanks largely to Wingate, there were now many more transport aircraft in the theatre; and thanks entirely to him a number of gliders as well. I shall have something to say about his plans in the next chapter; but during the latter half of 1943 not only his but everybody's varied incessantly. What remained constant was his intention of flying in a large proportion of his force, spear-headed by Mike Calvert's Brigade. Mine was to march in over the high hills between Ledo in Assam and Singkaling Hkamti far up the Chindwin, a good hundred miles north of where we had crossed it the previous year. This was in the operational area of the peppery American General "Vinegar Joe" Stilwell and his Chinese, and I had to seek him out to ask his permission. He was supposed to have a pathological dislike of all British officers. He took a lot of finding, since as usual he was improperly far forward encouraging with oaths some of his reluctant Chinese platoon commanders; but I found him in the end, and convinced him that, despite my Limey eyeglass, my intentions were honourable. He clinched the deal by giving me a note to his Chief of Staff which, long afterwards, I was privileged to see. It read: "Help this guy. He looks like a dude, but I think he's a soldier."

The trek over the Patkai Hills was a fair stinker. At one stage it took us nine days to cover thirty-five miles. The rainfall up there is about the highest in the world; the tracks were scarcely known, and inaccurately marked on the maps which included large blanks; and at moments the gradients for forty or fifty yards were literally one in two. Sloping tracks became butter-slides, and I had to employ hundreds of infantrymen as pioneers: building traverses, or cutting and putting down baulks of timber to give both mules and men a grip of the ground. These baulks had to be replaced every few minutes. The Brigade was stretched out over something like sixty-five miles from head to tail. In marching through jungle even on the level you have to go in single file, so you have nobody beside you with whom to have a cheery chat, while as like as not the chap immediately in front of you is a mule. Throughout that long haul over the Patkais sometimes at over 6,000 feet and lasting thirty-five days, nobody ever had a stitch of dry clothing; yet so attuned were the men to this life that they always got cooking fires going, by hacking at the outer, sodden bark of fallen trees and getting to the dry, dead wood within.

The head of the Brigade left road-head on 5th February and reached the Chindwin on 28th March. It wasn't quite the point where I had intended to reach it, but the detail of our journey was dictated by what tracks we could find. The hills were so precipitous that there was no question of making tracks of our own. We hit the River eventually about six miles upstream of Singkaling Hkamti, where we knew there was a Japanese garrison. I put John Fraser and a couple of hundred men across the River, on floats made out of their own clothing and equipment, as a bridgehead, and sent Jim Harman with a small party down the track on the far bank to lay booby-traps and set a flank guard in case any of the Japs from Hkamti should be disposed to interrupt us. Then – such were the technical advances we had made since the year before – I called up India on the wireless; and in flew American aircraft towing gliders which they cast off to land on a Chindwin sand-bank at my very feet. Out of them stepped my own sappers with my own boats and my own outboard motors, and soon the Brigade was chugging across the River under power. If all the men and animals of all the Columns could have arrived simultaneously, we could have completed the crossing almost in a day. As things were, nobody was kept waiting, and our southward march from the far side was resumed without interruption. Wingate himself flew in to see me, landing on my sand-bank, giving the troops of his rare praise and speeding them on their way.

The march was without incident for several days, until my leading troops bumped a patrol in the Uyu Valley and drew first blood. They captured one wounded man who greeted them with ecstasy: it was a Gurkha who had been taken prisoner on the first Expedition and pressed into service as a coolie; he thought his wound, a slight one, a trifling price to pay for liberation. Here we converted a stretch of paddy into a light aircraft strip, and summoned one of those new toys of ours. In it John Fraser and I flew south to choose from the air a possible site for our "Stronghold." For this year Wingate had produced some exciting new conceptions to match his new resources. Each brigade was to have a Stronghold, with its own garrison and defences, from which the troops based on it would sally forth to harry the Japanese, and from which they themselves would be supported. The sites would be chosen not only to suit us, but also to tempt the Japs into making ill-considered and costly attacks. They would be provoked into fighting us on ground of our own choosing, where we would dominate the approach-routes and select the ambush sites. Wingate illustrated his theory by pointing out what a nuisance Akyab, over in Arakan, had been to us: we were bound to capture it if we were to make headway in that part of the theatre, but all the routes to it were obvious and the Japs had them all taped. This was incontrovertibly true, and Wingate was turning to our tactical use a strategical lesson which was still being painfully rubbed in.

Mike's Brigade was to land from the air on a natural open space (two days' march east of the railway) which had been discovered by one of our Columns the previous year. From there he was to clamp a block across the railway line which was the main supply artery for the Japanese confronting Stilwell in the north. My job was to establish myself in the same district and, first, to capture the important airfield of Indaw twenty miles south of where Mike's block would be, and also, as a secondary role, harass the Japanese forces who would be trying to dislodge him. Unfortunately my march over the Patkais had taken longer than we had hoped. Mike had successfully flown in and established his block on the railway at a place called Henu by the 17th March, whereas the head of my long column only left the Chindwin on the 1st, leaving us many miles still to tramp before we could reach the effective area. It was about a week later that John and I flew our reconnaissance, and it was encouraging in one way, though heart-breaking in another, to be able to see in one side-to-side glance from the air at a mere 1,500 feet a stretch of country which it had taken us more than a week to traverse less than a year before.

I selected my Stronghold site. It was a Y-shaped confluence of two valleys, twenty miles west of Mike's block and twenty-five from my main objective of Indaw airfield. It was subsequently named "Aberdeen," for reasons best known to Wingate. We reached it on our feet a week later, cleared some of the paddy-lands to make rough runways, and within a few hours American gliders were planing down with bulldozers in their bellies. A few hours more, and Aberdeen was in business as an airfield, and another of Wingate's brigades, which included my own beloved 2nd Black Watch, was flying in. But I wasn't there to greet them. Wingate had flown in to see the embryo airfield rapidly growing, and I asked him whether I couldn't give my people time to get their breath back before attacking Indaw. The leading Column had had twenty-four hours' rest, but the other five – I had detached two for a special operation – and Brigade Headquarters were still puffing in, not having had a day's respite since beginning to tackle the Patkais seven weeks before. Wingate refused, partly on the grounds that I must take the pressure off Mike, who was being heavily attacked; partly because he wanted Indaw airfield quickly; and partly on the strictly practical grounds that if you let men have just a short rest after a long march they will stiffen up physically. There was nothing for it; on we marched; and that was the last time I ever saw Wingate.

I planned to attack Indaw with four Columns from the north and one from the south. This last was to attack first: I hoped the diversion would confuse the enemy as to the direction from which the main attack was coming, and make him face the wrong way. A sixth Column I set to ambush a road along which I thought reinforcements might reach him. Two others I had been forced to detach on a subsidiary operation as part of my bargain with Stilwell, and they arrived too late to affect the issue. In retrospect I am not enamoured of my plan, though it almost succeeded: we discovered later that the Japs decided to break off the action about the same time as I did, and if I had persevered I might well have got the airfield. I doubt whether I could have held it in the face of reinforcements who I now know arrived the following day; but this is mere guesswork.

Not for one moment would I blame ill luck as an excuse for failing to carry Indaw, but I had my share of it. So secret had been the plan that a Column of another Brigade, passing through a neighbouring area towards a different objective, gave out in all innocence to every village through which it passed, as its cover plan, that it was on its way to attack Indaw. This information reached the Japs, and they at once sent forward troops in the direction from which in fact I was approaching. Secondly, the Column that was to come in from the south, having decided to bivouac for the night, suddenly found itself astride a motor-road unmarked on the map (I suspect the same one, ten miles north, which I had stumbled on near Bon-chaung the year before). They were in the process of unloading their animals, and their muleteers therefore had no hold of their mules' headropes, when three lorry-loads of Japanese troops drove to their own surprise into the middle of the circle that was about to be the Column's bivouac. They opened fire, the mules stampeded, casualties were inflicted on both sides; but when all was over the Column had lost all its heavy weapons and most of its mules, and its commanding officer had been wounded. It was ineffective as a fighting force thereafter. Thirdly, I had failed to appreciate for the second time in two years that we would be operating in an area which was short of water. There were in fact a couple of streams running through it, but mostly with open paddy on either side; and the Japs, quickly realising their importance to us, held the approaches to them by fire. This was the principal factor in my failure.

Immediately north of Indaw airfield lay the Indaw Lake, and east of the Lake a ridge which ran parallel. I had planned to send the two Leicester Columns along the top of the ridge and so down to the Lake beside the airfield. Two other Columns were to advance directly on the northern end of the Lake, and my Headquarters to move along the ridge behind the Leicesters. I was giving out my final orders when we were fired on. For a few minutes I had no notion that this was no more than a patrol, so I hastily said to the Column commanders: "Well, you know what to do: away you go: good luck!" The Leicesters made good progress and reported a few hours later that they were on the Lake, being attacked but quite happy. By contrast the other two Columns immediately ran into trouble and everything went wrong for them through no fault of their own. One early disaster was when a container of fuel for their flame-throwers was set on fire by an enemy bullet. In its agony the mule on whose back it was blundered into their stock of mortar-bombs, which of course exploded. For two days those Columns tried to reach the Lake, but whichever way they tried they found the Japs dug-in in strong positions; and when in despair they turned away to seek water they found the Japs dug-in there as well.

Men can go without food for a surprisingly long time, but not without water: some time on the third day, at any rate in conditions of heat, they go crazy. Some men were so far past caring that they just rushed for the water regardless of streaming bullets, and were mown down, whereas there was no restraining the mules from the moment they could smell it. By the third day those two Columns had disintegrated, and I had nothing with which to reinforce the Leicesters. I had other worries at Brigade Headquarters as we sat helplessly on our ridge. Our own water problem we solved by having it dropped in containers from the air, but that was trivial compared with the others. From Aberdeen we heard that the tiny garrison I had left there in the expectation of the immediate arrival of a Nigerian battalion had been chased out by the Japs; and from Imphal we heard that Force Headquarters were having to move and were going off the air. From then on I could not raise them for forty-eight hours. Wingate had told me that the new Brigade reaching Aberdeen as I left would be directed against Indaw from the west, but there was no sign of it arriving and I had no means of communicating with it. It seemed to me after two days that I had no alternative but to pull out the Leicesters, and I did, receiving their signal: "Withdrawing slowly owing to wounded." Three days later Brigade Headquarters and the remnants of the four Columns engaged were back at Aberdeen licking their wounds. The Leicesters' tails were up; the others had had a hammering and a lot of casualties, but their morale returned with creditable speed. Wilkinson, the Leicesters' colonel, though he hadn't thought it necessary to tell me over the wireless, had a nasty wound in the shoulder and was flown out to India. I am glad to say that he was awarded an immediate D.S.O.

The various mysteries of the last few days were now explained. The rumour that the Japs were closing in on Aberdeen was without basis, and John Fraser, whom I had left in charge, had quickly exploded it; but his wireless set, a powerful R.A.F. one, had broken down and he could not transmit to me. The Nigerian battalion had landed at Mike Calvert's original landing-ground, and been ambushed while crossing the railway on the way to Aberdeen; they had now arrived and taken up their positions. The Japanese offensive had come so close to Imphal that Force Headquarters had been moved suddenly to Sylhet in India, which was why they had gone off the air at such a crucial moment. I am sure they would never have moved then had Wingate been alive.

Here was the biggest blow of all. Within twenty-four hours of seeing me at Aberdeen he had been killed in an air-crash. His staff had decided not to tell me for fear of putting me off my stroke, and I knew nothing of it until I got back to Aberdeen. This explained why there had been no intervention by the new Brigade from the west: presumably his orders had never reached them. Joe Lentaigne, commanding one of the Gurkha Brigades, was nominated as his successor; but he was in a particularly thick jungle area where it was impossible to land a light aircraft, and it would be some days before he could take over the reins.

Meanwhile my first priority was to give my men a rest. Except for the occasional supply drop – which was never much of a day of rest, for there was always a lot to be done – they had been marching, and latterly fighting, without a break for nine weeks, and the load on the man was about 70 lbs.: much more for whosever turn it was to carry the Bren-gun. We had been nothing like so short of food as we had the year before, but even so the men were dead-beat. I was able now to fly in quantities of fresh meat, bread, vegetables and other delights and to build them up a little. My other two columns had caught us up, and the whole Brigade was now concentrated either at Aberdeen or within ten miles of it.

Mike Calvert was firmly installed in his block astride the railway line. Each time the enemy brought up a stronger force to evict him, they found that his own position had strengthened since their last effort. By now he had the equivalent of ten Columns in and around the "White City," so called because of the innumerable parachute canopies hanging from all the neighbouring trees. Field guns and anti-aircraft guns had been brought in by glider, and he had mines and barbed wire in profusion. White City consisted of a horse-shoe of low hills, making three sides, while the fourth was composed of a railway embankment, parallel to which was 300 yards of paddy, making an excellent landing-ground for light aircraft. I flew in several times to see him, to compare notes and to concoct and co-or-dinate plans: never did I find him in anything but the most boisterous form. He even had people to stay with him, and once I brought our mutual friend Peter Fleming back with me in my aircraft. That was an especially hairy take-off, as the air-strip was being mortared at the time; but we had become inured to taking this sort of thing as all in the day's work.

I was able to relieve some of the pressure on the White City by sending Columns to operate between there and Indaw and harassing enemy concentrations; we also made further feints at Indaw to make them tie up troops in its defence. With Win-gate's death our directives had been altered, and I was no longer required to capture the airfield. A team of doctors, flown in from outside, reported that my men were too exhausted to be called on for a further major effort. Anti-climax though this was, I think they were probably right. But when a senior staff officer, an old friend with whom I had been both a cadet and an instructor at Sandhurst, was flown in to tell us that White City was to be given up, and the domination which we had established over the Indaw area surrendered, and the whole Force – there was now the equivalent of five brigades in the heart of Upper Burma – moved north to help Stilwell, we were all appalled, and protested bitterly. Joe Lentaigne, by now securely installed as Force Commander, agreed to fly in and talk with us.

Japanese air intruders were frequent during the day, and all aircraft movement in and out of Aberdeen, apart from light aircraft evacuating wounded or flying reconnaissances, was by night. We had an efficient system of landing-lights, which were flicked on and off as required for as short a time as possible: even so, they were occasionally shot-up. Visitors from India used therefore to arrive after dark and leave before dawn, unless they were prepared to spend some time with us. Joe arrived soon after dark, and we settled down to the last of several conferences in what I used to call "Meza House," after the river that flowed close by, and in which I used to do my daily ablutions. I remember that evening well. We had dined off local delicacies plus some goodies which Joe had brought in, eaten off the blue china of which the headman was so proud, and washed them down with rum, also provided by Joe. And then, by the light of the pressure lamps, Joe and Mike and Tom Brodie of 14th Brigade and I discussed what should be done, the other two brigade commanders not being able to get there. Tom Brodie was new to the game and kept fairly silent.

Mike and I argued ferociously that we should not pull out of the area altogether. We admitted that the monsoon would soon be upon us, with its risks to health and the increased difficulties of air supply; but neither of these, we maintained, was insuperable, and it would be folly to give up so much. Furthermore, we could do Vinegar Joe just as much good by continuing to block the Jap supply line from where we were: more, in fact, since to move into the same area as that in which he was operating would simplify the enemy's problems. From the knowledge of the Kachin Hills which I had gained on the way out the previous year – Mike's route had lain farther south – I was convinced that we could establish ourselves there and make one vast stronghold of them on either side of the railway. The Kachins were tough fighters and fiercely on our side; the tracks were few and steep, and easily held against attack; at that height the risks to health from malaria or blackwater would be negligible; and even in the monsoon you could count on quite frequent days for supply-dropping. Mike backed up these arguments with others, but to no avail. Joe just said that we had been ordered north, and that was that. The White City and Aberdeen were both to be abandoned; some of my Brigade would fly out from Aberdeen; the rest would march east across the railway, making one or two final diversions, and fly out from Mike's original landing-place.

So, rather tamely, ended the 1944 campaign of 16th Brigade: the only brigade, I like to recall, in either British or Indian Army that fought against all our enemies in the war: Italian, German, Vichy French and Japanese. By the 6th May we were all back in India, and under orders to go to Bangalore for a long period of rest. I remained for a few days at Force Headquarters at Joe's request as a sort of expert commentator on the news as it arrived from inside Burma, and then followed the others to Bangalore.

8

MORE than a quarter of a century has passed since the two Wingate Expeditions into Burma. It should now be possible to assess the concept and the balance sheet dispassionately. So far as I was concerned, the first expedition was infinitely the tougher of the two, but on the second all the brigades other than my own had to endure the monsoon, which we were spared. And as I have said, the first expedition was a watershed in my life, a spiritual as well as a physical experience.

Wingate's basic idea was a simple one, which others have had as well as he, including his kinsman T. E. Lawrence. A comparatively small body of troops at the heart of the enemy's communications system can cause havoc out of all proportion to their numbers. If you supply them by air, most of the difficulties of introducing them fade away. Everybody knows this now, but until Wingate demonstrated the potential of air supply in Ethiopia it had never been resorted to except in emergency. The first example of it that I can remember was just before the war, when an aircraft had to make an emergency landing somewhere in remotest East Africa, and supplies were dropped to its crew and passengers by parachute. The public reaction was: – "How marvellous! Whatever will they think of next?"

It is most unlikely that Wingate's ideas would ever have been realised but for Wavell's unswerving patronage. It was Wavell who gave him his first chance in Palestine in 1938, when he allowed him to form his Special Night Squads of Jews to protect the oil pipe line and their own colonies in Galilee from Arab marauders. On the twenty-fifth anniversary of Wingate's death, a symposium was organised in Israel in his memory. The leading military figures of the country paid remarkable tribute to him as the founder both of their tradition and their tactics: saying with truth, among other things, that while the British Army paid lip-service to the virtues and advantages of night-fighting, only Orde Wingate exploited them to the full. Dayan, Allon, Kollek, Yaffé, Akavia: most of the Israelis, other than the elderly, whose names are best known in this country first learned their trade as soldiers under Wingate. Avram Akavia, indeed, was afterwards his Adjutant in Ethiopia.

Wavell was well aware that he was playing with fire when he allowed Wingate to raise his Jewish levies, and when he was C.-in-C. Middle East he would not allow Wingate to revisit Palestine, as it still was. Lesser commanders wouldn't trust Wingate at all. General Bob Haining, who took over from Wavell in Palestine in 1938, hoofed him out of Palestine bag and baggage, for all that they were brother gunners. Wingate was eating his heart out in an anti-aircraft regiment in England in 1940 when Wavell summoned him to Cairo and gave him a licence to raise merry hell in Ethiopia, which he successfully did, nonchalantly bluffing at one moment an army of more than 20,000 Italians into surrendering to him, when he had virtually nobody at his back.

Then, in Cairo, there happened the mysterious business of his cutting his throat. The authoritative account of this episode is in Christopher Sykes's excellent biography *Orde Wingate**. I know nothing of the matter, except what follows.

When in 1944 my Brigade was setting off across the Patkai Hills our starting point was from somewhere away up the embryo Ledo road, then being built by American construction companies. Wingate wanted to see the leading Columns start, so he and I and his A.D.C. had been driven up the Road in a Jeep. The so-called Road was a mass of mud and shingle, and we had had to dig out our vehicle time and again. The rain was lashing down. I was afraid that we might over-shoot our destination, and at two o'clock in the morning I persuaded Wingate to stop. We sat on a trio of tree-stumps while the rain

Orde Wingate: Christopher Sykes: Collins: 1959 pp. 329-33.

thinned into mist, and recalled some of the memories which we had in common.

Orde was in one of those confiding moods which sometimes came on him. On this uncomfortable occasion he was ruminating aloud in the dark both about the past and the far future. I let him ramble on; he was not a man whom you could interrupt with impunity; but once or twice when he paused I put in a question.

"Are these rumours true: that after the war you might offer to the Jews your services against the British?"

A long pause; and then: – "I wouldn't be surprised."

He then began to talk about his time in Ethiopia, and his troubles in Cairo afterwards. He ended up by saying: – "Don't you believe those people who tell you that I cut my throat because I was annoyed at the way I was being treated." I was aware of him looking at me balefully, even through the darkness and the drizzle.

"Well, if that wasn't the reason, why *did* you cut your throat?"

"Mind your own business!"

We had had two much more loaded conversations a few weeks before: the first in the station hotel at Gwalior, where he had his training headquarters, and the second in Delhi. I had been haunted for months past by the sufferings of my men on the first expedition. Our rations had been grossly inadequate. They were on a scale designed originally to sustain parachute troops for three days; they weighed only 2 lbs. for each day; they included no meat. Out of the eighty days for which we had been behind the enemy lines, my own column had received only twenty days' worth of these already insufficient rations during the fifty days before I lost my wireless set in action: no wonder that the men had wasted away so fast physically, nor that I had had to abandon some by the trackside. The other thing that worried me was the exposure of those Burmans who had helped us – mostly Kachins and Shans, but a fair number of Burmese too – to reprisals.

After we had got out, and while we were piecing the lessons

together and compiling Wingate's Report, I had made it quite clear to him that I wouldn't take part in any further expeditions until these two things were put right. The men's rations must be adequate, and we mustn't go back into Burma unless we were going to stay in: otherwise we couldn't give protection to those who helped us. He accepted both these conditions, and on that understanding I agreed to have another go. He then went off to Britain and America, made a great impression not only on Churchill and Roosevelt, but also on General Marshall and General Arnold, cajoling out of them all sorts of aids which made the second expedition more effective: from our own force of bombers and fighters and gliders and light aircraft, down to flame-throwers and special rations. Arriving back in India, he fell sick with typhoid, contracted probably in Algiers. He recovered at a speed which astonished the doctors as well as everybody else, but he wasn't able to give as much attention to the detailed preparations as he would otherwise have done.

I discovered that the special rations, the famous American "K" ration, though ingenious, were going to be little or no more nourishing than the previous ones. I discovered also that there was no kind of guarantee that this time we were going to "stay in." Neither of my two conditions had been met. I realised neither of these things until the four battalions of my Brigade were already in their trains, and on their way up to that point in Assam from which we were to march over the Patkais into Burma. I had arranged to fly up to Assam in two of the American light aircraft, with me in one and John Marriott, my admirable brigade major, in the other, staying for two nights in Delhi on the way: I had been promised a bed by the Wavells. (Wavell was no longer C. in C., but Viceroy.) I arranged to stop off at Gwalior to see Wingate, and I put these points to him.

He was still looking desperately pale: it was less than a month since he had been taken off the "Dangerously Ill" list; but I hardened my heart and put it to him bluntly that neither of my conditions had been met, and that I was not prepared to take my Brigade into Burma until they were. Few sentences passed between us, and there were long pauses between each. The first thing he said was: –

"Who are *you* to make conditions with *me*?"

That was a tricky one to answer, and I don't remember how I dealt with it. Eventually he pushed across the table a mill-board with sheets of foolscap attached to it with a bull-dog clip, and said: –

"Write out your resignation."

I did.

"You are forbidden to mention or discuss this conversation with anybody. I understand that you are going to Delhi. You are specifically forbidden to mention it to General Wavell. I shall be in Delhi myself to-morrow. I will see you there, and give you instructions then about handing over the command of your Brigade."

I obeyed these orders more or less. I said nothing to Wavell, though bursting to do so; but I did warn John Marriott, who knew what I was planning to discuss with Wingate, that he might soon have to adjust himself to a new boss.

The following day I met Wingate by appointment in Mount-batten's office. I have always claimed for Lord Mountbatten that if he put his mind to it he could charm a vulture off a car-cass. Orde Wingate had already told him what was in the wind, and Mountbatten put to me a completely accurate *résumé* of what had passed between Wingate and me. I confirmed that this was exactly the situation. He then said, flatteringly but I hope sincerely, that my name had been so closely linked with the Chindits that if I were to leave them now my departure would give rise to every sort of speculation; it would under-mine the morale not only of my own brigade but of the rest of the Force; it would also strengthen the hand of Wingate's many enemies, and give them the chance to say: – "Even Bernard Fergusson can't stick him any longer." For his own part, he would do his damnedest to see that our ration scale was im-proved; and although he couldn't guarantee that we should stay in, he took my point and would do his best in this direction too. I let myself be persuaded, and am glad I did.

Outside his office afterwards, I said to Orde: "I'm coming this time, but not again."

"Nonsense," he said: "you're going to be one of my Marshals!" I still don't know what he had in mind when he said that. Did he see himself as Napoleon, and Bernard as Bernadotte? I have no particular aspiration to the throne of Sweden.

One element entirely lacking from Wingate's character was the quality of gratitude. He could and did reward loyal service, particularly service loyal to himself, and Heaven knows I am grateful to him for all he did for me. But I was shocked at his callousness when Wavell was relieved of his appointment as Commander-in-Chief in India; he said to me something like: – "He wasn't up to the job anyway." He owed everything to Wavell: his chance in Palestine, his second chance in Ethiopia, this third and greatest in Burma. Even the account of his life in the *Dictionary of National Biography* was written by Wavell in generous terms, though he was well aware that Wingate had not always been generous about him. Nobody else would have given him any scope at all, whereas Wavell not only befriended him but fought his battles for him with staff officers whom he had alienated by his studied rudeness. Yet now he took the line: – "I needn't be bothered with him again," and set out instead to woo Mountbatten, whom he had met at the Quebec Conference. Slippery as he was, and wholly unscrupulous in his view that the end justified the means, Mountbatten and Slim were both able to handle him, Slim calling his bluff on at least one major occasion.

At times the truth was simply not in him. When he sent me into Burma with 16th Brigade in 1944, he told me categorically that when I had captured the main airfield at Indaw Slim was going to fly in two divisions to fan out on a broad front. I failed in my attack, though I was later able to occupy the satellite airfield a few miles farther west. During the weeks between these two operations Wingate was killed, Joe Lentaigne was nominated to succeed him, and the whole direction and purpose of the Chindit campaign was changed, its new object being geared entirely to levering forward Stilwell's reluctant Chinese in their attack on Myitkyina and Mogaung in the north. Some months after the war was over, I was invited to lecture at the Royal United Services Institution on our campaign, and as a matter of manners I sent my script to Bill Slim to give him a preview. He wrote back: – "It's a free country, and you can say what you like; but when you talk about 'Wingate's Plan,' it is one that I never acquiesced in, and he knew it."

I went to see Slim, that embodiment of truthfulness and integrity, about whom Wingate had often been vitriolic in his comments. I found that Wingate had indeed put that plan to him, and that it had been turned down weeks before I started on my march. I didn't doubt Slim's word, but when a few years later General Kirby and his team were working on the *Official History* and calling me in from time to time I was able to confirm from documents that it was precisely as he had said. Either Wingate still hoped that a success at Indaw might induce Slim to change his mind, or he thought that I needed an especially juicy carrot to screw my resolution to the sticking-point.

At that misty meeting on the Ledo Road which I have already described, Wingate told me that if anything should happen to him Mike Calvert would be his successor. I warmly approved of this, because Mike Calvert, apart from his fighting qualities, had a mind almost as fertile as Wingate's own. (He was also the only man with any sort of influence on Wingate.) In the event, which was so soon to happen, Slim chose Lentaigne. I quote from his book: –

I knew him to be the most balanced and experienced of Wingate's commanders. It is an interesting sidelight on a strange personality that, after his death, three different officers each informed me that Wingate had told him he was to be his successor should one be required. I have no doubt at all that they were speaking the truth.*

The other two, apart from Mike, would be Derek Tulloch the Chief of Staff, and George Symes the Deputy Commander. The latter was a most unlucky officer. When the command of 70th Division fell vacant after the relief of Tobruk, George

Defeat into Victory: Cassell: 1956: p. 269.

Symes was selected out of all the major-generals in the Army to command this, the only British division then engaged in fighting the enemy. Within weeks it was switched to India and its three brigades sent to different places; then they were converted into Chindit brigades, and Symes appointed Deputy to Wingate. I know from his own lips that Wingate had told him that he was heir apparent. As soon as he heard of Wingate's death, he flew up to take over, only to learn that the lot had fallen on Lentaigne.

Lentaigne was a first-class officer, who had shewn his worth in the appalling withdrawal in the spring of 1942; but he had never come under the spell of Wingate, on whom he had been imposed and to whom he was anathema. Indeed, almost the only time that I was able to dissuade Wingate from doing something he proposed was when he wanted to protest to Wavell about Lentaigne's appointment to command one of his brigades: I knew that he was Wavell's own choice, on the advice of Indian Army members of his staff, whom he had asked to nominate the best brigadier available in India. Slim was quite right in regarding Lentaigne as "balanced"; he was also extremely brave; not least important, Slim knew him much better than any of us, and could trust him to conform.

I have set down at length these criticisms of Wingate because they are relevant to a proper assessment of him. The orthodox were scandalised by him, and a number of people saw nothing dishonourable in trying to wean away from him that small handful of Regular officers who took service under him. On the first expedition I think there were only six of us, of whom two were killed. The writers of the *Official History* devote two pages to an analysis of his character; I know they thought they were being both generous and merciful, and I can subscribe to much of what they wrote. The national press, hungry for a hero, believed that at last they had found one, and inflated him to a ridiculous degree. Perhaps after this lapse of time it will not be improper for me to quote from a letter Slim wrote to me from Australia soon after his book appeared (surely the best first-hand account of his campaigns written by any general): –

I gather that the *Daily Express* regards the book as a deliberate attempt to belittle Wingate. It certainly isn't that and between ourselves I think I have been rather restrained in any criticism of him. He was an odd fellow, and like most of us a mixture.

Churchill described him in a famous phrase as "a man of genius who might have become a man of destiny." Wavell wrote in his foreword to one of my books: – "I have better cause than anyone to recognise his genius, and to be grateful for it." And again in his contribution to the *D.N.B.*: –

He was no haphazard marauder; his operations were always most carefully planned, his training thorough, and his administrative arrangements as complete as possible. He had undoubtedly a high degree of military genius.

To those who served under him, Wingate was a very different person from the scourge of the staff or the idol of the press. We held him in awe, certainly. His standard was perfection, nothing less. We were expected not only to study his voluminous training memoranda, but to apply our wits to them, to make deductions from them, to expand them logically. One of his tactical maxims was: – "Don't be predictable," and it was difficult to predict what he himself was going to do or say next. Early on in the first expedition, when we were about fifty miles beyond the Chindwin and threading our way between known Japanese garrisons, he saw something which displeased him. Brigade Headquarters and five of the seven columns were moving in single file along a track, covering at least twenty miles. He called a halt and summoned all the officers from the three nearest columns, less one officer per column, for a talk which ranged far and wide: not only whatever it was that had annoyed him two hours before, but the decadence of the British race and the iniquity of pretending that Dunkirk was anything but a disgrace. He then dismissed us, saying that there would be no further move until dawn, and we returned to our columns rather puzzled, and greatly relieved to find that they had not been attacked in our absence.

On Christmas Day 1943, a few days before my battalions were to entrain for the front, I declared a holiday, and went round to visit each unit in turn. I was summoned back by radio to Brigade Headquarters to meet Wingate, who had arrived unexpectedly by light aircraft. He had been met by "Katie" Cave my second-in-command with the appropriate words: – "Merry Christmas, Sir!" He replied: – "How many mules have you got, and are they fit for hard service?"

Another time when the second expedition was preparing to go in, I heard him giving orders to the commanders of eight patrols, who were to probe across the River Chindwin at various places to pin-point Japanese positions. He directed one to pass through a forest near Tamanthi, which the local forest officer from pre-war days had assured me could not be negotiated even with elephants. I said: – "Excuse me, Sir, but I have been told that that particular bit of jungle is quite impenetrable." He rolled a cold eye over me, and went on dictating his orders:– "No patrol will report any jungle impenetrable until it has penetrated it."

It may sound daft, but the effect on all of us of his unbounded confidence was inspiring, almost hypnotic. Or on almost all of us: I can think of two cases where subordinate commanders failed to succumb to his spell. In both, their doubts seeped through to their own subordinates, and both units suffered disaster, the ultimate reason being want of confidence. Boldness was everything. The nettle must be grasped, not stroked. When our columns blew up chunks of the railway in 1943, the enemy deduced that this must be our object, and deployed his forces so as to cut off our retreat. When instead we pressed on across the Irrawaddy he was taken utterly by surprise, and initially we got away with it completely. Thereafter for various reasons we lost our momentum, and lingered too long in that Shweli-Irrawaddy bag of evil memory. It was miraculous, looking back, that so many of us got out of it.

For my own part, I thought that few of us would. After taking prolonged counsel with myself, I talked at length to my then second-in-command, John Fraser, and adjutant Duncan Menzies. I adjured them that if either of them got out and I didn't, they were to insist on seeing Wavell personally and telling him from me that although our venture had ended in disaster I retained complete faith in the concept, and hoped that it would continue and expand. My morale was low at that moment, what with hunger, my wound and the sand-bank episode, and I reckoned that our chances of getting out of that enclave on the wrong side of the Irrawaddy were five to one against. John Fraser and I survived; Duncan was killed a few days later. John Fraser, alas, was himself killed in a car crash in 1965.

A Scottish rhymester called Robert Crawford who flourished in the 1920's produced an imaginary epitaph:

> Here lies the Captain.
>   He wis unco clever.
> He could hae dune onythin' –
>   But he never.

Thanks to Wingate, that was the exact opposite of us. Wingate had an extraordinary power of making us feel that nothing was impossible; that each of us was like an organ, containing all sorts of stops that hitherto we had never pulled out. I myself would never have dreamed of taking my Column across the Irrawaddy in 1943 unless Wingate had told me to; and he told me in so matter-of-fact a fashion that it never occurred to me to query it. As we drew nearer to that formidable obstacle, I had plenty of time to think over how it might be done, and there seemed several feasible ways of doing it. It was therefore a shock to get a signal from him when I was within eight miles of the River saying: – "Crossing of Irrawaddy possibly hazardous leave it your own discretion." By that time I was morally and mentally over it; the actual physical feat I have already described.

He injected into us also, as well as resolution, a certain ruthlessness. I certainly stood in need of this, having had such a sheltered war, and indeed such a sheltered life, so far. This was a quality which was beginning to run dry at that stage in the

war. There were not enough Wilfred Lloyds about, to say: —
"If you won't do it, I'll have to find someone who will." Wingate hacked away at the deadwood without mercy before the
first expedition went in. Those whom he deemed too old, like
a certain colonel whose dismissal almost broke his heart – but
Wingate was right – were sent away with their dignity un-
diminished. Those who groused, the idle, the one who drank
too much and told bawdy stories to his men, got short shrift.
It was fascinating during the training period to watch that
first expedition growing daily smaller and more sinewy as he
cut it down pitilessly to those who he thought could stay the
course.

I doubt if there were any other commander of British troops
in India in December 1942 who would have dared address his
troops as Wingate did on the eve of our departure from Jhansi.
We had concentrated there and had ten days' rest after a gruel-
ling manoeuvre, during which we had marched 180 miles in
nine days with full packs, and gone through the motions of
fighting as well. Every officer and man who failed to finish the
course had been dismissed already. Wingate summarily disbanded one complete column, attaching its survivors to others
to replace individuals found wanting. He then addressed each
column in turn, saying that by his reckoning each man had an
even money chance, no more, of getting back alive. This was
when he told us what would happen to the wounded, and gave
us all our chance to withdraw.

That first year Wingate was known to every man in the
Force. This was not so the second year, chiefly because of his
illness, which prevented him from getting round to all the units
and columns as he would certainly otherwise have done. But
the legend of him infected even those who never saw him, just
as the legend of Victor Fortune spread throughout the prisoners of war in Germany: who knew he was present, who retailed
and realised the stories of his defiance, and who probably em-
bellished and enlarged them in the telling. There were in-
gredients in Wingate which were never understood by his
detractors. They never saw him, as I did, with his ridiculous

topi tipped over the back of his head supping a mess-tin of rice brought him by Bachchi Ram, the Indian bearer who went everywhere with him in the best tradition of Beachcomber's character Carstairs: with his backside all covered with sand from the *chaung* bank against which he was leaning. They never saw him, as I did, under fire. This was a very different Orde Wingate to the sullen, simian figure shambling round G.H.Q. insulting everybody, putting all their backs up, and being deliberately provocative and offensive. I imagine that this was the backlash from having been odd man out both at Charterhouse and Woolwich. When he reached his zenith as Commander of Special Force, he reached back into the past and brought back into his orbit two men, both startled at being rapt away from whatever they had been doing, who had been kind to him at Woolwich when others had been less so: Derek Tulloch and Lancelot Perowne, the one to be his Chief of Staff, the other to command one of his brigades.

It has never been widely realised that the Chindits, unlike the Commandos, the parachutists, the L.R.D.G., submarine crews, and so on, were not volunteers, except for a few of the officers. The volunteer principle is all very well, and those who volunteer deserve honour; but it skims the cream off units. It is far better in my view to select a unit and say: "You're Chindits: congratulations!" or alternatively: "Bad Luck!" and then shape it by trimming off the unsuitable elements. Later in the war the 2nd Black Watch became a parachute battalion overnight, and their failures were few. Thereby hangs a tale. General Montgomery was passing through Karachi, where the Battalion was, on his way to Delhi, and objected because they were still wearing Balmorals and Red Hackles instead of the red beret. He ordered them to conform immediately. That wise bird John Benson, who was commanding, asked him if he would mind delivering a letter to Wavell, with whom Monty was to stay at Vice-Regal Lodge, which he agreed to do. Little did he realise that it contained a report from John about this outrageous order, which was of course cancelled by Wavell immediately. I still maintain that ordinary infantry battalions should perform parachute, S.A.S. or Commando functions in turn for a period of so many years, rather than that special units should be created for the purpose.

Wingate's detractors maintain that his achievement in neither expedition justified the high casualty rate, particularly in the first, or the immense investment of resources, particularly in the second. One can claim for the first a boost for morale generally, such success as we had being exploited to the full both by Wingate himself and by all the organs of propaganda; the first demonstration of deliberate air supply; the amassing of useful intelligence; the diversion of Japanese effort. There was one much stranger result which became known only after the war, when the Japanese documents were in Allied hands. The Japanese said to themselves: "If the British can operate across the grain of this country, so can we"; and this was the genesis of their suicidal invasion of Imphal and Kohima, which shattered their strength for ever.

The scale of allotment of resources to the second expedition is certainly hard to justify if Wingate's Plan were not to be adopted. The clamping of a block across the road and railway at "White City" failed to throttle the Japanese force in the north as we thought it would. The fact that for two months they diverted several battalions in an attempt to liquidate it proves that it was a major embarrassment to them, but they managed to develop an alternative route through Bhamo. (I am a little nettled that the success of my own people in blowing up their vast petrol, ammunition and rice dump, which a patrol stumbled on near Indaw, rates no mention in the *Official History*; we were terribly pleased with ourselves at the time, and the loss of the ammunition especially must have been a serious blow.) It must be conceded that as things turned out the dividend did not justify the investment of five brigades. The brigade which rightly won most glory was Mike Calvert's 77th, which held the White City and bore the brunt of the attack on Mogaung; but I doubt whether White City could have been held without the help of other brigades, which harassed and broke up concentrations of Japanese attacking it. The fighting there was hard and bitter, and the only time any Japs got in they failed to get out again.

Wingate's success in getting hold of these resources naturally aroused jealousy. When a signal reached G.H.Q. from Quebec, warning them that 70th Division was to be converted into Chindits, I was acting as second-in-command to Joe Lentaigne's brigade, which was itself in process of conversion and greatly resenting it: I had been imposed on it, and was probably the most unpopular man in Central India. I was summoned to Delhi and found myself before the Commanders-in-Chief, with Auchinleck in the chair. (South-East Asia Command under Mountbatten had not yet been formed, though the decision to establish it, had we known, was being taken at that moment.) They were extremely upset, especially Auchinleck, at the prospect of that crack and battle-hardened division being lost, as they regarded it, to Wingate, whose nickname in staff circles was sometimes "Tarzan" and sometimes "Robin Hood." Could I throw any light on it?

I had of course no inkling of what an enormous expansion was being planned, and was therefore not able to comment usefully. But I did feel bound to confess that I had been urging Wingate to ask for battalions from 70th Division with which to rebuild his shattered original brigade. When Wavell had decreed a year earlier that Wingate was to be given two battalions, one British and the other Gurkha, plus the only battalion of The Burma Rifles that had reached India, he had failed to oversee which battalions were chosen; and Wingate had been fobbed off with two second-rate ones: hence the vast wastage in terms of deadwood during the training period. But when the Cs.-in-C. told me that Wingate was now to get the whole of 70th Division, I quoted to them the story of the Scotch minister who was praying for rain during a drought, and was interrupted by a cloudburst: he interrupted his intercession with the words: – "O Lord, I ken fine I was praying for rain, but this is fair ridiculous!"

Wingate's eloquence made a profound impression not only on Churchill, but also on Roosevelt, Marshall and Arnold. He returned from Quebec a major-general with a command the size of a lieutenant-general's and something approaching *carte blanche* (or so he wrongly thought) in its employment; he brought with him such endowments for his own exclusive use as had never been dreamed of in India Command, which had for so long been on short commons. He even had that object of every soldier's desire, the mere mention of which has been known to induce apoplexy: "a private air force." It comprised a squadron of D.C.3s, to enable us to be totally independent for our supply-drops; a squadron of Mustang fighters; a squadron of Mitchell bombers; a number of gliders; and a squadron of light aircraft for the evacuation of wounded. Arnold had been haunted when he heard that on the first expedition any wounded man who could not walk had to be left behind. Two helicopters and a Nordin Norseman communications aircraft had been thrown in for good measure.

Hitherto there had been two lots of transport aircraft operating from India. By far the larger had been the American "ships," as they called them, flying over "The Hump": the mountains between India and China, carrying supplies into Chungking. The armies in the field had no call on these at all. The second had been the puny fleet of R.A.F. Dakotas or D.C.3s, whose crews were as willing and gallant as professionally skilled; but they were terribly few. It is true that another R.A.F. Transport Squadron, and an equally good one, reached the theatre at about the same time; but it was Wingate who had proved that air supply was feasible as the major system, and a better alternative than the long and vulnerable lines of communication over surface routes. The extra transport aircraft that Wingate had brought into the theatre through his persuasiveness were to be a major factor in the winning of the war there, not only because of supply dropping, but because they enabled Slim to switch formations from one part of the theatre to another at crucial moments, especially from Arakan to Imphal. And hundreds of wounded men other than Chindits were to owe their lives to evacuation by these light aircraft and their superlative American pilots.

With the American fighters and bombers we were able to evolve our own techniques for support from the air. The Royal Air Force, perhaps partly because of their need to husband their aircraft, took the line that "the field is not the place for experiment." Not so the Americans under their remarkable commander Colonel Philip Cochrane and his Number Two Colonel John Allison. To them the field was the ideal place for experiment, and they had no inhibitions about "bomb lines" and so forth. Each column had an R.A.F. officer on the ground whom the air-crews trusted implicitly; and they would "talk them in" to any conceivable target.

The architect of these techniques, and the joint architect of our supply dropping system – the latter was adopted with only minor modifications as standard practice – was Bob Thompson; his co-architect for supply dropping was a reservist officer of The Border Regiment, Captain H. J. Lord, who was staff captain the first year, and who has never received full credit for his ingenuity. When the war broke out, Bob was aged twenty-three and a cadet in the Malayan Civil Service, which he had joined via Marlborough and Cambridge. At Cambridge he had learned to fly with the University Air Squadron, and had therefore contrived to get himself into the R.A.F.V.R. He was learning Chinese in Hong Kong when the Japs gate-crashed the war; and when Hong Kong fell he was with an irregular unit harassing the Jap supply lines on the mainland. He made his way to Kunming, whence he was flown to India and attached to Mike Calvert's column the first year, and his brigade the second. He had unlimited courage and an agile imagination; he was the perfect foil to Mike, and had much influence with Wingate. Like Lord, he has never had his due for the contribution he made to the harnessing of the air to the winning of the war in Burma. After the war he played a major part in the "emergency" in Malaya, remained on as Defence Secretary for some years after independence, headed the British Advisory Commission in Vietnam, and is now as Sir Robert Thompson a leading authority on the Far East. When he wrote once that

Wingate is more likely to be remembered after the turn of the century than many more conventional generals whose names are better known now, he may well have been right.

Certainly the substitution of the air for the ground as the main supply route owed more to Wingate than to anybody else. Some time after I had brought my brigade out of Burma in May 1944, I was summoned to a conference at Dehra Dun. It was an enormous affair convened by Slim, whom I now met for the first time (though a year before, recovering in a convalescent home in Simla from my wound, malaria and malnutrition, I had been looked after wonderfully by his wife, who was running it). I think all the Corps Commanders and Divisional Commanders of 14th Army were there; Brigadiers were six a penny. We sat on terraces, so to speak, on either side of a large room, with Slim presiding from a table at one end, flanked by Giffard as C.-in-C. Land Forces. There was a lot of talk, much of which sounded to me almost defeatist. I remember but will not reveal the identity of a divisional commander who said – and not without support from others – that to prevent the Japanese cutting the road behind one a force of at least a brigade would be needed every x miles; there were only y brigades in the 14th Army; it was z hundred miles to Rangoon: – *ergo*, it would be impossible to capture Rangoon overland. Down in the forest of my memory, something stirred. Where had I heard this or something precious like it before? The Rawlinson Hall at Camberley in the spring of 1940, *à propos* of how many A.A. batteries would be needed to protect the advance of the B.E.F. into Belgium!

This was frankly too much for me. Had these boobies really no knowledge of what Wingate, whom they all affected to despise, had demonstrated and achieved over the last eighteen months? Didn't they realise that he had shewn that the road, which had been our Achilles heel in Malaya and Burma in 1942 because it was so easily cut, was entirely out-dated as the lines of communication and supply? It made me almost physically sick to think that all we had learned so painfully, and at considerable cost in lives and suffering, was being ignored as an irrelevant music-hall stunt, and that people were still talking as though nothing new had been learned since those dreadful days of early 1942. Something like a brainstorm broke over me; I got to my feet, and I gave them an earful.

I sat down again, shaken by my own outburst; and in the hush that followed a tall, languid, fair-haired Brigadier whom I had never seen before got up on one of the terraces opposite. He was obviously much less awed by all the rank and fashion than I was. "I don't quite know who the last speaker was," he drawled, "but obviously he was talking sense. I mean, it's obvious, isn't it? I mean, it's obvious to anybody who uses his brains, and has been for a long time." He continued in an almost Bertie Wooster fashion, but illustrating what he had to say from his own experience as a brigade commander in the field. He sat down, and I got up again to comment on a point he had made. He got up to comment on my point; and we might well have gone on like this, but for a dry interruption from Slim at his table: – "Brigadiers West and Fergusson having left us in no doubt as to their views, they will now kindly keep their mouths shut for the rest of the conference." But it was nicely and jocularly said; the laugh it raised was sympathetic; and West and I subsided virtuously into our respective seats, and took no further part.

At the next break I sought him out. He was Michael Alston-Roberts-West, – he has since trimmed his name to West, *tout court* – formerly of the Oxfordshire and Buckinghamshire Light Infantry, commanding a brigade in the 2nd (British) Division. In 1952 he commanded the Commonwealth Division in Korea, another theatre where failure to use air supply at the right moment nearly caused disaster; and the French would have fared better in their calamitous war in Indo-China if they had applied these lessons also. Before the conference ended I was cross-examined at length by Slim about certain details of our methods. He and his staff, at any rate, were fully alive to the potential of air supply.

I have tried to assess Orde Wingate fairly and dispassionately. In case some of what I have written may be thought disloyal

to his memory, let me make it clear that I stand by every word
of what I wrote six months after his death: –

No other officer I have heard of could have dreamed the dream,
planned the plan, obtained, trained, inspired and led the force.
There are some who shine at planning, or at training, or at leading:
here was a man who excelled at all three, and whose vision at the
council-table matched his genius in the field.

9

I HAD hoped and expected to be sent home, but no such luck.
I was summoned to G.H.Q., to the office of the Director of
Military Training, who turned out to be General Gurdon, my
first-ever company commander. I was to head one of two
"training teams," each consisting of a brigadier and half a
dozen officers whose job was to run courses in jungle warfare,
and to set and umpire exercises for newly raised or newly
arrived formations. My base was at Ranchi, and I also had a
perch – "office" would be too grand a word – in Calcutta.
There I found an old French army friend of mine had
been made Governor of Chandernagore, the suburb of Calcutta
which was still anachronistically a French colony; and I stayed
a night with him in that beautiful Governor's house on the
bank of the Hooghli which had once been lived in by Dupleix.
He and some of his officers looked in on one of my courses.

I twice went down to the Arakan front to study the form
there, and on one trip had an absurd adventure. I had arranged
to stay the night at Cox's Bazaar with Paddy Bandon the Air
Commodore, an old acquaintance, and found with him Colonel
Clinton B. Gaty, one of Phil Cochrane's American pilots, with
whom I had had a lot of fun in Burma. Paddy had a couple of
bottles of Scotch whisky, and in the course of the evening with
their help Clint Gaty and I got braver and braver, until he said:
"Let's you and me go and knock hell out of Akyab (he pronounced it *Ack-Eye-Ab*) first thing in the morning."

I felt less brave when at 6 a.m. I climbed into the co-pilot's
seat of a B 25 Mitchell bomber, beside Clint, and we took off
down the coast. Akyab had been in enemy hands since April

1942, and every attempt to recapture it had failed. It lay on a diamond-shaped island of the same name, stretching ten miles from corner to corner. It was tricky to capture overland, since the routes to it lay along rivers with high ranges in between; and every advance was vulnerable to attack from the flanks. I knew it intimately from the map and from models, having pondered it daily in my Joint Planning days; I recognised every feature of it as it came into view that memorable morning. By this stage of the war we knew that the Japanese had withdrawn some of their troops from Arakan, and a new assault was being planned on Akyab for about six weeks later; but it was still supposed to be strongly held, with lashings of anti-aircraft artillery. Clint and I therefore approached it cautiously at 10,000 feet, while he blasted off a few cannon-shells at the harbour-side warehouses. To our surprise, nobody returned our fire.

Puzzled, we went gradually lower and lower, until we could see weapon-pits galore, but unmanned, and the sand silting up in them. Finally we were steaming up and down the streets at 300 feet, and it was quite obvious that there was nobody there. This was intelligence of the utmost importance, and we flew back to Cox's agog with our news. As we taxied along the tarmac to Control and switched off our engines, we could see Paddy looking worried, with an Army captain beside him.

"I'm afraid we're in trouble," he said as Clint and I clambered down. Somehow the news of our sortie had got to the Corps Commander, who required my presence immediately. Corps Headquarters was two hours' drive away. I exclaimed that I must get back to Calcutta that morning, at which Paddy said: "I'm afraid this officer has a message for you." Licking his lips with apprehension, the captain said that he had orders to tell me to consider myself under arrest. There was no officer handy of equivalent rank to escort me, as the rules required; but I bowed to my fate and suffered myself to be driven, boiling with anger, to wherever it was. The B.G.S., whom I knew from Cairo days, warned me that his general was furious. I was duly marched in, and told that my conduct in taking an unauthorised part in an unauthorised reconnaissance flight over an area in which we were deliberately trying to avoid shewing interest was a breach of both manners and discipline, and inexcusable on all grounds. Considering that we had been trying to recapture Akyab for two and a half years, and that our conspicuous failure to do so had been public knowledge throughout that time, I didn't feel that that particular charge was valid: though on reflection I realised that I was guilty of a breach of manners, which I might well have resented myself if our roles had been reversed. I tholed my rocket with the best grace that I could call on, was released from arrest, and told that I might go.

I then told the general the result of our reconnaissance: that I was certain that the enemy had evacuated Akyab. Instead of shewing interest or being grateful he was extremely angry, and I thought for a moment that he was going to put me under arrest again. I told the B.G.S. my story in the outer office, but it doesn't seem to have got any farther: certainly Mountbatten told me some years after the war that it had never reached him. A few days later I was joyfully on my way home to Britain and had rather lost interest, but later still I heard that the farce had been played out to the end. On the 3rd January, some six weeks after my inadvertent discovery, an assault was launched by two brigades, and there wasn't a Jap on the island. Indeed, the troops were beaten to it by half an hour, by an air force officer landing on the airfield without incident in an Auster. Not many people have been put under arrest as a Brigadier, and I take a twisted pride in being one of them. Poor Clint Gaty was shot down and killed over Shwebo in Burma the following March.

I was running a jungle warfare course in some delightful country close under the Himalayas, not far from Darjeeling, when I got a signal ordering me to report to Cocanada *en route* for the United Kingdom. Cocanada is a small, obscure port 300 miles north-east of Madras; and going home *via* Cocanada sounded like going to Bannockburn by way of Brighton Pier. But mine not to reason why, especially if I were homeward bound. I made hasty arrangements for such heavy luggage as I had, and for the soldier servant – a ploughman from Kilkerran called Bob McClung – who had succeeded Peter Dorans the previous year, to be repatriated too, and set off for Cocanada in an aircraft borrowed and piloted by Robin Sinclair. Sinclair was an Air Force student on the course, son of the Secretary of State for Air, and normally employed in the secret and hazardous business of photographing Japanese shipping in Singapore from an unarmed Mosquito at 30,000 feet. At Cocanada I met Bob Laycock, who had succeeded Mountbatten as Chief of Combined Operations after his appointment to South-East Asia Command – he was inspecting some Combined Ops training there – and learned that I was to join his staff in London.

We flew home by easy stages, stopping in Cairo where we saw Paget, and Caserta where we saw Alexander, and buying large quantities of bananas on the way; I was told that they hadn't been available in Britain for years. I discovered how true this was when on arriving in London my taxi-driver preferred two bananas to hard cash for his fare, and my six-year-old nephew to whom I gave one tried to eat it without peeling it: he had never seen one before.

For four years and more I had promised myself that I should spend my first night in London at the Ritz, a hotel which hitherto I had always been too impoverished to frequent. I presented myself at its portals; they said they were full; I spun them my yarn; they relented and gave me a room. I went down to dinner. Even in wartime conditions it looked gloriously civilised. I glanced round the dining-room from my table and saw nobody I knew; but a waiter brought me a note which read: – "Welcome Home! Come up to Room X when you've finished your dinner, and have coffee with us. H.M.W." I didn't know who H.M.W. might be, but when I got to Room X it was General Jumbo Wilson and his wife. With them was Lord Gowrie, V.C., and *his* wife, who had done their courting under my parents' roof many years before. It was from this room that I rang up my parents to tell them that I was back; I had cabled from India to tell them to write no more letters, so they were not completely surprised. It was a good moment.

Next day I made my number at C.O.H.Q., got a ration card and an identity card, and that night caught the train for Kilkerran, where I had a full month's leave.

My twenty-two months at Combined Operations Head-quarters, from January 1945 till November 1946, were frankly not very exciting, though I enjoyed immensely the first few months of being back in London, meeting friends, and filling in the gaps of the four years I had been away. I felt very much a Rip Van Winkle. My colleagues kept quoting to me incidents that had happened and lessons that had been learned in battles or on beaches that I had never heard of. I didn't know there had been fighting at Caen; I had never heard of the Falaise Gap; and what was all this talk about Mulberry and Pluto, L S Hs and L CT(R)s, of Buffaloes and Weasels, of Habakkuk and Lilo?

I had been there for three months and had just about mas-tered all this jargon, when I was suddenly invited to stand for Parliament, for the safe Tory seat of Galloway. I had never had the slightest thought of becoming a Member of Parliament, and I would certainly not have been tempted by a constituency with which I had no affinity; but I had known and loved Galloway all my life. And like many other people in that year of 1945, I had a feeling of conscience that having been lucky enough to come through the war intact I ought to acquiesce if I were really wanted by my neighbours. There might be a chance to do something positive and constructive. In this exalted mood I went to see Bob Laycock, who tried to dissuade me; when he failed, he sent me along the passage to see Antony Head, with whom I had also been at Camberley, but he too failed to dis-suade me, even when he said that I was behaving like a hys-terical schoolgirl. By the end of the week not only I but they had been adopted as Tory candidates: I for Galloway, Bob for his own native constituency of Bassetlaw in Yorkshire and Antony for Carshalton in Surrey. Furthermore, the Assistant Scientific Adviser was standing somewhere for Labour, and the Assistant Camp Commandant for the Liberals. It is hum-bling to reflect how well C.O.H.Q. got on throughout the election period without these supposedly key people.

Not all the Tories in Galloway were delighted at my adoption, and indeed I would never have let my name go forward if I had known that I was featuring in a feud. Among the non-enthusiasts was the sitting member, who had represented Galloway for fourteen years and had every intention of continuing to do so. He offered himself as an Independent, and it was soon evident that I would find myself at the foot of the poll. But I had my compensations: two months footloose in the most beautiful corner of Scotland; the right for the first time in my life since joining the Army to say what I thought about everything, whether I knew anything about it or not; and the prospect of a full month's holiday before the declaration of the poll, since the servicemen's votes had to come in from overseas. Everybody, even my political opponents, was nice to me; and indeed, after it was all over, the biggest branch of the Labour Party in the constituency invited me, "to shew there is no ill-feeling," to address them one evening on my experiences in Burma, which I did. I spent the period between Polling Day and Declaration Day sailing down to Dublin and back in the 4-tonner which my brother Simon and I had built a few months before the war. As my crew consisted of Murray Sinclair, who had been severely wounded in the foot in Normandy, and Pat Tweedie, who had lost his right arm at the shoulder in Sicily, I had to do most of the work myself, which is all wrong for a skipper. But we had a wonderful sail, and I got back in time to Kirkcudbright to hear the Independent declared the Member with 13,000 votes, 2,000 ahead of the Labour candidate, with me another 2,000 behind. I returned to C.O.H.Q. to find the Chief of Combined Operations, the Assistant Scientific Adviser and the Assistant Camp Commandant all back at their desks. Antony Head had been the only successful runner out of the stable, and he went on in due course to be Secretary of State for War – a portfolio which he held for longer than anybody since Haldane – and Minister of Defence.

Inevitably C.O.H.Q. was running down, and we were concerned chiefly with ensuring that it would have a secure footing in peace-time so far as training and experiment were concerned.

Training was my responsibility, and I set out to find three sites: one in Britain, one in Germany and one in the Middle East. I found one in Britain, I found one in Germany, and took my team to look at a possible site at Salamis, just north of Famagusta in Cyprus. It would have involved spending a good deal of money on the port of Famagusta, but we reckoned this would be a sound investment anyway, both for the economy of Cyprus and for strategic reasons. It doesn't matter to us now, but if our recommendations had been accepted it would have made the Port Said operations of 1956 much easier to mount.

On the way out to Cyprus, we had an overnight stop in Marseilles, where we were housed in an Air Force mess; and there I met Alan Saunders, the former Inspector-General of the Palestine Police, who was now running the police in Tripolitania, soon to become independent as Libya; he was on his way back there from consultations in London. "Talk of the devil!" he exclaimed as he saw me. His successor in Palestine had been seconded from the Metropolitan Police, to which for family reasons he now wished to return. Saunders had been asked while in London to suggest a replacement. The authorities had decided to bring in somebody from outside; Saunders knew that I had become fond of the country, and not least of the Police; he knew that during a lecture tour which I had done in the Middle East from India between the two Wingate expeditions I had renewed for old time's sake my contacts with the Force; and he had proposed my name. He was very insistent, and I toyed vaguely with the idea for the next three or four nights, when left to myself after the day's work; but I didn't take it seriously until I got home, and found a definite invitation from the Colonial Office to be Inspector-General of the Palestine Police. At that I sat up and took notice.

I was thirty-five, and so far as I could see going on quite well in the Army. On the other hand, retrenchment was squeezing: all round me contemporaries whom the fortunes of war had promoted, like myself, ahead of the normal age were dropping back into more appropriate slots. I hoped that I wasn't unduly ambitious personally, but I didn't want to drop too low in the hierarchy after having been a brigadier, with one short break as a colonel, for more than three years. Also, I was indeed enamoured of Palestine; I admired the Police and had many friends in it; and the problems of that country were certainly a challenge. I therefore accepted, with the provision that the appointment would be for a limited period, and that I would be free to come back to the Army in due course. The reaction to this stipulation was unfavourable, and this gave me pause: if I were only thirty-five, I had at least another twenty years of service to run; and I was sure that it wouldn't be good for anybody, either me or the Palestine Police, to take on the job at the summit for anything like so long, apart from the fact that I certainly didn't want to leave the Army for good. The exchange had got to that point when the War Office applied the hatchet by saying, a little ungraciously, that in any case I was "Not Available." That was that, I thought with regret, and turned back to the problems of Combined Operations.

In October 1946 I received two communications within days of each other. The one was from Neil Ritchie, who was Commander-in-Chief in Scotland, and acting as Colonel of the Regiment in the absence of Wavell in India. It offered me command of the 2nd Battalion, which was then in Karachi under John Benson, who wanted to retire and farm his acres. The other was from the War Office, to say that the Palestine Police had asked for an officer to command the Police Mobile Force in the rank of Assistant-Inspector-General; and that as I had volunteered for the Palestine Police some time earlier I had been nominated for the appointment. I pointed out that the job which I had previously been offered, and for which the War Office had refused to release me, was the top one; and that I would infinitely rather command my own Regiment than be one of three A.I.G.s, with a Deputy I.G. between me and the summit.

The Inspector-General was in London at the time, and we met. He was a highly-decorated war-time Commando and a protégé of Bob Laycock, who had backed him strongly for the job when the War Office wouldn't release me for it. He pressed me strongly to come. The Police Mobile Force had been formed during the war, with the task of reinforcing the ordinary static police in any area where things had got out of hand. It was being commanded at present by a retired Indian Army Officer, whom the I.G. thought too old. Some gross misunderstanding arose at this stage between the I.G. and me, which may well have been my fault. I understood that although my nominal job would be to run the P.M.F. I would in fact have a specific responsibility for all anti-terrorist activities. Now this as a job did sound extremely interesting.

I was summoned by the Military Secretary to talk it over. It was General "Boy" Browning, who had had an exciting war since I had last met him: he had raised and commanded all the airborne forces and been Chief of Staff to Mountbatten in S.E.A.C. He was as elegant as ever, with the same quizzical look on his handsome face.

"Which do you really want to do?" he said: "command your Regiment or go to the Palestine Police?"

"Both," I said: "that's just my difficulty."

"Well, why shouldn't you do both?" he said, thoughtfully. He went on to suggest that I should go to the Police for a couple of years and then command; I was still quite young, and by the time I had finished command I would be back in step with my contemporaries and ripe for a peace-time brigade. He undertook to discuss it with the Adjutant-General, and to let me know the answer in a couple of days. His solution was adopted: two years with the Police, and then command. I handed over my Combined Operations chair to my deputy; got myself measured for my smart blue police uniform; went home for two weeks' embarkation leave; and one sunny morning boarded an aircraft for Palestine. I was under no illusion: I knew I was going to a thankless and tricky job; but it was to a problem which constituted a challenge, in a country I loved, and with a Force that I admired.

Somebody met me at Lydda Airport, and drove me through the Bab-el-Wad and up the familiar Seven Sisters road to Jerusalem. I went straight to the Inspector-General's office at Police

Headquarters in the Russian Compound, where he received me with some embarrassment. Sir Charles Wickham, a former Inspector-General of the Royal Ulster Constabulary, had just completed a report on the Palestine Police at the request of the Government, and among his recommendations, which had already been accepted, was the disbandment of the Police Mobile Force which I had come to command. I suggested an immediate cable to Browning to say that I was available to command our 2nd Battalion after all, but the I.G., while apologetic about my job having folded up, was still very pressing that I should stay; he was insistent that he needed a soldier, and if I went he would have to start all over again looking for another one. We decided to think things over for twenty-four hours, and to discuss it again the following day.

I decided to stay. It would have been an anti-climax to go. We got down to devising a job and a name for it. I was to be called "Assistant Inspector-General (Operations and Training)"; the other two A.I.G.s were respectively in charge of the C.I.D. and of Administration. The Operations side we left rather undefined for the moment; on the Training side I would take over the various depots for recruits and the general responsibility for courses. Meanwhile I was to look around and get the smell of things, and also to arrange for the absorption of the Mobile Force back into the main body of the Police.

The Palestine Police had changed considerably, and not for the better, since I had first known it nine years earlier. In those days its British element had been only 700 strong, and the standard high. Every constable had done six months' recruit training at the Mount Scopus depot; spoke either Arabic or Hebrew, and possibly both; and had a good knowledge of the law, as well as all the usual professional police procedures. During the war it had expanded considerably, and now it was expanding faster still. On the whole we were getting a good stamp of man, varying from those who had found it difficult to settle down after the war to young men in search of adventure. But in my view many of them were too young; they were allowed to join at eighteen, and I was appalled to find that the duration of the recruits' course had been reduced to one month. Instead of the former certainty that the man in blue would know all the answers and be a competent interpreter, most of the new policemen had had far less training than the average private soldier. The old hands were naturally upset over this, and at the end of my first look round I expressed my own disapproval in strong terms to the I.G., recommending fewer recruits and a longer training period. I found that we didn't agree about this, and increasingly, alas, I found that there were many things about which we did not see eye to eye.

My oldest and closest friends in the Force had made me welcome; but Jock Munro, who was now their liaison officer in London, had warned me that I would not find it the happy ship I remembered. The introduction of a non-policeman from outside to be Inspector-General had been resented, and Jock said that I could thank my stars from my own point of view that Alan Saunders's plot for me had not come off. After what he had said, it did not come as a surprise to find a certain chill as I travelled the country. The former P.M.F. officers were angry at the supersession of their A.I.G., and having met him I could see why. He was a charming man, one of whose brothers was a High Court Judge in England and the other a P. & O. Captain. He received me with kindness, but his officers with suspicion, owing partly to doubts about their future.

The P.M.F. had been raised entirely from within the Force, except for a few officers who had been brought in direct from the Army. Some of its constables had come straight from the training depots, and had never been proper policemen at all. As it expanded, so its officers had been promoted; in many cases they had outstripped by two ranks their contemporaries who had preferred to remain genuine policemen. It looked as though it had been a daft idea from the start, but its genesis was in the days towards the end of the war, when the troubles were beginning and there were no troops to deal with them. There was naturally much jealousy between the P.M.F. and the Force proper, and whatever one did was sure to be wrong.

After looking at the problem for some weeks, I recommended

that all P.M.F. officers should be reabsorbed into the main body, dropping one rank in every case; and my recommendation was accepted. This left some of them still ahead of where they would have been, and put some others back into their proper place. All lost financially, but one couldn't let them be better paid than their colleagues in the same rank. A few were reasonable enough to say that this seemed the best of several bad solutions, but most people took it ill. My unpopularity with both sections of the Force was now well-established, resting as it did on two sure foundations: my solution to the P.M.F. problem, and the fact that I wasn't a proper policeman. I did my best to be one, insisting among other things on being addressed as "Mr" and not as "Brigadier" or "Colonel," mastering the text-books, and struggling with my Arabic. In the end I was accepted by most but not by all.

Not only did I fail to persuade my superiors to slow down the rate of recruiting: they speeded it up. In the old days the Depot at Mount Scopus sufficed for all needs, for technical courses as well as recruit training. For some years past there had been a second Depot based on the abandoned railway station at Jenin. The Jewish entry was trained at Sarona, the Arab at Bethlehem under a splendid character called Suleiman Said Suleiman. I now had to establish and staff a third training depot for British recruits. There was a large Tegart police station no longer fully used near a Druze village near Haifa, called Shafr 'Amr, and I took it over, adding some Nissen huts to accommodate the overflow. (Tegart, like Wickham, had been called in to advise from outside in 1938, and on his suggestion vast forts had been built all over Palestine instead of the rambling old Turkish police stations that I had known. They fulfilled their function of affording protection to the police and their families, but psychologically they were all wrong; nobody going with a civilian complaint to the police wants to put his head inside the sort of castle one associates with Beau Geste.) I put in charge Assistant Superintendent Hamish MacLeod, a fine Gaelic-speaking Highlander with red hair and moustache who had been several times decorated for gallantry. He was most reluctant to leave proper police work, and he took a lot of persuading; but he proved to be just the man for the job.

The internal security problem in Palestine in 1946 was totally different from that of before the war. The trouble-makers were Jews, not Arabs, and their activities were urban, not rural. The terrorists' planning was much more subtle, and their techniques more sophisticated. "Terrorist," by the way, was recognised as a silly word: until then, its *nuance* suggested somebody who terrorised his own people and, by implication, successfully. "Rebels" or "enemy" were unacceptable politically. The word "thugs" was officially adopted; but it was so obviously inappropriate that in fact everybody continued to talk about "terrorists."

Another difference was the scarcity of information. In the Arab troubles there was never any lack of informers to tell the tale. Their stories had to be carefully sifted, and often there was an ulterior motive behind them, such as the furthering of an old feud or the paying off of old scores; but there was usually a valuable sediment left after processing. In addition there were many responsible Arabs with a genuine loyalty to the Administration, whose motives in bringing us intelligence were honourable. Now we got very few tips indeed, and from what little we got it was difficult to make deductions. Many Jews disapproved of terrorist activity, but those that did had no knowledge of terrorist plots and plans; and even if they had, would not have given them away. Their attitude resembled that of the many Frenchmen in Occupied France, who wished that the Resistance would cease its activities but were not prepared to denounce or reveal what they knew of them. There were not to be found among the Jews of Palestine the equivalent of those Vichy supporters who were prepared to collaborate with the occupying power, as we had now unfortunately come to be regarded.

The official mouthpiece of Jewish interests was still the Jewish Agency, as it had been for many years. It included such well-known figures as Ben-Gurion, Mrs Myerson (now Mrs Meir) and – technically in a subordinate capacity but actually very influential – Teddy Kollek. Of the three organisations whose names were on everybody's lips, the Hagana, though illegal, was so to speak respectable; it was the secret army preparing for the show-down between Jews and Arabs which both were certain would come, but the British still hoped would not. The other two really were terrorist bodies to whom no holds were barred: the Irgun Zwai Leumi, led by Menachem Beigin, and the much smaller Stern Gang, now led by Avram Yellin, Stern having been killed by a policeman while resisting arrest in Tel Aviv; his sister Hannah was still involved. Yellin was a newcomer to Palestine, a civil engineer from Poland who had only arrived in the course of the war. He had once been in our hands, but had got away in a mass escape from an internment camp near Latrun, and was again on the run. The Hagana did not perpetrate murder, but were not above stealing arms and ammunition, or bribing venal soldiers or officials, of whom there were only a few, but considering all things disgracefully many: most of them riff-raff left over from the war.

At the top of the Administration was the High Commissioner, General Sir Alan Cunningham, who had succeeded Lord Gort at the beginning of 1945; Gort had only held office for a few months after MacMichael's retirement, and had to resign owing to ill-health; he died in March 1946. Cunningham was then still a bachelor, as I was; and I often dined with him *tête-à-tête* in that beautiful Government House, redolent with memories of Wauchope (who died in September 1947). The country was still divided into the same six Districts, each under a District Commissioner: Galilee, Haifa, Samaria, Jerusalem, Jaffa-Tel Aviv and Gaza; and the Police pattern followed that, the senior policeman in each District being a Superintendent. At Police Headquarters, in addition to the D.I.G. and the three A.I.G.s, were several staff Superintendents and the various heads of the specialised branches: signals, bomb-disposal and so on, plus the subordinate wings of the C.I.D., the Flying Squad, fingerprints and the rest. The D.I.G. was a former officer of the Egyptian Police, born and bred in the Middle East and bilingual in English and Arabic; it would have been a miracle had he not resented the penetration to the higher ranks of the Force, including the topmost of all, by a lot of amateurs. He was friendly and jovial, but I always suspected him of being a *faux bonhomme*, and he made no attempt to conceal his satisfaction at my eventual downfall. Number Two in the C.I.D. was Dick Catling, then a Superintendent, a brilliant policeman with a penetrating mind whom nothing could rattle, not even the many attempts on his life; he ended his police career as Inspector-General in Kenya with a thoroughly well-deserved knighthood. He, with John Briance in the C.I.D. and Ben Shaw, Superintendent of Jaffa-Tel Aviv, both excellent Arabists, became my closest friends in the Force: a dubious distinction for them.

On the military side, the General when I arrived was Sir Evelyn Barker, an old ally from when he was commanding the 6oth in Tel Aviv before the war; he was succeeded by Sir Gordon MacMillan of MacMillan of the Argylls, whom I had known on and off for most of my service. There was now no lack of troops in the country, which was the main reason for disbanding the P.M.F. All the professional policemen, with whom I found myself more and more in sympathy, wanted to put the emphasis on proper police duties rather than to rival the Army at its own game. On the other hand, Police sources of information, such as they were, were better than the Army's, which suffered from want of continuity; and Special Branch responsibilities had clearly to remain with the Police.

Britain's role in Palestine was now more thankless than ever. Throughout the world, and especially in the United States, sympathy for the Jews, largely because of their sufferings in occupied Europe, was clamorous. The annual quota allowed to enter by the British was pitifully small, and this was exploited to the full in adroit propaganda. It was hard to see what solution would be least inequitable to both sides. One looked back over the years to the many which had been propounded at different times, every one of which had been hailed with protests of: "Impossible! Unthinkable!" and yet each time, when the problem had become still more difficult from the extra secretions of a year or two, one was tempted to say: – "Why didn't we adopt that when it was first suggested? Too late now!" One such was the recommendation of Partition by the Peel Commission in 1937. It raised a howl of objurgation from every quarter; but a few years later it looked as though it would have been a possible answer, and a few years later still it imposed itself as the result of a bloody war.

Not long after I returned to Palestine, a Commission of Investigation arrived from the United Nations. It was the first such body I had met. It had a respectable Chairman in the person of a Swedish Judge, and there was a man called Hood, either Australian or Canadian, and one or two others who were all right. Most of the rest were poor stuff. There was a shortage of hotel accommodation, and great difficulty in finding billets for them all. Two had to be accommodated in a religious hostel, of which they evidently mistook the function, since they brought back a couple of prostitutes with them, and were ejected from the place in the small hours of the morning. Two were reported to have left the country considerably richer than when they came. Many other bodies and individuals investigated the problem on the site; all of them seemed to be *parti pris* in favour of the Jewish case before ever they arrived, and they would depart with their brief-cases bulging with exquisitely produced printed propaganda emanating from the Jewish Agency. Not for one moment am I suggesting that this was sharp practice on the part of the J.A.: they were fully entitled to grasp at every opportunity to indoctrinate, and they certainly never missed a trick.

Then there were the illegal immigrant ships. The Jews bought up every sort of craft, often ill-found and leaky, and crowded them almost to the waterline with their refugees; these ships made their way to the shores of Palestine and disembarked their passengers on the beaches. They were accused of deliberately choosing such vessels in order to exploit to the full the pathos and the hazards of these voyages and so enlist still more sympathy: there may well have been truth in these charges. One ship at least had to be succoured and towed in by the Royal

Navy at the request and on the confession of the Jewish Agency. A chain of camps had been established in Europe to bring refugees to the various embarkation points. General Sir Frederick Morgan, who as "COSSAC" (Chief of Staff to Commander Supreme Allied Forces) had played a major part in the planning of the "D" Day landings in Normandy, was now Chief of U.N.R.R.A. (United Nations Relief and Rehabilitation Activities) in Germany. He reported officially that he had found his organisation being used without his knowledge to channel Jews and their families into this system, their ultimate destination being Palestine, regardless of the quota. His reward was immediate dismissal by Fiorello La Guardia, himself a Jew, who doubled the jobs of Mayor of New York and Head of U.N.R.R.A. Illegal immigrants continued to flood in. Some eluded capture; those who were caught were interned in camps near Athlit to await their turn in the quota, at the expense of those who were scheduled to come in by legitimate channels.

Both soldiers and policemen had to school themselves to be completely impartial. In this context I have clear memories of one particular day. It was the policy of the Palestine Administration to settle Jewish immigrants on former State lands: lands which had belonged to the Government under the Turkish régime, and which had no registered owners. It was my duty one morning to witness the installation under Police protection of an advance party of Jews on some lands in the Beisan valley which came into this category. They were technically State-owned, but had been cultivated since time immemorial by Arabs. We had a large-scale map, and the acres on to which the Jews were to be put were clearly defined; and the Jews, a party of sturdy, determined young men, had arrived complete with tractors to plough a furrow round the ground allotted to them. The local Arabs were there in full strength; and I am still haunted by the memory of one old woman who sank to her knees, grasped the slack of my trousers at the calf, and pleaded with me not to expel her and her sons from the lands of their forefathers. My orders were clear and my heart had no option but to be hardened. The young Jews began to plough their furrow; the stones began to fly; the Jews – who were by no means unmoved by the anguish of the Arabs – protected themselves with large dish-covers which they had had the forethought to bring for use as shields; and I myself got a dunt on the back of the head from a stone which was fortunately at the end of its trajectory.

I then drove off to Haifa, where I found that yet another illegal immigrant ship was about to be boarded by a Port and Marine launch, under Inspector Fox (whom I was to meet again years later in a similar job in Aden). Purely to widen my experience, I joined the party, and got another dunt on my head, which this time left a scar, from an angry would-be immigrant who attacked me from behind with a china plate which he broke over my skull. They were duly brought ashore, and I accompanied them to Athlit, so as to be able to bear witness that no undue force had been used. I went to bed that night with a thumping headache, but confident that nobody could ever accuse me of partiality for either side. As usual I was wrong.

Even after a quarter of a century, I find that I still harbour a lingering resentment against those people who damned us without giving us credit for trying to hold the ring impartially. They ranged from blundering British sentimentalists to thundering American Zionists. I have never been able to conjure up much affection for the shade of Ben Hecht when I remember how he said at this period: "There is a song in my heart whenever I hear of a British soldier being killed in Palestine." I have sympathy on the other hand for the shade of Ernest Bevin, Foreign Secretary, uncommitted, ailing, approaching his death and hard-pressed, who was provoked to burst out in the House of Commons: "The Arabs are not represented in this House, as the Jews are." A great snarl of protest burst out around him: unreasonably, because what he had said was perfectly true. It would be a poor sort of Jew who didn't stick up for his own people.

At that time, however, the direct responsibility for Palestine rested not with Bevin but with Creech-Jones. There is etched on my memory one of my bachelor evenings at dinner with

General Cunningham the High Commissioner, when, encouraged by his confidences, I ventured to urge on him shyly some particular course of action. He said that he had been asking permission to do this, but could not get an answer out of Creech-Jones. After dinner we went into the drawing-room as usual, and he picked up a copy of a magazine to read, but switched on the wireless to hear the news before doing so. There was a report that the very question I had just asked had been put to Creech-Jones in the House of Commons; and Creech-Jones had replied that this was "entirely a matter for the High Commissioner." I do not feel free to record Cunningham's reaction. I myself would have found irresistible the temptation to resign, and to be quit of all the passing of the buck that was going on in those days. Cunningham stuck it out to the bitter end, and a bitter end it was.

After I had been in Palestine for about three months, it was all too obvious that successful terrorist actions were increasing rather than diminishing in number, yet I found myself almost destitute of ideas. I seemed to lack, and my colleagues seemed to lack, the sort of intuitive thinking that was inspiring our opponents. I tried to translate into the urban and suburban areas of Jerusalem, Haifa and Tel Aviv the kind of ideas that my subordinates had dreamed up for me in the jungles of Burma; but all I got was the sort of echo that you might expect in an empty squash-court. My Burma experience might have helped if we had still been operating against Favzi Kawokji or Issa Battat, but it seemed to have no relevance against Beigin or Yellin, whose plots were hatched in back rooms, whose battle-fields were the streets, and whose security was informer-proof.

It seemed to me, baffled as I was, that we needed people with experience of terrorism or something closely allied to it: people who would foresee the sort of plan that might occur to the imagination of terrorists: people, in short, who had been something like terrorists themselves: not to terrorise or to repay in kind, but to anticipate and to give would-be raiders a bloody nose as they came in to raid. I sold this idea to my superiors, and it tied in nicely with a plan which the Inspector-General had for me: to go back to Britain and negotiate the buying of a hundred new police cars, for which he had just had sanction from the Administration.

Never before in my life – and indeed never again – was I entrusted with buying a hundred motor-cars. I was delighted with the assignment, and with the prospect at the same time of two weeks in London: but I did venture to say that the idea of equipping ourselves with a hundred new police cars, all identical Humbers with a left-hand drive, was daft. In a country like Palestine, where new cars were a phenomenon anyhow, and where police cars should be unrecognisable as such, surely what we wanted was a fleet of every kind of car, of every type and age and vintage, which could only be spotted individually over a period of years as belonging to the Police, and of which we could change the number-plates every quarter of an hour if need be. I was overruled, and I shut up.

However, for my other idea I had full sanction. I was authorised to recruit in great secrecy up to four officers with the sort of qualifications set out in my specification: who had planned and successfully executed behind-the-lines operations during the war. Three would raise and train a small team from the Police; the fourth would be my staff officer. The knowledge that I was going to contrive this during my short visit home was restricted to fewer than half a dozen people.

The purchase of the cars, much as I disapproved of them, was easy. To my astonishment the engagement of the officers took little longer, because I had the sense to go immediately to consult "Boy" Browning. From his war-time experience he had an intimate knowledge of the specialists in the field in which I was interested. I interviewed several and chose my four. Two whom I had particularly hoped to hook I failed to get: the one because he was already employed in a "Greenmantle" sort of job in Central Asia; the other for the excellent reason pithily given in the 20th verse of the XIIIth Chapter of the Gospel according to St Luke: he had just married a wife.

Among several other suggestions to my superiors which failed to find favour was the purchase of three light aircraft.

I had been impressed in Burma by what could be done with them, both in the way of reconnaissance and of rapid communication. Obviously there did not exist in Palestine the prime reason for which we had first acquired them in Burma, the evacuation of wounded; but for the two supplementary uses, reconnaissance and communication, there was every occasion, and a third also: the aerial surveillance of villages and settlements which were being subjected to search. We could buy three Austers for the price of four cars, out of the hundred cars for which we were budgeting; and within the Force there were several former pilots and no end of former ground crew. It used to irritate me sorely to spend three hours on the road between Jerusalem (where I had now acquired a tiny house and an all-round Sudanese servant who had once been cook to a friend of mine in the Sudan – the best investment of the kind that I ever made) and Jenin, where I also had a modest lodging, or Haifa, where my business often took me, when I could have done the same trip in an aircraft in a third of the time or less. I had just published a book, which had brought in precisely the money I needed to buy an Auster for myself. While I was in Britain buying these cars for the Police, and interviewing clandestinely these possible new colleagues, I also negotiated from my private purse the purchase of a brand-new three-seater Auster. I arranged with an acquaintance, David Oldman, a gunner officer with long experience of flying, to deliver it to me in Palestine, accompanied by an old friend from the Durham Light Infantry, "Crackers" May, as co-pilot.

I now loftily told the Palestine Government that as they could apparently not afford any Auster Aircraft for the Palestine Police I was prepared to put my own at their disposal, free and for nothing, provided only that they would pay for the petrol and be responsible for the insurance while they used it, and would surrender it for my own use on Saturdays and Sundays, should I happen to need it. I gave them no time to think it over, and as a result they agreed at once. I was an idiot not to get the agreement in writing; in the end I had to pay for every pint of petrol used on their behalf, which ran into several hundred pounds. So much for a gentleman's agreement with a Government department.

I advertised in Force Orders for qualified pilots, and was astonished to find how many we had in the Force without knowing it. I interviewed more than a dozen from a short list selected from written entries, and finally picked three. As "Captain of the Flight" I chose Crowe, a slim, dark, former Warrant-Officer and flying instructor in the Royal Air Force, who had been shot down and made a prisoner over Kiel a few days before the war ended. All three were posted to Mount Scopus to await the arrival of my tiny aircraft, and to be handy to the Qalandiya airstrip: that hazardous landing-ground which straddled the main road where the ground crew, by kind permission of the Air Commodore, had agreed to look after and maintain my aircraft when it arrived, on private financial arrangements.

And arrive it did, one afternoon at Lydda, and bang on time. Far up in the air it looked no bigger than a dragon-fly, but it came down to land in a few short yards on what I had once known as a mere grass runway, and had seen grow to be one of the main air junctions of the world. Time was when I could wander in to the cluster of wooden sheds which constituted Lydda Airport, and there was nobody to challenge one, or to ask for a look at my identity card. Now it was highly sophisticated, with an excellent restaurant which I often patronised.

I had taken Crowe down with me. Now I ejected poor Crackers May and sent him up to Jerusalem in my car with the luggage and my driver Constable Baynton (who had been the M.T. serjeant of that unfortunate British battalion which was overrun at Quneitra in 1941). Crowe climbed into the co-pilot's seat, and I got in behind. It took us only eight minutes, including the climb to 3,000 feet, from Lydda to Qalandiya, instead of the hour and more which it took by road. This first experience alone was enough to satisfy me that I had made a good buy.

From then on the aircraft was in great demand and constant use. One of its earliest trips was to take Darling, the Deputy

Superintendent in charge of signals, down to our remote police post at Aqaba and back in a day, having spent several hours there, a jaunt which would otherwise have taken him the best part of a week. I think every District Superintendent borrowed it in turn to fly him over his area; I recall one telling me with enthusiasm that he had learned more about the geography of his District from an hour in the air than from a year on the ground. Our first opportunity for what I called "aerial surveillance" came when the Irish Guards were throwing a cordon round an outlying suburb of Jerusalem; Crowe and I circled it so as to spot anybody who might be trying to get away: to our disappointment nobody did. Once on a flight from Jaffa to Haifa we saw men drilling in a cranny of the hills south of Mount Carmel, who could only have been Hagana: we alerted the Army, but the birds had flown by the time they got there. A terrorist leaflet appeared announcing that A.I.G. Fergusson had taken to the air because he thought it was safer than travelling the roads, but they would get him all the same. They can't have known what a rotten pilot I was proving to be.

With infinite patience Crowe was teaching me to fly. We used to take off from Qalandiya early on a Saturday morning and go down to an abandoned war-time strip near Gaza, close to a settlement occupied by Belgian Jews. The children used to come down to watch, and I offered them flights: I had forgotten that orthodox Jews must not use any form of transport on the Sabbath, and the children were not even allowed to climb into the aircraft and "pretend." We would then fly back to Jerusalem and put in a day's work. I soon switched to a much more congenial system. A battalion of the 60th Rifles under Lyon Corbett-Winder was stationed beside an unused concrete airstrip – the Gaza one was sand – at Aqsa. Crowe and I took to flying down there on Friday evenings, spending the night in the officers' mess, and flying at first light, when conditions were quiet and there was no turbulence. One proud morning after a couple of circuits and bumps Crowe got out of the aircraft without warning, in the traditional instructor's manner, and walked away, telling me to carry on by myself. I went round faultlessly, reminding myself through chattering teeth that one's first solo flight was the happiest moment of one's life. There was no sign of Crowe when I landed, so I went round again and this time did a ground-loop (a ground-loop is when you get your braking wrong on landing and spin round in a circle). That brought Crowe out of hiding all right, but I went round again a couple of times, before going back to breakfast with the 60th, very pleased with myself.

On Sundays I used to fly up to Acre, that most beautiful of Arab towns, with its old *Khans* and narrow streets and paved waterfront. I have always thought that it would make the perfect setting for a film of *Sinbad the Sailor*. There I kept a sailing-boat jointly with John Marriott my erstwhile brigade major, who was commanding the Airborne Division's school there, and two or three of his brother officers. She was an old plug of a thing, but we had a lot of fun out of her, lazing our way up to Ras-en-Naqura and back, eating and drinking local wine and sun-bathing and sleeping and toppling over the side now and then into those blue Flecker-like waters, with that superb back-drop of reddish hills. The early flight up from Jerusalem was glorious every time, though I used to feel guilty at not attending the Scots Church. I can remember every landmark on the way: Beit Rima, the Arimathea of the Bible; the deep gully at Kilo 41 which we used to leave to starboard; the plain of Esdraelon opening out, also to starboard, with the Sea of Galilee beyond, and the Mount of the Transfiguration springing out of the low ground; Mount Hermon with its snows to the north; the ugly towers of the Haifa cement-works to bring one back to the present sordid century; the placid and sluggish River Kishon, which one could never believe capable of a spate wild enough to "sweep them away, that ancient river, the river Kishon." Every time on those early Sunday morning flights, I remembered the verse from Whittier's hymn: –

> O Sabbath rest by Galilee,
> O calm of hills above,

Where Jesus knelt to share with thee
  The silence of eternity,
  Interpreted by love.

There was no love whatever about the place: only implacable hate.

Acre was the scene of one of the terrorists' most brilliant exploits. On the northern edge of the town lay the old fort, which one would have thought almost impregnable. It was now a jail. It was rectangular in shape, with an empty moat on its northern side, where its main gate opened on a road running north, parallel to the beach. At that end were the administrative offices. South of them, and beyond a formidable iron fence, was a large open space within the walls where the prisoners exercised. All round were the cells, and a covered passage running between the open space and the massive ramparts which gave out on to the narrow vennels of the town. On the south-eastern corner was an excrescence, not part of the main fort, where were housed those unfortunates who were lunatics as well as criminals.

One day we heard that a hole had been blown in the wall, and that almost all the prisoners had escaped. The Prisons Department was separate from the Police, but it looked as though the blame for the escape and the failure to corral the prisoners before they all got clear of the town might involve both of them, and the Army as well. There was to be an immediate enquiry, and I, as part soldier, part policeman, was to conduct it. I do not remember who my two colleagues were, but I was briefed by the High Commissioner, the Chief Secretary (Sir Hugh Gurney, who was afterwards assassinated while High Commissioner in Malaya), the General and the Inspector-General, and flew up at once in the Auster. It took us two days to unravel what had happened, and to produce our report.

Both plan and execution had been superb. The terrorist plotters had managed to get word to their comrades inside the Jail that on a certain day, during exercise time, they would blast a hole in the south wall. They could not name the day, but they would give warning by setting off a small preliminary explosion near the lunatic wing, which should have the additional effect of diverting the attention of the warders. This was exactly what happened. There was a Turkish bath in the street across from the south wall. They climbed on to the roof of this, and shoved some planks across the street, which was only a few feet wide. This gave them access to a barred window; they blew out the bars with a small charge, got into the passage, and laid a much more powerful charge against the thick wall opposite. Warned by the sound of the explosion from the lunatic wing, the prisoners in the know surged up against the iron fence near the administrative buildings to avoid the blast; and the prisoners not in the know, including the large Arab majority, though puzzled, followed suit. Such warders as were still available, thinking that it was just one of those inexplicable riots which happen in jails from time to time, pumped tear-gas through the grille. At that the main charge went off at the far end of the enclosure, blowing an enormous hole in the wall. The prisoners in the know rushed for it as one man, followed by the others, Arabs and all, in an effort to escape the tear-gas. Finding this yawning gap, the whole lot poured through, leaving the Jail practically empty except for the bewildered warders and one poor wretch, an Arab, who being under sentence of death was being exercised separately in a little cage of his own.

It was a Sunday afternoon, and only the minimum of Police and Army were on duty. The Police station was a quarter of a mile up the road to the north; the Army camp, belonging to an airborne unit, a little way to the east. Many troops and a few constables were bathing in the sea, and some of the quicker-witted among them nipped back on to the road, where, dressed in the incongruous rig of bathing-trunks and revolvers, they intercepted a few of the escapers who had unwisely chosen to go that way. Most of the others had either gone to ground in the nooks and crannies of the town, where they hastily exchanged their prison garb for something else, or nipped out across country. Some hastily-mounted road blocks and search parties recaptured a few, but all the most important terrorist prisoners were spirited away according to arrangements already made. I was sitting in the unfortunate Commandant's office – he had been enjoying a quiet Sunday off at the time of the break – hearing evidence, when the telephone rang, and I answered it. The voice at the other end said in Arabic that its owner, who was under a life sentence for murder, had taken advantage of this unexpected opportunity to have a few days at home with his wife, but he'd be back on Saturday. He was, too.

I had one other major court of enquiry to conduct, into the blowing up of the Haifa Police Station. This had been done in broad daylight by a single man, who must have been as courageous as he was cool. It was a triumph for the terrorists; it made the Police look very silly; and the High Commissioner was not surprisingly hopping mad. So was I, but for a different reason. When I was being briefed before flying up to Haifa, I found that for once we had had a tip that it was going to be done, and that I had deliberately been excluded from the secret, in the interests of keeping it as close as possible. According to my understanding, this was exactly the sort of operation that was my business. I seriously considered resigning in protest, but decided that this would be petty; I contented myself with being very rude instead.

The tip had been surprisingly accurate, though it made no mention of a specific day. A car would be driven in through the wire, and a heavy charge of explosive inside it would be blown. I do not know who was in the secret apart from the I.G. and the Superintendent of the Haifa Division; but six British constables were briefed to mount a special guard, taking it in turns, on the compound, and to shoot without hesitation anybody who looked like setting off such an explosion. The Haifa Police Station was a several-storeyed building round three sides of a square, in the middle of which was a small building used as a sort of duty office. The ground floor was used for offices, the lock-up and so on, and the living accommodation was on the upper storeys. The whole thing was heavily wired, with an ela-

borate entrance. Some weeks had passed, and those few in the
know were beginning to lose faith in the tip. One Saturday
afternoon things were quiet, an Inspector was sitting in the
duty office, and British Constable Murphy, a young fellow with
not much service, one of the six specially briefed men, was
hanging about in the square with his Tommy-gun duly loaded.
He noticed a black Police car drive up to the wire, where it was
challenged by an Arab constable, who then waved it through;
it drove on to the square, and the driver switched off his engine.
Suddenly Murphy spotted that the driver, who was in Police
uniform, had no escort. One of the strictest of all rules at that
time was that every driver must have an armed man with him,
to keep his eyes skinned while his mate concentrated on the
driving.

Murphy, who apart from wild shooting came well out of the
whole thing, strode to the car, and asked the driver, who had
just got out, who he was and where he had come from. For
answer, the driver reached into the back of the car and pulled a
switch; straightening up, he gave Murphy a shove on the chest
which threw him off balance and sent him reeling; he then ran
for the wire while the Arab constable goggled at him. Murphy
fired six shots at him; the first five missed, the sixth hit and
wounded the Arab constable. He then looked in the car, from
which a thin trail of smoke was rising, but couldn't find the
bomb which he guessed must be there; so he doubled to the
duty office and told the Inspector to sound the alarm. The
Inspector, who was not in the know, said: – "Now, now, what's
all this?" Murphy, rightly deciding that this was no time for
explanations, pushed him aside, pulled the switch that sounded
the siren, and lit off for cover, telling the Inspector to do the
same. The Inspector, following more slowly and not fully convinced, was still on the square when the bomb went off a little
later.

I forget what the time-lag was, but there was time enough
for most of the men in the building to get out of it. There were
some who had been playing football, and were in the showers
when the siren went. They dallied long enough to make them-

selves decent, and the three fatal casualties were all from this group; they were passing a window as they ran downstairs, and caught the full blast. A number of others were injured, including the Inspector, and the building was badly damaged. One of the luckier ones was a boy I had recruited from Eton when I had been home in March, and invited to lecture to First Hundred there; several had chosen to do their National Service in the Force as a result of my line-shoot. My court of enquiry established nothing useful, beyond the exact sequence of events. It was very much one up to our adversaries, and there was nothing to be done about it. I could only hope that my special squads, when they got going, might do something to even the score.

IO

It is hardly the job of a Police Force to talk in terms of "going on to the offensive." At the same time, I was not alone in thinking that we had been purely defensive for far too long. It seemed to me that on those rare occasions when we got a tip we ought to devise a sort of ambush. One morning in Jerusalem we heard from some source or other that there was an intention to kidnap a prominent figure that evening and hold him as a hostage for a convicted terrorist then awaiting execution. The first reaction at Police Headquarters was to issue a warning to take special care, but when I heard of it I thought that this might offer the sort of chance which Dick Catling and I had often discussed, of allowing our opponents to put their heads into a noose. We thought of a plan, and the I.G. approved of it.

The best restaurant in Jerusalem was, and for all I know still is, Hess's: it was certainly as good as ever when I last had a meal there in 1967. It had been a favourite rendezvous of the Regiment before the war, and as a policeman I often ate there still. We had learned to be chary of discussing future plans on the telephone, which we knew to be tapped. It struck me that if we could get word to our opponents that somebody worthwhile would be dining that evening in Hess's they might lay for him, and that we in turn might lay for them. I flattered myself that I was worthwhile. Hess's had only one door, which gave on to the street; there were no back doors or side doors, and the far side of it looked out on a cemetery: anybody who had been kidnapped could only be got away through the front door.

The plan seemed to me splendid, and still does, though perhaps in retrospect it looks a trifle naive. The idea was that I should book a particular table with the maximum publicity in Hess's, where the dining-room was upstairs: the table by the window at the far corner of the room. I would gently contrive to put a plate on the window-sill, in the dark. If and when the kidnapping group came in to collect me, I would have ample warning, since they would have to walk the whole length of the room. I would push the plate off the sill so that it crashed in the street, and Dick Catling's boys would close in on the front door. As I emerged from it with my captors, I would suddenly duck and run up the street to the left; Dick's boys would open fire; and a neat little operation would be over. It would all happen so quickly that there would be little risk for me, and if it came off it would be a considerable score. I rang up Hess on my office telephone, hoping that the telephone tappers were on the job, and booked that table; went round in person to confirm that I'd got it; rang him back to cancel it because of some unexpected clash of engagements; rang him back again to re-confirm. Hess was and is a friend of mine, and I hope will remain so even after reading this, if he does. I knew that *he* would never tip anybody off, but I hoped that with all this telephoning and so on I might have succeeded in establishing myself as a bait.

I cannot claim not to have been nervous as I set off in my car through the labyrinth of wire which one now had to negotiate when driving in Jerusalem. The idea of all this wire was to facilitate the rapid closing off of streets when an "incident" happened; I felt and feel that actually it helped the terrorists, since it channelled our own movements so much. I was barely half-way to Hess's when the sirens went off, and I said to myself: – "Damn it! They've kidnapped somebody else!" And so they had: some unfortunate British judge, whom they kept locked up for weeks with nothing to read but Arthur Koestler's *Darkness at Noon*, over and over again. I am an admirer of *Darkness at Noon*, but not to that degree. My beautiful plan had failed as flatly as when a photographer's flash doesn't go off. I still don't know whether or not my telephone talks had been overheard; but when I met Yellin of the Stern Gang years later in Paris I found that he had in fact had several transcripts of calls I had made, though he had no knowledge of this one.

This hostage business was beastly. There was the horrible case when two young Education Corps serjeants were kidnapped while enjoying the hospitality of a Jewish family in (I think) Tel Aviv. They were both mere boys of twenty or so. They were held against the threatened execution of two terrorists under sentence of death. The sentence was carried out, and the British were told by telephone where they would find the serjeants: hanging from trees in an orange grove near Nathanya. That was bad enough: but their bodies had been booby-trapped, and that was worse. The last remnant of sympathy for the terrorists as brave and potentially chivalrous opponents was snuffed out when that happened, and every decent Jew in the country – who far outnumbered these monsters – shuddered with shame. That night, I must confess, some British troops and policemen made their way into Tel Aviv and knocked a few people about as a reprisal; but I will always be proud of the fact that that happened so seldom. One American journalist in Jerusalem – and he was a Jew himself – expressed to me his respectful amazement at how much our people, involved in a quarrel which was not theirs, seemed able to tolerate without exacting revenge. "Our boys could never do it," he said. Thank God, I have never had the occasion to test whether they could or not.

The Nathanya incident was too much for one eye witness at least. We received an anonymous letter whose authenticity we were able to establish by means I will not reveal, even after this lapse of years. Its writer had been present when these two hapless young men had been condemned to death. He revealed the name of the twenty or so men who had been present, including his own. We arrested the whole lot, as we were empowered to do under the then emergency regulations, knowing that we would be including him, but that his identity would be secure. We locked them up in pairs all over the country, certain that sooner rather than later some of them would talk, whether from loneliness or from such remorse as had inspired our unhappy and haunted informant: they had obviously been dominated by a few toughs. I anticipate any suggestion that they might have been subjected to mishandling, a prettier word than torture, by the assurance that we did not go in for that sort of thing. There may have been lapses in this respect from time to time at some junior level, but it was never condoned at any respectable one. Within forty-eight hours, there was a deafening outburst in the House of Commons. Why were we detaining these respectable citizens (some of them were very respectable in the public eye) without either evidence or trial? We were ordered peremptorily to release our prisoners, and those two wretched boys went unrevenged. They were both disobeying orders when they accepted the invitation to that friendly Jewish household; they did so because, improperly, they were taking sides in a dispute which was none of their business, and sympathising with the Jews. It was at the hands of certain ruthless and unscrupulous Jews that they lost their lives: condemned to death in a kitchen, and hanged on a couple of orange trees.

One day I called, as I often did, on Bill Conquest, the burly head of the C.I.D. in Haifa, for whom I had great admiration. Many attempts had been made on his life, and that of Inspector Wheatley his Number Two. I begged Conquest, not for the first time, to take more care of himself, and among other things to quit his house in the city and sleep behind the protection of the wire. Bill said impatiently: – "How the blazes do you think I'd get any information if people had to come through the wire to look for me?" He explained that he went to his office by a different route and means and at a different time each day, but that there was now so much wire about the place that it had become difficult to vary it. I flew on down to Samakh, at the southern end of the Sea of Galilee, where I had planned to spend the night with Bill Manger, the local commander of the Trans-Jordan Frontier Force, who was doing something for me in connection with a planned operation. Next morning I was called to the telephone, and told that Conquest had been killed. On this occasion, as on others, he had driven his car to a garage and switched to a taxi to get to his office. As he walked from the one to the other he was shot in the back of the head.

The first two of my special squad commanders arrived in due course at Lydda Airport, where I went to meet them. The name of one I will not disclose, because it never became widely known: let us call him Angus. He had been a pupil of mine at Sandhurst, although I had scarcely known him there. Since then he had had a curdling sort of time, being parachuted with great enjoyment behind the enemy lines here, there and everywhere. In Italy he had stolen the King's bullet-proof motor-car, and driven it around for three weeks before being ambushed in it, a predicament from which he had shot his way out. He had also been dropped on to a German Corps Headquarters, with a view to blowing it up: by a miracle of R.A.F. precision he had landed by mistake on its roof, and had had to shoot his way out of that predicament too. In Yugoslavia he had bought a herd of goats off a goat herd, and the goat-herd's clothes as well, and driven his goats through a village where another German headquarters was, wreaking damage to it as he passed and disappearing afterwards. None of these activities was in the Sandhurst syllabus as I remembered it. The other chap's name I can disclose because, like mine, it became notorious for his and my activities in Palestine at that time: it was Roy Farran. He too had been my pupil at Sandhurst, where he was himself an instructor when through Boy Browning I recruited him to join me in Palestine. His war had been as dramatic as Angus's, and at one time the Germans had put a price of £10,000 on his head. He had been forbidden to take part in an operation over Italy which he had planned, but he had pleaded successfully to be allowed to fly a reconnaissance over the area. The aircraft came back without him; but a radio signal from him reached base that night. It read simply: – "Sorry: I fell out."

We three dined that evening in the King David Hotel. I then let them loose to wander round the Force – they were both old Palestine hands and acquainted with the country – to cast their eyes over potential members of their respective squads. After two weeks they returned with a list of names of people they wanted, on whom I checked up. They had evidently chosen well, and I got the men released, the reasons for their sudden postings not being revealed. It was more important to get them thoroughly trained than to get them into the field quickly; and for reasons both of secrecy and convenience I got them up to Jenin. From there a track ran up into the hills to the westward, giving access only to a single village: it included every type of country other than urban in which they were likely to operate. I declared it a closed area for two hours every morning, and we converted it into the equivalent of a clay-pigeon shoot, where we were able to erect devices corresponding to the sort of ambush they might easily encounter. The one thing I was not able to produce with my limited resources without giving the game away was a village street. If I had been just a trifle more ruthless, I could have done that, by commandeering a length of street in Jenin; but I didn't.

One morning at Jenin just after dawn I was shaving, when I saw a policeman on a grey horse riding at a walk down from the hills just west of the Depot, with an Arab walking beside him. I strolled down to the fence in my pyjamas with my lather on my cheeks to greet him as he went past, and saw that the Arab's wrist was tied to his stirrup. The constable was very young, nice-looking, smart and smiling.

"Good morning!" I said. "What have you got there?"

"I'm not sure," said the constable in a cultured voice, "but I hope and think it's a murderer."

"I hope you don't mind my asking you, but what were you doing this time last year?"

"This time last year I had just become captain of my house at Wellington. I enjoyed that, but this is much more interesting!"

I went up to Jenin again on the eve of the squads going operational to give them a pep talk. By now I knew them all as individuals, and a first-class lot. Most of them had been in the armed forces at one time: one was an ex-cavalry serjeant, two had been commandos, one Irish-American had been a fighter-pilot. They were all fit as fleas, and had been taught to shoot the Tac-Tac way, since Roy and Angus had both been Tac-Tac's pupils. Roy's squad was to operate in the Jaffa-Tel Aviv-Jerusalem area, Angus's around Haifa. Both had been found unobtrusive accommodation for a base, though they would be out of doors most of the time; both had been issued with quantities of clothing such as young Jews were in the habit of wearing; both had been given battered cars and an old truck, though if anybody had lifted the bonnets they would have found first-class engines. The biggest snag was that none had more than a smattering of Hebrew, and few had even that; but the concept as a whole wasn't quite so amateurish as it sounds. Each squad also had a radio, and could communicate with me through Jerusalem.

The first success went to Roy's team. It was basically a Trojan Horse operation, involving the temporary commandeering of a laundry delivery van. The colonel of the Argylls, Cluny Macpherson, was an old friend of mine, who willingly agreed to detain its driver at a road block on suspicion of something naughty being in his vehicle. He was well treated, being regaled on a series of cups of tea in the Argylls' guard-room; and after two hours his van was handed back to him, with an explanation that it had all been a mistake. Good use had been made of it meanwhile, and as a result a terrorist courier was picked up with some useful and informative documents on him. He was only a boy. Captured terrorists ran the risk of heavy punishment, including the death sentence if they were armed; but nobody under eighteen could be executed, and for this good reason the gangs used people under that age, girls as well as boys, whenever possible. This was not a startling *coup*, but it did seem to indicate that we were working on the right lines. It was all the more of a body-blow when the whole business crashed about our ears.

"The Farran Case" was a *cause célèbre*. In brief, a young Jew disappeared from the streets of Jerusalem, and Farran was at first suspected, and eventually accused, of having murdered him. Heaven knows that plenty of British had been murdered, resulting in many songs in the hearts of Ben Hecht and others; but British policemen and British soldiers are not supposed to

go around murdering people, whatever the provocation. Roy
Farran was called into Jerusalem for questioning, and I put him
up in my house. I had staying there already a former member of
his team, the Irish-American ex-fighter-pilot, whom I had pulled
out of it to be groomed for a special solo operation; he had just
finished a long process of being schooled in an obscure corner
of the country, and was about to be launched. His Christian
name was Bill, and "Bill" he will be for the purpose of this
story.

As soon as the rumours of a scandal began to circulate, I
was ordered to stand down both squads, to suspend all operations in progress or pending, and to cancel the arrival from
Britain of the third member of the team. Roy's squad was
ordered back to Jenin; Angus's to concentrate in their base
accommodation near Haifa. Plaintive queries of "Why?"
reached me over the radio from Angus, and I flew up to meet
and tell him at a secret rendezvous on an abandoned airstrip
which was known to us both. I got back to Jerusalem in mid-
afternoon and found no sign of Roy in my house: only a series
of urgent summonses from the Deputy Inspector-General to
go and see him. The I.G. himself was away in Britain at this
critical moment.

"Where is Farran?" asked the D.I.G. aggressively. Apparently Roy had been interrogated that morning; and as a result
orders had been issued an hour or two later that he was to be
put under arrest. All I could say was what Bill had told me: that
he had come back to the house from Police Headquarters, and
announced his intention of driving up to Jenin to collect some
clothes, since he had practically nothing but his pseudo-Jewish
outfit with him here in Jerusalem. Two of his men had gone
with him. A telephone call to Jenin confirmed that he had indeed been there, picked up some clothes and left. A quick calculation shewed that he ought to be back at any moment. The
D.I.G. issued an order there and then that the frontiers were
to be watched for him, and Lydda Airport too.

The hours wore on, with no sign of Farran. Then a report
came in from the frontier that before the D.I.G.'s signal had

arrived he had driven across it into Syria, accompanied by two men, all three of them in plain clothes, bluffing his way out of Palestine and into Syria with his familiar persuasive charm and identity cards which were in order. I went sadly back to my house, where I could see that Bill was ill at ease. Over a drink, talking almost to myself, I pointed out to Bill some of the implications of what had happened: not least of them the fact that the United Nations were about to debate the whole Palestine problem, that the Jews were already putting about the story that the British were covering up the scandal, that they would certainly allege that Roy's flight had been connived at, and that the whole thing could bubble up into something really disastrous. Bill, who had been very close to Roy, was obviously getting more and more uncomfortable. At last, under great stress, he confessed that he was torn in two about where his loyalties lay; but if the crisis was as important as I said, perhaps he should tell me that Roy had revealed that he was going to Damascus.

The D.I.G. had shed any pretence of friendship that afternoon, and had been overtly hostile. I had no wish whatever to confide in him. It was now about dinner-time. I rang up Sir Henry Gurney the Chief Secretary, a man whom everybody trusted, and asked if I could come and see him as soon as he had finished dinner, to which he said yes. I drove up there, and joined him and two male guests – Lady Gurney was away – over their coffee. He was as friendly and calm as ever. He said: – "I know you've come to talk shop, and I can guess what it's about; but there's no hurry. We're going to see a film after dinner, and you and I can have a chat after that."

I can't say that I was able to pay much attention to the film. I had been due to dine with Dr and Mrs Weizmann down at Rehovoth that night, and had been looking forward to it; but I had cried off the day before, knowing that the storm was about to break, knowing that I would certainly be needed in Jerusalem, and also not wanting to involve those two nice people in the renewal of an acquaintance which might soon be an embarrassment for them. At last the film finished, the other guests went, and Gurney without any apparent sense of urgency took me through to his study, where we settled down to another drink. I told him most of what I knew, including my grounds for belief that Farran had gone to Damascus. I asked for a breathing-space of forty-eight hours to try and find him, with the help of my aircraft, and bring him back. He gave me his blessing for this, and saw me to the door with the greatest kindness. His final words were: – "Things may have gone wrong for you, but I'm sure you've nothing to reproach yourself with. Don't worry more than you have to. Good luck!"

Before going to bed I alerted Crowe for a fairly early take-off; and first thing in the morning I went to see the D.I.G. to tell him what I was up to, and of my talk with the Chief Secretary the night before. He was not friendly. He was adamant that my squads would have to be broken up, and I was in no case to argue otherwise. All I stipulated was that their individual members should be posted in twos and threes and not as singletons, so that at least they could keep each other company, reminisce with each other, and not be tempted into any possible indiscreet revelations out of sheer loneliness. I clearly understood him to agree. With that I took off and flew to Jenin, *en route* for Damascus.

At Jenin I found to my fury that the whole of Farran's squad had been herded half an hour before into a single room under guard. This had been done on telephoned orders from the D.I.G. since my interview with him less than an hour earlier. They were surly as hell. One of them reminded me that in my "pep talk" in that very camp a few weeks before I had said: "Don't be afraid to take risks: my shoulders are fairly broad." "Fat lot of good your shoulders are!" he said. It was a long time since I had been spoken to like that, but I was in a mood to agree with him. I couldn't tell them where I was bound, or on what mission. All I could say was that I would be back in a couple of days. I rang up the D.I.G. in Jerusalem to protest about what had happened to the squad, but he refused to take the call. My Depot officers in Jenin were acutely embarrassed at having had to put the D.I.G.'s orders into effect, knowing that they must be entirely contrary to my own wishes; I could not embarrass them further by giving them counter-orders which they could not in propriety obey. I drove back miserably to the airstrip, where Crowe and Bill were awaiting me. I had taken Bill with me partly because his operation, like all my others, had been cancelled, and partly because I thought there might be a job for an extra hand in whatever awaited me in Syria. We flew on to Damascus, over the country which had become so familiar to me in 1941, and landed at Mezze aerodrome, on the fringe of which I had been shot up with Pat Bourke and Peter Dorans.

Here I was in trouble again. My departure from Jerusalem had been so precipitate that I had forgotten all about passports, *carnets* and all the other documents needed for the three of us and for the aircraft: I was so accustomed from war-time to both countries being under the same administration. The Syrians were surprisingly accommodating about this, and by noon – what a lot had happened in the course of that morning! – I was in the office of Patrick Scrivener the British Minister: the same office as that in which I had had such a cool reception from MacKereth ten years earlier. Scrivener by contrast was glad to see me, since he was feeling in need of enlightenment. Farran had called on him two hours before and had poured out a story which to Scrivener, knowing nothing of the background, had seemed incoherent, all except the sting in the tail: nothing would induce Farran to return to Palestine unless he were guaranteed freedom from arrest and immunity from trial. It was virtually an ultimatum. The Minister pushed across to me a copy of a signal which he had sent to this effect, and we concocted together a follow-up one in the light of what I had been able to tell him. Meanwhile Farran had arranged to call back in person at 6 p.m. to hear what reaction had been received from the Palestine Government, and we decided that I had better lie low all afternoon until Scrivener summoned me by telephone to confront Farran when he came back. I therefore booked in for the fourth time in my life at the Orient Palace Hotel, taking rooms there also for Crowe and Bill.

At 6 p.m. the telephone rang. It was Scrivener, saying: –
"You'd better come along. I'm afraid the bird has flown." I
went, and heard that Roy Farran had rung up from Aleppo,
more than 200 miles north of Damascus, asking what reply
there had been to the Minister's signal, and pointing out that at
Aleppo he was well poised to cross into Turkey, a country
which had no extradition treaty with Britain. The Minister
had given an evasive answer, playing for time, telling him to
ring up again next morning. Jerusalem had in fact said that
they were not prepared to bargain, but that the Minister was
to use his good offices to persuade Farran to return. This was
probably the only reply open to them, but it wasn't much help
to the Minister. We agreed that I should fly up to Aleppo in the
morning, try to trace Roy, and do my best.

At Mezze Airport in the morning, it was blowing great guns,
and the sand was swirling. An Iraqi Airlines aircraft came in
with a British pilot, Captain Banks, a well-known character
who had been flying around the Middle East for years. He took
one look at my little Auster, trembling in the wind, and said: –
"I've just had one of the most hair-raising flights of my life;
and if you take off in that little thing you'll be committing
suicide." I changed my plans; told Crowe to fly up to Aleppo
as soon as flying conditions improved; and hired a Damascus
taxi for myself and Bill. It was a trip that I would normally
have thoroughly enjoyed, through such famous towns as Homs
and Hama, and past the great water-wheels of the Orontes
river with its leaping fish, like Tobit's in James Bridie's play.
Again Flecker's verse came back into mind: –

> Thou hast not many miles to tread,
> Nor other foes than fleas to dread:
>   Homs shall behold thy morning meal,
> And Hama find thee safe in bed.

Unfortunately I did have other foes than fleas, and some of
them seemed to be on my own side.

We reached Aleppo at dusk. After booking in at Baron's
Hotel, I went round to see the Consul, an excellent chap who

long ago had served in the Palestine Police. He too had had a
visit from Farran, who had used his facilities for ringing up
Scrivener; he too was puzzled about what was going on, but
was both understanding and helpful when I filled in the gaps of
the story. He thought it possible that Roy might smell a rat at
the Minister's delay in passing on to him any reaction from the
Palestine Government. So far as we knew, the Syrians had no
knowledge as yet of what all the fuss was about. The Consul
was on good terms with the local authorities, and was confident
that he could persuade them to close the exits from the city
from dawn onwards, and intercept Roy if he should try to drive
on towards the Turkish frontier, which was only forty miles
away by road. Roy had refused to divulge where he was staying.

Bill and I were sharing a two-bedded room in the hotel. He
was already in bed, and I was smoking a last cigarette on the
verandah, when I heard the unmistakable tones of Roy's voice
in the street below, and saw his small trim figure disappearing
down a side street just opposite the hotel, and into a door on
the right-hand side. It was close on midnight. I got Bill out of
bed and on to the verandah, indicated the door, told him to
dress and follow, and nipped downstairs into the street and
round the corner. I pushed at the door, and found myself in a
dubious hotel full of dubious people: "hotel" is a euphemism.
There was Roy, looking black as thunder. He claimed to have
seen me on my verandah, and to have called up to me deliberately: that could be true, but up till then it had not been my
impression.

He took me to his dingy little room. He was on edge and
drink-taken. I found myself very sorry for him, knowing what
a wonderful record he had (which incidentally had brought him
two D.S.O.s and three M.C.s before he was twenty-three) and
how keen we had been together on the ploy we had been
sharing. He was now in a mess where he would not have been
but for me, who had lured him away from teaching Cadets at
Sandhurst. The conversation began with his saying that I would
not get out of that room alive. I replied to this gambit by saying
that it was hardly fair: he had a gun, and I hadn't. He answered

with perfect truth, and all the confidence of a Tac-Tac man, that I was no damn good with a gun anyway. He knew his own mind, and for the three hours that our talk lasted he expressed himself and discussed his situation with increasing clarity. The first interruption came from Bill who opened the door and revealed himself as being in the custody of the two members of Farran's squad, his own former colleagues, who were unquestionably drunk and in an ugly mood. Farran said: – "Hallo, Bill! So you gave me away!" and enjoined on them to do him no harm. But – and this is only funny now, when looking back on it – these two were determined to execute both Bill and me before we left; and every now and then throughout my talk with Farran they would put their heads in through the door and, in increasingly mumbling voices because they were knocking back the booze next door, would say to him: – "Shall we do him now, Sir?" for all the world like Mrs Mopp.

Farran and I drank a bit too, as that long night drew on. I besought him to come back and stand his trial, and at last he agreed, provided it was recognised that he was doing so of his own free will. He asked me for a promise that his movements in and around Aleppo would not be interfered with, as he would need to cancel the arrangements which he had already made with contacts there for crossing the frontier into Turkey. I agreed to both these conditions, and we arranged to meet at the Aleppo airport at 9 a.m. in the morning, Crowe having arrived with the aircraft that evening. Bill and Roy's two henchmen would drive back to Palestine in the police car which Roy had purloined. By now the henchmen had fallen asleep, and at 3 a.m. Bill and I walked back the few yards to Baron's Hotel, both very shaken men and reckoning ourselves lucky to be still alive. Of the many things that Bill had been called by his former chums, "rat" was the mildest. In fact, in very difficult circumstances not unlike those in which I found myself, he had behaved impeccably.

I now had to fulfil my obligation to Farran that his movements about Aleppo would not be interfered with, and before going to bed I went round and knocked up the long-suffering British

Consul. Like a good former Palestine policeman, he didn't appear to mind, his only worry being about whether I could trust Roy to keep in the later morning the undertaking he had made in the small hours. By this time I was in the same mood as I had been with the war correspondents before the attack on Damascus: dog-tired and ready to take a chance. My heart sank a bit the following morning when Roy was half an hour late at the airport; but he turned up in due course, explaining that he had had trouble in tracing his contacts.

Bill and Roy's two men, who had almost tangible hang-overs, started off south on their long journey with Bill driving: the trip shewed no promise of being a friendly one. Roy climbed into the back seat of the Auster, to all appearance his usual smiling, frivolous, Hibernian self. I got into the co-pilot's seat, Crowe into the pilot's; and off we set. For the benefit of those who don't know it, Syria consists of a long spine of mountain down its western side, flanked with lower hills just east of them, and then miles of desert, out to Palmyra and beyond. To start with, we took the direct route over the mountains; but the weather there was so turbulent that Crowe turned south-eastward to fly over the desert. It was no less turbulent there, and we found ourselves doing what cavalry people would call a "bending race," steering between *haboubs*: the sand equi-valent of water-spouts, swivelling upwards from the desert and swirling unpredictably about in the sky. I timed them, and noticed that a *haboub* could start from scratch at desert level, and reach us at our ceiling of 7,000 feet in a couple of minutes. Neither Crowe nor I could forecast which way they would spin, and we could fly no higher than we were flying already. At one moment, Roy tapped me on the shoulder from his place in the back seat, and shouted against the roar of the en-gine: – "You know, they'll never hang me! We'll never get there!"

Crowe, grimacing, tapped with his finger at the fuel gauge, and throttled back the engine so that I could hear him. We hadn't enough petrol left to get back to anywhere in Palestine, and would have to land at Damascus to refuel. We did so, but the mood of the Syrian airport authorities, which had been so co-operative the day before, had changed. Evidently they had heard at least a whisper of a rumour. Roy Farran was led away with something resembling V.I.P. treatment; Crowe and I were incarcerated for some hours in a small room. By mid-afternoon Crowe and I had been released, and sped on our way back to Jerusalem; Roy, whom I hadn't seen again, had been offered a commission as a colonel in the Syrian Army, and had opted to stay in Damascus. As I flew back disconsolate with Crowe to Qalandiya, having so nearly succeeded but finally failed in the sortie which Gurney had allowed me to try, I couldn't help thinking how beautifully Farran's names would transliterate into Arabic: Roy Alexander Farran into Ruhi Iskander Farhan.

Two efforts were made to induce Farran to come back: the first by me, which failed, entailing an uncomfortable interview in Damascus at which he insisted on Syrian officials being present to hear him accuse me of being pro-Jewish; the second by two officers of his own Regiment, which happened to be stationed in Palestine at the time, who went up to Damascus to plead with him. This second approach succeeded; but as soon as he returned he was put under arrest, in flat contradiction to the terms which I had agreed with him during those memorable night hours in Aleppo, and those which had been put to him by those two officers of his own Regiment in Damascus. I protested. I was told first that he had abrogated that agreement by leaving my custody at Mezze Airport, and secondly that I had no authority to negotiate it on those terms in the first place. Both these points were bogus. He had not been in my "custody" at Mezze Airport; he was returning of his own free will and at my request through a foreign country where our writ did not run, as a result of a mission on which I had verbally been given a free hand; he was wanted back in Palestine to stand his trial, and – despite a few days of lingering in Damascus while considering what might be a better offer – he had come. Putting him into close arrest was a clear breach of an undertaking which I had given, and which was morally binding even if, in excess of zeal, I had exceeded my authority. Neither Cunningham nor Gurney would ever have initiated this, and the orders must have come from London.

Inevitably he slipped his cable, and found refuge, as we afterwards discovered, with a Bedu Sheikh with whom he had been put in touch some months before in connection with an operation. As usual, the Sheikh's nomadic tribe was moving almost imperceptibly over the face of the earth, and this time it carried Roy Farran with it, across the border into Saudi Arabia: he was lost to all eyes, swathed in the appropriate dress. The wretched officer who was supposed to be guarding him when he escaped through the lavatory which he had asked to visit was ignominiously dismissed from the Force, and I was suspended from all duties other than the nominal supervision of the recruit depots. It was nothing like a full-time job. Angus was paid off and sent home, and his squad broken up as Roy's had been. The terrorists threatened a programme of reprisals and began to put it in hand; and Roy returned voluntarily from his sojourn in the "black houses" of his friends. This time he was put under strict Army guard at Sarafand, to await his trial. He was deemed to have reverted to the Army, to enable the trial to be by court-martial. He whiled away the time by starting work on his memoirs. I was not allowed to see him. Nor was I allowed to go on leave. At one stage it was suggested that I should not be allowed the use of my aircraft, but this prohibition was withdrawn on my undertaking not to cross any frontier.

So began four unhappy and lonely months, relieved only by the loyalty and sympathy of friends, both Police and Army. I got both a cable and a letter from Wavell, expressing sympathy. I will always be grateful to General MacMillan for one special act of kindness. It was at some big cocktail party out of doors. MacMillan sent his A.D.C. across to fetch me, and stood talking to me at the top of some steps in full view of the gathering, indicating thereby that he at any rate did not intend to regard me as a pariah. But there was nobody I could confide in completely, and I badly needed legal advice. In the end I got special leave to go down to Cairo – though for some twisted reason they wouldn't let me use my aircraft for the trip – to consult a British lawyer, and I came back much happier.

The lawyer was John Besly, legal adviser to the British Embassy, who had served in the Seaforth in the First War. To him at last I was able to speak freely. Although I had not been involved in whatever Roy Farran might have done, I had sailed pretty close to the wind in an effort to cover up for him; my chief concern at that stage of the game was to keep the squads in being. John Besly seized on this, and it stood me in good stead.

At last the trial opened, some time in October, Farran having been in custody since June. It had been a long, weary wait. I got a cable that morning from my parents, directing my attention to Psalm 37, verses 5 and 6: a good sort of cable to get in the circumstances. I knew most members of the Court, and many members of the press, who were there in force. The Judge Advocate General was Melford Stevenson, a future High Court Judge. The proceedings took only a short time. When I was called, they first established my identity and then asked me whether I recognised Roy. I looked at him, and got a grin back. Then they asked me to recall a conversation which I had had with him on a certain date, and this was my cue for refusing to reply, on the grounds that it might in certain circumstances tend to incriminate me. There was a sort of *frisson*, and the pressmen all scribbled away, like the jurymen in *Alice in Wonderland*. The prosecution counsel had evidently thought I might take this line, and he reached for one of several books on his table with markers in; he had the misfortune to knock them all over, and they fell face down on the floor. He picked one up, and began thumbing through it.

"Were you going to quote Regina V. Somebody?" asked the Judge Advocate General.

"Yes," said Counsel.

"I thought perhaps you were. I've looked at it, and I rule that it doesn't apply. Colonel Fergusson, have you taken legal advice?"

"Yes, Sir," I said.

"In that case, you may stand down."

After luncheon I was allowed into Court to hear the sum-ming-up, and found myself sitting next to the Sheikh who had been Roy's host during his wanderings. The members went out to confer, and came back in again. The Sheikh said in Arabic: – "It must be all right: they don't look like people who are going to punish somebody." His guess was correct. Farran was found Not Guilty, and whisked away so fast that I never got speech with him. The ordeal was over.

So was my career in the Palestine Police, and I thought it more than likely that it was over for good in any context. That afternoon I was invited to resign, which I did, and told to be out of the country for the sake of my skin within thirty-six hours. I got a note bidding me to Government House at 6 p.m., and General Cunningham the High Commissioner was excep-tionally kind and understanding. So was Gurney. Several Police friends and Jamal Tuqan came to my house; and we had as cheerful an evening as was possible in the circumstances. My Sudanese servant was in tears and saying unkind things about Jews and all their doings. The first thing next morning, he went out and got hold of a photographer, so that we could have our pictures taken together.

Some of the press reports of the trial were vitriolic, one American paper describing it as "a British floor-show." I can only testify that the prosecution case was compiled with the utmost thoroughness, and that the Police authorities, smarting at the scandal, had leant over backwards to make it stick.

As for me, I was taking the greatest care of myself. My telephone rang, and a man whom I knew both socially and as a member of the Stern Gang – but he didn't know I knew this – asked me when I was leaving.

"Leaving?" I said; "I've no intention of leaving!" and I accepted an invitation to dine with him a few nights later. I was determined as a security precaution not to go back to Police Headquarters, and I thought it wise to avoid going to my own bank for the money I would need to get me home. I went in-stead to another one in Allenby Square, where the manager was the man who six years before had knocked on my door at midnight in the Taurus Express, and whom I had supplied with money in Istanbul. I reckoned it was his turn now, and he advanced me £300. As he was getting it, I looked out of the window and saw two sinister men standing on the pavement. In my jumpy mood, I thought they were after me, and rang up Police Headquarters to suggest they might be pulled in. The manager and I watched it happen. I was quite wrong: they were not after me; but they proved to be two men we had been seeking for years, so my final dying kick was a lucky one.

By chance, Franklin, one of the pilots, had bought his discharge from the Force, and we had planned to fly home together in the Auster. An hour before sunset we drove out to Qalandiya for the last time: Steed (who had replaced Baynton as my driver), Crowe and O'Rourke my escort, who was to be killed by terrorists a few weeks later as he came out of a cinema. I said good-bye to them and to the R.A.F. maintenance crew on the darkening airfield, and with a heavy heart I took off, with Franklin piloting. I was turning my back on a disastrous episode, one on which I had embarked with high hopes of being effective. Far from doing any good, I had inadvertently done positive harm. However, I was not prepared to tolerate criticism of any of my actions, except from somebody who had at some time found himself in a like position, and I wouldn't wish my worst enemy that.

We landed unannounced just after the sun had set on the airstrip at Aqsa, where we were warmly welcomed by Lyon Corbett-Winder and his officers, who had naturally been following the case eagerly; they had no notion we were coming to them. Next morning I got up at dawn, and saw a couple of N.C.O.s of the 60th just outside my hut, both armed. I was more touched than I can express to find that a self-mounted guard of serjeants and corporals had been taking turn, two by two, all night to watch over me in case of any funny business. It wasn't necessary, as not a soul in Jerusalem, not even Crowe, O'Rourke and Steed, knew where I'd gone; but it was jolly nice of them, all the same.

II

FOR obvious reasons, I wanted to disappear for a bit, and this
had been agreed to by all concerned. Before going to Palestine,
I had been detailed by Wavell, as Colonel of the Regiment, to
write its war history, in a form which might appeal to the
general public. (When it appeared in 1950 as *The Black Watch
and The King's Enemies*, a rude friend of mine in the Royal Navy
said: – "But I always thought The Black Watch *were* The King's
Enemies.") Meanwhile a talented girl in London, a former
Wren Secretary of Bob Laycock's at C.O.H.Q., had been
"devilling" for me, with access to War Diaries in the Historical
Section of the Cabinet Offices; and thanks to her labours I had
with me detailed accounts and maps of all the actions in which
battalions of the Regiment had taken part in North Africa,
Sicily, Greece and Crete. So I flew home slowly with many
stops, some of several days, with my longest pauses in Tripoli
(where David Rose was stationed), Tunis, Athens, and Crete.
To this last I went in a Greek Air Force plane, returning to the
Piraeus in a cockroach-ridden tramp-steamer. I finally reached
London the day before Princess Elizabeth's wedding, to which
I escorted my mother, impersonating my father and borrowing
his invitation card and morning suit, he having been stricken
with 'flu. I had been off the map, so to speak, for some six
weeks.

A day or two later, I went along to see General "Boy"
Browning. I was just in time, as he had been appointed Treas-
urer to the newly established Household of Princess Elizabeth
and Prince Philip, and this was his last day as Military Secretary.
He greeted me warmly, commiserated over my misfortunes,

and said: – "Well, anyway, things have turned out fine so far
as time is concerned. The command of your 1st Battalion falls
vacant in March: so you can have three months' leave, lucky
dog, and then take over."

Thrilled at this news, I went off to the Adjutant-General's
Branch. I knew the Battalion was at Duisburg, in Germany, and
that Berowald Innes was commanding, like his father before
him; but I didn't know which officers were serving with it, and
this the Adjutant-General's Branch would be able to tell me.
I was received with embarrassment, and after some beating
about the bush I was told that it had been decided, after all the
trouble in Palestine, that I was not to be given command after
all. My immediate thought was to demand to see the Adjutant-
General, but this was succeeded by a better one: to go back to
Boy Browning. He swore a little oath, and rang up the Adjutant-General. I made as if to go, but he restrained me, so I
heard his end of the conversation, and could guess at the other.

"Yes, but we promised him command after he'd done the
Police. . . . Yes, I know 'circumstances have changed,' but
what's the good of a promise which doesn't hold good when
circumstances change? . . . Well, after all who sent him there?
We did. . . . And who gave him Farran? I did! . . . As you know,
I'm leaving this job, *and* the Army, to-day, but I'm not leaving
either until we honour our word. . . . Right; and I can tell him,
can I? Actually he's here with me now! . . . And no going back
on it? . . . Right . . . Good-bye."

He turned to me, and said: – "Congratulations. That's my
last act in the Army; and I think I've done worse in my time!"
I went back to the office I had just come from, and it is pleasant
to recall how pleased on my behalf those officers were who had
given me such a shock half an hour before.

At the beginning of March 1948, I flew out to Germany in
my little aircraft, circling Duisburg and the barracks before
landing a few miles away. Duisburg was still in a dismal mess
from war-time bombing, and from the air I could see many
ruined factories and houses, twisted cranes and gantries. The
barracks, by contrast, looked luxurious; they had been rebuilt

on a lavish scale, and proved to be the most comfortable I was ever in. I had not served with the Regiment since being kidnapped back on to the staff at Ahmednagar six years before, and this was a real home-coming. The more senior officers were all friends of pre-war days, and many of the others were sons of officers whom I had known in the past: indeed, at one time during my three years in command out of thirty-two officers in the Battalion seventeen were "sons"; and much the same applied in the Serjeants' Mess. Patrick Campbell-Preston was second-in-command, and David Rose the senior company commander. I was delighted to find that the names of the eight most senior officers formed themselves into an elegiac couplet:

Campbell-Preston, Rose, Rowan-Hamilton, Burnaby-Atkins,
Fortune, Wingate Gray, Sutherland, Pollok-McCall.

No fewer than five of these were "sons," and Rowan-Hamilton, whose father had been my first Commanding Officer, had two brothers in the Regiment as well.

There were plenty of complications to commanding a battalion in Germany in 1948-51. In few respects was the Army back to pre-war shape. In matters of discipline, for example, there were strict orders against "fraternisation" with German women and against black-marketeering: both were extremely difficult to enforce. For a long time, men were forbidden to have anything to do with German women. Then the pendulum swung, and not only was marriage with Germans allowed: we got into trouble if we sought to discourage it.

As for the Black Market, a conquering army had now become an army of occupation. Every advancing army in history has looted, and ours had been no exception. Nobody was looting now, but the Black Market had come to be regarded by many otherwise respectable people as a permissible alternative. The only currency one was allowed was the so-called BAFs, which could be spent only in NAAFIs or NAAFI-run clubs. One had no access to marks, and German shops were out of bounds. Rations were meagre and dull: so admittedly they were at home, but by 1948 there was lashings of cheap food in the German shops, much more varied than what we were getting.

Married families with children were especially tempted. The one thing the Germans were short of was cigarettes, which commanded fantastic prices in the Black Market. To discourage misusing them, our own cigarette rations were cut to a drastic minimum, and one was not allowed to supplement them with extra supplies from home. I used to be irritated, as a heavy smoker, by seeing non-smokers drawing their due in cigarettes, and knowing that these could only be intended for barter in the Black Market. People had been living so close to it for three years that they had come to regard it as normal; only innocent newcomers like me were shocked, and even I was infuriated at not being allowed into any German restaurant, for instance. I made myself unpopular trying to enforce the rules. They were relaxed later, and a certain amount of German money allowed; but they should have been eased long before they became a strain on discipline to the degree that they did.

The pre-war and war-time effort to introduce the "Group System" – cross-posting of officers and men between regiments – was now resumed more determinedly than before. We had some sturdy allies in the Adjutant-General's Branch who did their best to defend us, and in this context I give honourable mention in despatches to Aubrey Sibbald and Dudley Grist. The former was a Service Corps lieutenant-colonel who had risen from the ranks; his father had been a serjeant-major in the Grenadiers under my father forty-five years before; he was regimental-minded to his finger-tips, and had an astonishing memory of the past, present and probable future of every officer in the many regiments he looked after. It wasn't his fault that the rot was so difficult to stop. As for Dudley Grist, a Gloster, he used to send me helpful personal signals, prefixed Personal Fergusson from Grist. When one arrived owing to an error in transmission headed "Personal Fergusson from Christ," my prestige with the Royal Corps of Signals and others rose tremendously.

The rats were really trying to get at us now. It is my belief that if Wavell, who had been relieved as Viceroy of India in 1947, had not been with us to thunder away with all the majesty of a national hero and a Field-Marshal in the House of Lords, we might well have been defeated. At one moment I was told that three of my company commanders would be posted away, and three from other regiments posted in to replace them. I said I would accept one and no more: Dugald Macfie of the Camerons, who I knew would fit in, as he did: I had to invoke Wavell to avert the other two. Later I was told to give command of a company to an officer who had been reported on adversely *by his own regiment*: he was to be given another chance at our expense. He was a nice enough chap, but not of company commander timber. I employed him in some other way, and in due course received the written "displeasure" of the Army Council; I also incurred the spoken displeasure of Wavell, who asked me why I had not referred the matter to him in the first instance instead of putting my head in the noose. The answer was, of course, to mix a metaphor, that I preferred to keep my trump card on ice for real crises.

One such was when a policy letter came round of which the purport was the levelling out of seniority among all the warrant officers and serjeants in the Highland Brigade; it contained a warning that cross-posting on a massive scale would be needed to achieve this. I gave this long thought, and then addressed the whole Serjeants' Mess. I explained that the only way round it that I could see was for individuals to express their willingness to drop a rank, if necessary, in order to stay with the Regiment; that I wanted a statement from each, which would be seen only by me and the Adjutant, as to how each one felt about it; and I promised that nobody would be thought any the worse of if he expressed a preference for posting rather than going down a rank. The result was illuminating. Out of fifty-two, forty-eight said they would prefer to drop a rank than be posted; of the four exceptions, two were men with large families who could not face the drop in pay. In spite of this, two serjeants were posted against their will, one a bachelor, the other a married man with two children: both bought their discharge, and re-enlisted in the Regiment as private soldiers. I reported all this to Wavell, and my letter reached him at a lucky moment, on the eve of a debate in the Lords: he made the most of it, the press took it up, and we were left in peace for a long time thereafter. It was thoroughly distasteful having to resort to this sort of thing to defend ourselves against those who should be defending us.

Another source of irritation was the War Office Selection Boards. We were required to choose from the ranks young men whom we deemed fit to be commissioned, and the commanding officer to sign a certificate that he was prepared to accept the individual after training as one of his own officers. I was naturally sparing with such signatures, and expected them to carry weight. It was therefore maddening to have the signatures ignored and the candidates rejected. There was one case where a boy who had been President of Pop and Captain of the Boats at Eton was turned down because he "lacked the qualities of leadership," without which he could hardly have reached those eminences. When I protested, I was invited to spend three days of my next leave attending a W.O.S.B., in order that I might see for myself how fair and how scientific their methods of selection were. I thought they were rotten. The decent modest boy who had been brought up not to thrust himself into the limelight was at a disadvantage. By this time, the boy I have mentioned had got through at his second try, but two others, both first-class, had been rejected: one from farming stock in the West of Scotland, the other the son and grandson of officers in the Seaforth Highlanders. I went to the Adjutant-General's Branch and concocted a plot with a brigadier who I discovered shared my views to the full. He arranged things so that these two should be sent to an Officer Cadet Training Unit as though they had passed the Selection Board. They emerged respectively fourth and eighth from their course. My fellow-conspirator and I then confessed our crime, and I understand that the psychiatrists did all sorts of unpsychiatric things like biting their finger-nails. The boy of farming stock came to us, did well, and afterwards put in eight years as a volunteer officer with our Territorials; the other went to his family regiment. I gather that these Boards have since improved out of recognition.

In 1948 we were nominated to be one of three guinea-pigs to test out the New Model for training National Servicemen, the others being an armoured Regiment and a gunner Regiment. We were given an outline syllabus, but beyond that a free hand. I remembered how Wavell used to bewail the system under which we took keen young men from civil life, drilled the heart out of them on the square, made them conform in every way, and then complained that they didn't show initiative. We pondered how to parry this tendency, and after some gestation produced a system which became known as "scallywagging." I formed a Training Company under Bruce Fortune who, after being severely wounded with a bullet through the liver in the Desert, had become A.D.C. to Wavell and infected with his ideas. I gave him first-class officers and N.C.O.s and one good private soldier for each section. As a draft arrived from the Depot, it was dumped straight away in the admirable forest covering many square miles which lay just east of our barracks. The men were told that they were a Maquis in process of formation, in country where a ferocious enemy was hunting for them; they were then introduced to their N.C.O.s, and weapons, who and which had notionally just arrived by parachute. For five days, winter or summer, they roughed it and got along as best they could, cooking for themselves, avoiding their pursuers, and attacking selected targets. Thereafter they were brought into barracks; it was pointed out to them that they hadn't been as effective as they would have been if properly trained; and that now they would understand the purpose of the training that lay ahead of them. By this time, certainly in theory and I believe in practice, they were throwing quite a chest at having fended for themselves and tholed these days in the forest, and were reconciled to square-bashing, weapon-training and the rest.

There had been an outcry at home about the iniquity of sending these young men to the moral cess-pool that Germany was supposed to be. There were three especially outspoken critics: a peer and an M.P. whose names I forget, and Canon Raven of Cambridge, who was a pacifist anyhow. I wrote to each inviting them to come and see for themselves what we were doing, and the manner in which we looked after the young soldiers. All three said they were too busy, and Canon Raven ended his letter by saying that he "would continue to watch the situation from Cambridge." This was too much for me, and I sent an article to Ivor Brown, who was then editing *The Observer*, and was kind enough to publish it, describing our endeavours and telling how these three invitations had been refused. I included a phrase which gave me pleasure: "They are all busy men; in fact they are all busybodies." The result was a rush of visitors including Wilson Harris, the talented Independent M.P. who was also Editor of the *Spectator*, and John Wolfenden, not yet Sir John, who had been another critic. I handed the latter over to Bruce Fortune's subalterns, who gave him stick, which he took very well. We did go to great lengths to look after these boys. Possibly we even overdid it, such as when I made their platoon commanders write to their parents; but we were sensitive to the widespread criticism of what Canon Raven had described as the "devilry" of sending young men to the Army in Germany. It may be some criterion of our success that in two years in Duisburg, we had only three cases of venereal disease, of which only one was a National Service man.

Each year Wavell came to visit us as Colonel of the Regiment, staying for anything up to a week. One year I induced Eric Linklater to come with him: by dint of telling a tremendous lie, Eric had served from 1915 to 1918 in the Regiment on the Western Front as a private soldier before his eighteenth birthday. Wavell wanted to see where three battalions of the Regiment had crossed the Rhine in March 1945, when both Thomas Rennie and Richard Boyle had been killed: we organised a picnic on the river-bank, with about twenty officers and N.C.O.s who had taken part. When the Berlin airlift was on, he expressed a wish to fly up with it, and I fixed this: he flew in the co-pilot's seat, while I sat on a sack of flour in the back.

We ourselves moved up to Berlin as a Battalion in March 1950, after the airlift was over. Wavell planned to visit us in May, but in April he wrote to say he was ill, and would have to postpone it. Then we heard with a shock that he was dangerously ill and fighting for his life. Daily bulletins sent us by his son Archie John gave him a chance at first, but became more and more ominous. On the 24th May, just as I was leaving the Orderly Room for luncheon, a signal arrived to say that he had died.

It was a grievous blow to the country, where his counsel though sparingly given was heard with the more respect because of his dignity and the feeling that he had been given a raw deal. It was a hammer-blow to the Regiment: a file of letters which I still have shews how seriously he was taking his duties as our Colonel, and how tirelessly he was fighting the battles of the infantry as a whole. To me it was devastating: I had been so close to him for so long. And he was barely sixty-seven.

I was ordered to London by the War Office to help with the arrangements for the funeral. The offer had been made to bury him at Westminster Abbey, possibly beside his former Chief Allenby; but Lady Wavell preferred the Chantry Garth at his old school. He was devoted to Winchester. He had incorporated its name in his title, Earl Wavell of Cyrenaica and Winchester. When he matriculated his arms, he had chosen a Winchester scholar as one of his supporters, and a Black Watch soldier as the other. When he had been received *ad portas*, the highest and rarest honour that Winchester can bestow on an Old Wykehamist, he had applied to it in his speech those words of Horace: –

> *Ille terrarum mihi praeter omnis*
> *Angulus ridet.**

Now he lies in it, with the one word WAVELL on his grave.

Soon after I reached London, his body was moved to the Chapel of St John in the Tower, of which he had been Constable for the past two years; and there it lay, watched day and night by Yeomen of the Guard. I had already called Bruce Fortune over to help me; now we were further reinforced by thirty-five Jocks, and the Pipes and Drums, under my Signals

*Odes, II, vi, 13. "That spot of earth smiles on me more than any other."

Officer Andy Watson, and accompanied by Nobby Clark the Quartermaster. This detachment relieved the Yeomen of their vigil.

Although he was not to be buried in the Abbey, there was to be a State funeral service there. There were many questions to be settled, such as who were to be pall-bearers; who were to be allotted special places in the Abbey and who mere tickets for unreserved seats; what troops would take part; timings; and the route to be taken by the cortège when it left for Winchester. The body was to be brought up-river from the Tower Pier to Westminster Pier in an R.A.S.C. launch escorted by two naval ones, while the Honourable Artillery Company fired a salute of nineteen guns. The long procession from Westminster Pier to the West Door of the Abbey would be led by our Pipes and Drums, with a detachment of Household Cavalry bringing up the rear.

The pall-bearer question was complicated by a cable from Mountbatten, who was on leave in Sweden pending his assumption of his new appointment as Fourth Sea Lord, claiming a place as pall-bearer. This was hotly opposed by his brother Lordships in the Admiralty, on the grounds that he was only a Vice-Admiral. He rightly retorted that for this occasion he was a former Viceroy, and characteristically got his way.

The service was due to begin at noon. The coffin was carried from the Tower by the Black Watch bearer party at 11.15, and the guns began to boom. On board the launch, with the coffin and the bearer party, travelled Archie John Wavell, Andy Watson and General Arthur Smith, who was not only Wavell's former Chief of Staff but also Lieutenant of the Tower. At bow and stern stood a Yeoman in full dress. On either side of Westminster Pier the procession was already formed up, except for the great, who were still standing round in small groups talking. I asked them to take their places, which they obediently did. Then Boy Browning, bless him, who was representing Princess Elizabeth, observing that I was under emotional stress, decided to relieve the tension for me, and called across: – "Bernard!"

I went over, saluted and said: – "Sir?"

"You're *fat*!" he said, with his usual mischievous smile; which did the trick completely. My emotion was further relieved when one of the Field-Marshals also called across: – "Bernard!" I went over to him, saluted and said: – "Sir?"

"How do I carry my baton? I've never done it before!"

"I don't know, Sir. I'll ask Lord Wilson." I did.

"I dod't kdow, dab it. Fidd out quick and tell be."

I went over to Monty, and asked him, but he had forgotten his baton altogether. The other Field-Marshals broke rank for a moment, compared notes, settled on a common procedure and adopted it. The explanation of this seeming ignorance was that large-scale ceremonial parades had been rare since the end of the war, and even on this day everybody was still in drab khaki.

I have described elsewhere and at length* that wonderfully moving service in the Abbey, the drive down to Winchester through the June countryside, and the actual burial in the Chantry Garth as the shadows were growing long. The following morning General Arthur Smith came and talked for five minutes about Wavell to the Jocks at their billet in Wellington Barracks, as they sat around polishing their equipment before going to Buckingham Palace in the afternoon. There in the garden the Queen, as Colonel-in-Chief, spoke to each one of them individually, referring to Wavell as "Our Colonel," and reminding them that her own brother had been killed as a Regular officer in the Regiment in 1914. That evening they went off for a short leave, while Bruce and I returned to Berlin.

Towards the end of 1950 I went on leave to Scotland, had a heart attack, spent two months in hospital, emerged, got engaged to be married, and got married. My engagement provoked an insolent telegram from the officers of the Battalion which read: "Congratulations on happy issue of heart attack." I was married in London, with Pat Tweedie as my best man. This was the last time I ever saw my father alive, and I could hardly get speech with him: for most of the reception he was locked in reminiscence with two guests, neither of whom he had seen since they were serving under him in the First War.

*Wavell: Portrait of a Soldier, pp. 91-93.

One was Lord Gowrie, the other General Carton de Wiart: both were V.C.s. I returned to Berlin with my wife, whose elder sister was married to Patrick Campbell-Preston, for the last two months of my command. I then handed over to Patrick, who had so suddenly and so surprisingly become my brother-in-law. All too soon we were being seen off one chilly evening from the Charlottenburg railway station. The serjeants sang "*You're no' awa' tae bide awa'* "; the pipers played, headed by Jenkinson from Dunfermline, who had lost an eye in Tobruk and had played in Westminster Abbey at Wavell's funeral; and the train whistled and steamed away into the snow, past the checkpoint and through the Russian Zone.

My father died while we were on our way home. He was eighty-six years of age, it was sixty-seven years since he had joined the Grenadiers, his life had covered a great span of the Army's history. If he had died a few years earlier, his death would have been to me like the clanging down of a shutter. Now, as he had been granted good health and had aged only gracefully and slowly, it was more like the gentle lowering of a curtain. My wife and I took my mother to Brittany for a change of scene, and on the way back I called in at the War Office to learn what my next job might be. I had hoped for a brigade, but was told that by post-war standards I was still too young at forty. I was to go instead as Colonel Intelligence, Supreme Allied Powers in Europe, better known as SHAPE, which was in process of being established. Early in May I reported at its temporary headquarters at the Hotel Astoria in Paris, within a cricket-ball's throw of the Arc de Triomphe.

The administration of SHAPE was entirely American, with American rules, American military policemen and American jargon. A litter-bin, for instance, was a trash-can. Within the office, the wearing of uniform was compulsory at all times. The only meals one could get on the premises were in an American-style cafeteria in the basement. Out of loyalty I went there for luncheon my first day, and being in uniform I was wearing the kilt. When I had finished, I rose to my feet and found something brown and sticky adhering to my bare knee. My companion identified it as a piece of discarded chewing-gum, which its owner must have stuck to the under side of the table.

This compulsory wearing of uniform was an appalling nuisance. The only relaxation of the rule that we could estab-lish was to be allowed to change before going out to lunch in a restaurant, but one had to change back again afterwards. One winter's morning at 8 a.m. I went with my wife to attend the Requiem Mass of an old friend of her family. As I was going on to the office afterwards, I had no alternative but to wear uniform. The church was dark, and it was not until we were well settled in our seats that I realised I was sitting on the women's side of the church, and that all the men were on the other side of the aisle. I sought to join them, but all the vergers could see of me in the dim light was my kilt; and they thrust me back ignominiously among the womenfolk, where they deemed I belonged.

Such matters as these local American rules within the head-quarters were only pinpricks. It came as a shock to me to real-ise, as I did not realise until after I had been at SHAPE for a month or two, that we, the British, were in very truth the junior partners of the Americans. It took me still longer to realise that this was now our position not only within SHAPE, but beyond it; and not just for now, but for good. This had not been evident to me in Palestine, nor in the British Zone in Germany, nor in the British Sector in Berlin, in all of which I had lived very much for the moment. The only Americans we saw in the British Zone were the occasional visitors or partici-pants in manoeuvres; and those in Berlin were in no greater strength than we. My reading of the newspapers, which must have been pretty innocent, had not schooled me to the thought that we were no longer Equal Top Nation.

I always felt that Lord Montgomery could have done more than he did for the British position at SHAPE. His official title was Deputy Supreme Commander. He lived in state in a Château put at his disposal by the French, and had his office at the end of one of the many stalks protruding from the main SHAPE building (after we moved into our permanent home near Marly). He spent most of his time touring, inspecting and lecturing, and was responsible also for the annual exercise held at SHAPE for all the subordinate commanders and their staffs. The Americans regarded him primarily as a distinguished pet. As the senior British officer in the Intelligence Branch, I used to screw up my courage every few months to go and implore him to do something positive about our say in matters of policy, but I never got any change out of him. Once he called me "a mental masochist!" Far more effective from our point of view was Ted Hudleston, who was Assistant Chief of Staff Operations. Although very young and only an Acting Air-Marshal, he was as forceful as he was able, and cut a great deal of ice with the Americans. I had worked closely with him in Cairo, and was to work closely with him again.

At the head of the hierarchy was Eisenhower. Whatever his shortcomings may have been as President, as the founding father of SHAPE he was superb. His great charm had a curious innocence about it, and his face had an endless variety of expression. Within a year he left to run for President, and was succeeded by Ridgway, who had a great reputation as a fighting general, both in Europe and in Korea. But SHAPE was not his métier, nor tact his strong suit: and it was a relief when he went fairly soon. To everybody's delight he was succeeded by Al Gruenther, who had been Chief of Staff to both Eisenhower and Ridgway, and had been SHAPE's real architect and guiding spirit throughout. A devout Catholic, a hard worker with an unfailing memory, one of the leading bridge-players in the world, a wit of the first water, genuinely interested in people, he was the ideal man for the job. He used to despatch from his office little slips of paper with orders, requests for information, rockets, written in his own spidery hand: these were known among the Americans as "Gruenthergrams." I got a Gruenthergram one morning, to which he had pinned a cutting from the Agony Column of *The Times*, in which somebody was advertising for a tutor with a Scotch accent to teach an intelligent parrot. He had scrawled at the foot: "It is my understanding that you intend to apply for this position as an extra-curricular activity. If I can be of any help to you, please let me know. I am confident you can handle the job, and will so state. A.M.G." I replied with some frivolous verses, which he caused to be duplicated for SHAPE-wide consumption.

Of the French officers at SHAPE I found I knew a surprising number, from my pre-war or Free French past. They included Boisseau, now a Colonel, and des Essars, now a Major-General. Poor des Essars was shortly to lose his only son fighting in Indo-China. Among the Turkish officers was Emin Dirvana, who had been our bear-leader and interpreter when I was with Marshall-Cornwall in 1941: he too was now a colonel. Other interesting characters included the Danish colonel who during the war had swum from Denmark to Sweden, and thence been flown to Scotland, with the earliest photographs of the V.2 Rocket, obtained by the Danish underground from Peenemunde; and the Dutch naval commander with two British D.S.O.s who had escaped with his submarine from Rotterdam in 1940 and, among other things, had torpedoed a German submarine from his own. These were both with me in the Intelligence Branch, and far more experienced in the work than I.

The problem facing us was formidable. At that time the Russians had in Germany twenty-two divisions, of which ten or twelve were armoured, plus another eight in the other countries which they occupied in Europe. In addition to these, there were the forces of the satellite countries, which varied in efficiency and in loyalty to the Soviet bloc. The consensus of opinion of the various NATO countries as collated by us was that the twenty-two divisions could be increased to eighty in less than a month; reinforcement could continue after that, but at a lower rate, since rolling-stock would have to return to Russia, where many other divisions were available if required. I forget now precisely what we had to oppose these twenty-two divisions, but it was fewer than ten, of which only three were armoured; and as most of our reinforcements would have to come from overseas our rate of build-up could not begin to emulate that of the Russians. I was sure then, and I see no reason to be less sure now, that our possession of the Bomb and of tactical atomic weapons as well, and the fact that we proclaimed our readiness to use them if forced, was the one thing that stopped the Russians in their then mood from rolling on westwards to the Atlantic. In those days, of course, the Russians had no nuclear weapons at all.

When we had been established for about a year, a mock exercise was held within SHAPE. We knew roughly when it would start, and had been warned that it would last for a week. It fell to me to organise the Intelligence Division, and I had divided it into shifts, to work eight hours on and eight hours off. I have always maintained that on any exercise, whether a paper one like this or large-scale manoeuvres in the open air, you must get your people into the rhythm of routine from the outset. A mere three-day exercise is of minor value, because it is too short: people pride themselves on being able to keep going without a break, as one can easily do for such a limited time. I remember being hauled over the coals on Salisbury Plain as a brigade commander by both the divisional commander and the C.-in-C. for being asleep in my caravan during the first night of a three-day manoeuvre. I still think I was right: I had applied the same rules to my staff, and there was a duty officer to waken me if I were needed. But one of my American colleagues, at least, was horrified when this particular exercise began, and I announced that I was going home, since I was on the second shift. "That's not the way we do it," he said: "we work till we drop." I couldn't make him see that we should function less successfully if we all got tired simultaneously. This was one lesson at least that I had learned as a brigade major in 1940.

I am in no doubt but that those early days were the best time to be at SHAPE: when everything had to be built up from the bottom, prejudices to be broken down, precedents to be set, ideas to be pooled, plans to be made. Thereafter it must have been largely a question of keeping things up to date and making occasional adjustments, apart from the upheaval when SHAPE had to find a new home in Belgium. Two and a half years of it were enough for me, and it came as an excitement and a relief to be nominated to attend the 1954 course at the Imperial Defence College.

The year at the I.D.C. is a precious oasis of leisure in lives which have been busy hitherto and are likely to be busier than ever thereafter. It is a year in which not only to stand and stare, but to exchange ideas and swap experience. You are not expected to work unduly hard, but rather to absorb like a sponge. Wavell expressed his regret to me more than once that he never got there. In my year we were a round dozen from each of the fighting Services, plus another dozen from various branches of the Civil Service. There were four students each from Canada and Australia; two each from India and Pakistan; and one each from New Zealand and South Africa. There were also four Americans. We included two future First Sea Lords, Varyl Begg and Mike Le Fanu, and future Permanent Heads of the Foreign Office and the Commonwealth Relations Office, Denis Greenhill and Morrice James.

Half-way through the year I was asked what I would like to do next. Having been abroad for five years out of the last six, and eight out of the last thirteen, I thought it would be pleasant to serve in Scotland for a bit. I knew that the command of the 153rd Highland Brigade of the Territorial Army, comprising two battalions of Black Watch and one of Gordons, would soon be vacant, and asked not very hopefully if I could have that. This sort of job was supposed to be, in the soldier's phrase, rather "cushy," and I expected to be told that after the I.D.C. I must do something rather more dashing. But the Military Secretary was in a benign mood, the appointment was mine, and for the next twenty months I had that splendid, almost feudal, command, stretching from the Firth of Forth to the Pools of Dee, and from Loch Rannoch to the Inchcape Rock.

AFTER the summer camp of 1956 was over, I tucked up my Territorial Brigade for the winter, and went off to London for two or three days, leaving my wife and year-old son in my army quarters near Coupar Angus. It was some time in late August. I had arranged to catch the night train north, and my wife was to meet me at Perth first thing in the morning. I had boarded the train, and was sitting down to a pink gin in the restaurant car before dinner with two fellow-travellers whom I happened to know when I felt the crook of an umbrella handle steal round my upper arm from behind. I looked round, and there was "Pooh" Hobbs, my former Number Two at C.O.H.Q., now a major-general and Commandant at Sandhurst. He was smiling, but he left no room for argument when he said: – "I have to tell you to get hold of your luggage, get off the train and come with me."

In the taxi, he explained that he had been to look for me at White's Club, where he had picked up my trail to King's Cross. There was the possibility of a military expedition to recover the Suez Canal; it had been decided to set up a special planning staff, and both he and I were to be on it. It was of course ultra-secret. The thing was in its infancy, and he himself didn't know much about it yet; but over a couple of drinks in White's he told me what little he did. Among other things, I might be required to fly out to Cyprus in the immediate future, where General Sir Charles Keightley, who had helped instruct us both at Camberley in 1940, and who would command the operation if it came off, had his headquarters as C.-in-C. Middle East. Meanwhile I had to ring up my wife to tell her not to meet my train in the morning, and I could hardly have expressed myself worse. I said: – "Something rather serious has happened, and I may have to leave the country." I put it rather better at my second attempt, and allayed her misgivings, though of course I couldn't tell her what was up.

It was in April 1956 that British troops left the Canal Zone, with mutual flowery compliments passing between the British and Egyptian Governments. The Suez Canal Concession still had twelve years to run, being due to expire in 1968. It was considered bad form to suggest that the word of Colonel Nasser might not be trustworthy. The Statutes of the Canal Company, as revised and agreed as lately as January 1956, proclaimed in Article 4 that "the duration of the company shall be equal to the duration of the Concession." On the 26th July, less than three months after the British troops departed, Egypt nationalised the Canal, occupying the Company's offices and installations forcibly with troops.

Only a tiny group was present when I reported to the War Office next morning. Keightley himself was there, and Ted Hudleston the airman (this was to be the fourth time we had served together), Pooh Hobbs, and Vice-Admiral Richmond, a New Zealander in the Royal Navy who was second-in-command of the Mediterranean Fleet. Pooh Hobbs had told me the evening before what my job was to be: Director of Psychological Warfare. For this my qualifications were nil. My only assets were my knowledge of the Middle East, my ability to speak French (since the French were to be in on this if it came off) and the fact that I was available. My Arabic was negligible. I was put in touch with some mysterious people who were supposed to know all about psychological warfare, and told what my resources would be. The whole project at this stage was still what Eisenhower used to call "very iffy," but planning was soon in full swing in a section of the War Office which was put aside for us and heavily guarded. It is surprising in retrospect that not a vestige of a leak occurred during the two months that the invasion was gestating.

I was guilty of one breach of security. I had been out to

Cyprus and back with all due secrecy, and walked into my club for a drink. I bought and paid for it at the bar, and wandered on with it into the room beyond. I was followed a few minutes later by the barman, saying: – "Which of you members has given me a Cyprus shilling?" We all speculated about how on earth a Cyprus shilling could have got into our change, while I tried to look innocent.

Our growing staff was joined by some French officers who, for all they wore plain clothes, looked to our guilty eyes unmistakably Gallic; and the French Admiral Barjot, who was to be Number Two to Keightley, just couldn't have been anything but French. He was fat and jolly, with a paunch which projected so suddenly that you could almost have stood a glass on it. He had been in Algeria at the time of the French collapse in 1940. Having made no secret of his dislike of the Vichy régime, he had been dismissed by Darlan, and for the next two years had scratched a living as a reporter on Alain de Sérigny's newspaper *Echo d'Alger*. In this capacity he had witnessed and reported the Allied landings on the 8th November 1942, before rejoining the Navy and rising to high rank.

I have before me as I write (as they say) a small black notebook full of my jottings from this time, most of them now quite incomprehensible: names, telephone numbers, addresses, notes for propaganda broadcasts, unexplained dimensions, times, appointments, records of conversations. It was a frantically busy period, and my task was made harder by lack of staff, the need for secrecy, and no money or means of transport. I ran up a bill of eighty pounds, much of it for taxis, which I was never repaid. I did one inspired piece of recruiting. Michael Wingate Gray, my former Adjutant, was between appointments and living in Edinburgh. I told him the discreet minimum of what was afoot, he jumped at the chance of joining me, and I got him posted to the War Office, where he tripled our efficiency within twenty-four hours. From the Foreign Office came Sidney Hepplethwaite and Valentine Reilly: the former a career man, the latter a war-time pilot with a D.F.C., working on contract in the Foreign Office Information Department. There

was a silly wrangle going on as to whether Sidney or I should
be the boss, about which neither of us minded; we forged ahead
in total agreement while the Foreign Office and Ministry of
Defence fought it out and finally settled on me. I tapped Peter
Fleming for some ideas, and when he heard what my job was he
said: – "I cannot think of a more certain way of bringing a
promising career to an abrupt end!"

I was told that the following would be my resources, apart
from my small Franco-British staff. A British broadcasting
station in Cyprus called Sharq-al-Adna, which had been mixing
entertainment and propaganda for Arab audiences for some
years, would be commandeered and become my property from
D-Day onwards. I knew the man who was running it from pre-
war days in Palestine, when he had joined the Palestine Broadcasting Service from Wauchope's staff: so I foresaw no difficulty
there. I would find a printing-press in Nicosia, already installed
and manned, by a detachment of R.A.O.C., to print leaflets for
me, which the R.A.F. were under orders to drop. They would
be packed in a special device which from barometric pressure
exploded 1,000 feet above the ground and scattered the leaflets
over a wide area. These would be all my resources before the
landings, but for afterwards I would have a "Voice-Aircraft,"
at present employed in Kenya where the Mau Mau disturbances
were in full swing, which could fly very slowly a few feet above
the ground, giving directions and exhortations from the air.
Finally, I would have a small unit of one officer and twenty-four
men with loud-hailers installed on trucks, which would cruise
along the streets, also delivering instructions and exhortations
either by voice or from prerecorded tapes. Mine might not be
a very glorious command, but at least it included some in-
triguing toys.

I had been authorised to recruit Arabic speakers for broadcasting, being warned that none of the Arab staff of Sharq-al-
Adna was likely to agree to mouthing anti-Nasser propaganda.
I had no contacts of my own, but after fossicking around I discovered the names of a few refugees from the Nasser régime,
and approached them. Not one of them would touch it, for fear

that their voices would be recognised and reprisals carried out on their families. I then tried the B.B.C., but my diplomacy had to be so delicate that it made little impact. I peppered them with "ifs," and "of course, it is most unlikely that such a situation will ever arise;" they agreed to earmark a few, regular Arabic broadcasters, but I could sense them saying in B.B.C. language:– "That guy's nuts!" almost before the door shut behind me. When the balloon finally went up, they said that as a result of the invasion the demand on their Arabic speakers had become so great that none of them could be spared, and I was left high and dry. I had to make do finally with a scratch lot of Arabic speakers, not one of whom was Egyptian. Their accents were recognisably Palestinian or Algerian, and I learned afterwards that their Egyptian audiences had decided they must be Jews – which was hardly calculated to "win friends and influence people."

After a few weeks, the odds against the intervention had become so long that none of us really believed in it any more. Our gradually gathered staff had begun to disperse. We were told that a cadre exercise would be held from Keightley's Headquarters in Cyprus with what remained, and then we would all stand down. On the afternoon of Friday the 28th October, I was called into Ted Hudleston's office, where he drew me pictures on the back of an envelope and talked so obscurely that I had to beg him to be more explicit. I then realised that the project was on. That night as we lay in bed, my wife – who had joined me in London – and I heard the sound of aircraft flying overhead even more continuously than usual, and I knew that these were bombers going to Cyprus. I flew out the following day with Keightley in his private aircraft, plus three or four more of his staff, including Ralph Murray the Political Adviser, who had been snatched up while on leave from being Minister in Cairo, where Humphrey Trevelyan was Ambassador. Trevelyan had been my great benefactor in the matter of lending me books when I was training my brigade in his jungles in India in 1943, and I felt a cad, conniving as I was at a bombshell which would burst so soon over his kindly head.

But it wasn't my business. It wasn't even my business to query the ethics of invading Port Said, any more than it had been the business of my father to query the ethics of invading Ulster from The Curragh in 1914, a parallel which was in my thoughts throughout that flight. I was a soldier, although saddled with an unaccustomed job. To be honest, I was enjoying myself. There was little straw with which to make the bricks required of me, but that wasn't my fault; and it was exhilarating to be engaged as we were. Whatever specious excuse might be given politically, so far as I was concerned we were out to recover the stolen Suez Canal.

As I have written elsewhere,* "tempers ran so high over the ethics of the Franco-British intervention at Port Said that its technical brilliance has been obscured." Although I was only a by-stander so far as the operations were concerned, I did know something about Combined Operations from my time at C.O.H.Q., and the execution of this particular "assault from the sea" was almost impossible to fault. In many ways, it was the most difficult ever mounted. It had to be planned from five different centres: London, Paris, Cyprus, Algiers and Malta. There was much political chopping and changing right up till the last moment, and indeed after. All the forces — land, sea and air – taking part had to set off from bases with vast distances between them. Many of the participants were reservists. There were so many postponements that it was late in the year by the time the final decision was taken. If the eventual touch-down time for the landing-craft had been eight hours later, it would have been much more difficult; twenty-four hours later it would have been impossible. The good weather lasted just long enough. There are still some who claim that the professional standard was low. They speak either from ignorance or from prejudice. Except for one bombing sortie which was only partially successful, it was first-class.

If on the other hand they like to say that the performance of my Psychological Warfare Branch was ludicrously bad, they will find nobody agreeing more fervently than I, though I hope

*The Watery Maze: the Story of Combined Operations: Collins: 1961: p. 392.

they may find it in their hearts to concede that it was not entirely the fault of me or my staff. We were bedevilled by short-handedness, lack of experience, hasty mounting, and the cocoon of secrecy in which we were swathed. Practically nothing went right, except that we can claim to have saved lives by our warning broadcasts from Sharq-al-Adna. Our sequence of set-backs was farcical.

First, the printing-press went wrong. The men manning it were Ordnance Corps reservists, trained printers for the most part but unfamiliar with this particular type of machine. Early on, some essential piece got broken, and a replacement had to be flown out from England, with a loss of several days. That held up the printing of the first batch of leaflets half-way through. Next, we thought we had better experiment with the scattering device for the leaflets, which had been tested some-where in Britain. We found that with the different barometric pressure of the Middle East, instead of exploding 1,000 feet up to scatter its bounty, it exploded at about six feet above the ground, at which height it might easily split open the head of some unfortunate *fellah*. We discovered that it needed to be heavier, so we added a quantity of sand to its load. Therefore, if anybody should ever tell you that my Directorate dropped sand on Egypt as part of its psychological warfare programme, he will be telling you the exact truth. Next, the Government of Kenya protested violently against having its "Voice-Aircraft" taken away from it, and asked why. It was told to mind its own business, and cough it up. The aircraft duly arrived, but all the loud-hailing equipment was removed from it by somebody in Aden when it stopped there to refuel, and it arrived bereft of its power of speech.

The next thing really was a disaster, which may well have had a major effect on the operation. To this day I do not know whose blame it was. For political and humanitarian reasons alike, the operation was to be as bloodless as possible, and con-siderable risks were taken with the lives of our own men, both on the ground and in the air, to ensure that Egyptian casualties, and especially civilian casualties, were kept to a minimum. Our broadcasting was to be a major factor in this. The population of Port Said, which was estimated at 180,000, included many thousands of non-Egyptians: French, Greek, Italian, Maltese and others. D-Day was to be the 31st October: one happy result of this was that D+1 was 1st November, D+2 2nd November, and so on, which was easy to remember. The Egyptians were known to have 160 jet fighters and forty-five heavy bombers; all the bombers and at least half the fighters were of Russian manufacture, and it was uncertain how many of the air-crew were Russian too. It was deemed unwise to risk our vulnerable convoys within their reach until the Egyptian Air Force had been wiped out, preferably on the ground. In fact, the Fleet Air Arm alone destroyed 200 Egyptian aircraft for the loss of three – two during the first phase, and one later. Hence the delay between the opening of the air offensive and the landing of troops, which was the subject of so much criticism at the time and since.

It had been agreed in London, and there was no shadow of doubt about this part of the plan, that the very first stick of bombs to be dropped, on the afternoon of the 31st October, would be on Cairo Radio, the most powerful in the world. Its vitriolic voice was heard all round the clock in every Arabic-speaking country, and amplified in every Arab *suq*. The first bombs would take it out like a tooth; and the moment it went off the air Sharq-al-Adna would come up under its new management, and on Cairo Radio's wave-length. Sharq-al-Adna, unfortunately, could not carry anything like so far, but at least it would be heard all over Lower Egypt, Libya, Jordan, Syria, the Lebanon, and with luck, though patchily, beyond. Suddenly, somebody somewhere in London lost his nerve – it may have been a collective somebody – and Cairo Radio was struck off the bombing programme altogether. At 4.15 p.m. on the 31st the first airfields were bombed, but from this programme also the important bomber base of Cairo West was excluded on urgent orders from London: American civilians were being evacuated from Cairo to Alexandria by the road that runs along the edge of the airfield as a result of the Franco-British ultimatum, which had been refused by the Egyptians some twelve hours before and accepted by the Israelis, to whom it had also been addressed. It will be remembered that the pretext for the intervention had been the desire to separate the Egyptians and Israeli armies in Sinai; but he must be innocent indeed who still believes that this was anything more than a pretext.

So for three days more Cairo Radio churned out its vitupera-tion, as it had every justification for doing, adding tales of the deliberate bombing of teeming cities, which again was perfectly fair as propaganda, even though there was no word of truth in it. The R.A.F. and the Fleet Air Arm had the sternest orders about fighting with one arm tied behind their backs. Sharq-al-Adna piped up its own version on its own wave-length mean-while, but it obviously had nothing like the effect that it would have had with the monopoly of the air on Cairo's wave-length that we had counted on. Protests at even the highest level at not being allowed to "take out" Cairo Radio had no effect.

I am almost sure that it was Tom Prickett, whose title was Chief of Staff, Air Task Force, talking with me in the Operations Room somewhere about the third day, who suddenly said: – "I wonder if they could possibly think that Cairo Radio is actually in Cairo, and are forbidding us to bomb it for fear of civilian casualties?" I buzzed off a signal at once, and his guess was right. The equivalent of Broadcasting House was of course in Cairo, but the transmitters were away out on the edge of the desert. Permission to bomb was now immediately granted. We alerted Sharq-al-Adna to stand by for a change of frequency, and began listening in to Cairo Radio: Sidney, Michael Wingate Gray, Colonel Lande the senior Frenchman, myself, and a few more. My Arabic wasn't good enough to follow in detail the fast, impassioned news bulletin which was being broadcast, nor, of course, did the news-reader's voice falter as the bombers approached: he would be in Cairo, well away from the trans-mitters, from which alone the sound of the aircraft would be heard. He went off the air as suddenly as though somebody had cut his flex with a pair of scissors; and up on that wave-length from Sharq-al-Adna came the voice of one of the few Arabic speakers we had been able to secure. Cairo Radio was silent for a couple of days, but unfortunately the raid had not been as precise as it should have been, and it came up again, though at lower strength, thereafter.

I had had major trouble, too, at Sharq-al-Adna. I had flown out weeks before to explain to its Director in veiled terms what would be required of him in the unlikely event of all this happening. His sympathies were deeply and genuinely with the Egyptians, and he was distressed at the very thought of it. We discussed the business on a purely hypothetical basis, and he was quite sure that none of his Arab or British staff would agree to broadcast our bulletins or propaganda. I had sent him several possible people for test, but he had reported adversely on all of them saying that either their voice or their Arabic was not up to the mark. I now suspect that, so *parti pris* was he, the Prophet himself would have been rejected for this purpose as unsuitable or unqualified.

Early on the morning of the 1st November, some fifteen hours after the first bombs had been dropped, I got an urgent signal from the Foreign Office, asking what I was doing about Sharq-al-Adna, and adding, in case I hadn't heard it – which I hadn't, nor any of my tiny staff – a transcript of what it had been transmitting in English and Arabic throughout the night, which had been monitored in England. I was appalled. It was a short message, frequently repeated. The gist of it was that the staff of Sharq-al-Adna was heart and soul with their Arab brethren; they dissociated themselves from the broadcasts of the night before; and Sharq-al-Adna was no longer to be believed.

Sharq-al-Adna, which was half an hour's drive away, was now once more putting my own stuff on the air, but, knowing nothing of radio or telecommunications, I had no idea what its technical staff might get up to next, let alone its editorial staff. They might even sabotage the place. It was no time for niceties or protocol. I asked for and was given a tough, sensible major of Signals with a quorum of technicians, plus some very untechnical armed infantry, and got them within ten minutes. I gave the major orders in writing, for his own legal protection if necessary later, and buzzed him off as fast as he could go. He was to put the whole staff under arrest; confine to his house the Director, cutting off his telephone; cause the technical staff to work, under duress if need be, under his own direction; and ensure that he got enough Royal Corps of Signals men to find out quickly how to operate the station. Some years afterwards I met a relation of this major, who had told his family that he had thoroughly enjoyed the whole proceeding. I remember his face; I wish I could remember his name. Nobody could have risen to the occasion better.

The next set-back was when the R.A.F. said they were too busy to drop my lovely leaflets. These varied from appeals in Arabic to see sense, to cartoons and caricatures drawn by Ronald Searle, a friend of mine whom I had persuaded by almost blunderbuss tactics to fly out with us for the purpose. I think he regretted it quite early on, since politically he was not in sympathy with the operation, (though he was a popular addition to our small circle, which included a former officer of the Egyptian Police, and a former Suez Canal pilot). In any case, most of his output was vetoed by the Foreign Office representatives on the spot as being too witty and near the bone; and hundreds of thousands of copies of his drawings, eagerly produced by the printing-press (which had now recovered from its malady), were committed to the incinerator. I believe the few surviving copies are now in demand as collectors' pieces, but alas, I had too much on my mind to collect any.

Another conversation which I remember with Tom Prickett, who was a good number, was also in the Operations Room. The Government at home was by now highly sensitive to Cairo's accusations of dropping bombs deliberately on centres of population, and of the degree to which these accusations were being accepted as true in other countries. Tom stormed into the Ops. Room using, I am sorry to say, bad language; and saying: – "I'm being asked to report where every single blanking bomb has dropped that we've dropped." I was inspired to say, gently and sweetly: – "Much easier for you to report where you've dropped every single one of my blanking leaflets." It is rarely that I think of the *mot juste* in time; mine is more often *l'esprit de l'escalier*. In all fairness, I cannot imagine anything more likely to qualify the Chief of Staff of an Air Task Force for admission to Bedlam than to be continually button-holed by a Director of Psychological Warfare, and to be asked in plaintive tones to fly off aircraft in conditions of danger to drop bits of paper over enemy cities. It is as likely to annoy him as Harold Nicolson's remark about stamp-collecting annoyed the whole world of philately, when he said that he could see no point in collecting little bits of coloured paper which other people had licked.

This was the first operation, so far as I know, when one was subjected to control and interruption from base by Telex con-versations. By now, perhaps, officers are so fully used to this that they are trained in it, and it no longer gives them any qualms; but in Cyprus in November 1956 it was a novelty, and an undesirable one. If one receives a signal, no matter how urgent, one has at least time to digest what it says, to compose a reasoned answer, and to have both questions and answers on the file for future reference. A Telex conversation has none of these advantages. Furthermore, there was a constant queue of people waiting to send or receive messages, and impatient for you to get off the line and make room for them. I had to spend several hours when I was badly in need of sleep awaiting my turn at that damned machine because I had been warned that a call would be coming through for me from London; and it was half a mile from where my alluring bed was awaiting me. For the uninitiated, this was how it worked. At either end, there were two typewriters. One was manned, and being typed on by a visible human typist to whom you dictated your mes-sage. The other was a ghost typewriter, tapping out with in-visible fingers the message being dictated and typed from the other end. I abominated this means of communication. My inquisitors in London knew what points they were going to put to me, and were no doubt quoting from notes they had already compiled and held in their hands. I, in the stuffy un-

ventilated dungeon which housed our terminal of the appara-
tus, was required to give snap answers, remote from my office,
my advisers, and such meagre papers as I had. I declined to
commit myself to anything that I was not sure about; and as I
was sure about scarcely anything, I declined to agree to almost
everything. The only such talk that I remember clearly must
have been conducted from the London end by a typist whose
knowledge of historical allusion was defective. People were
tugging at my elbow to get me off the line for more urgent
communications, as the ghost typewriter tapped off to me pleas
which I had already rejected; I was only too keen to finish the
unproductive conversation myself, and get to bed. London, in
a last despairing effort to persuade me against my inclination,
tapped out: – "I beseech you in the barrels of Christ to think it
possible you are mistaken." I replied: – "Roll out the bowels.
Good night."

At 8.20 a.m. on the 5th November, my old 16th Brigade from
Burma days, now parachutists, dropped on Gamil Airport two
miles west of Port Said, under the command of Brigadier Tubby
Butler. A few minutes later, the French parachutists under
Massu dropped on Port Fuad, on the eastern side of the canal.
Except for one minor bridge, which the Egyptians blew up
before the French could reach it, both lots had taken all their
objectives within the hour. Sharq-al-Adna was broadcasting
warnings to civilians to keep their heads down, just as, for the
last few days, we had been giving warnings about air bombing.
We did not wish to be too precise about targets; but we would
say things like: – "To-day we shall be attacking railway mar-
shalling yards, so keep away from them. Listen again at 2 p.m.
for any fresh news." "To-day you will be all right east of the
line X-Y-Z, but be ready to take cover at short notice anywhere
west of it."

At 3 p.m. the first approach was made by the Egyptians for
a surrender, and a Cease Fire was arranged for 3.30. It was
reversed, no doubt on orders from Cairo, and fighting began
again soon after dark. During the night, loud-speaker vans
toured the city, announcing that Russian help was on the way,

and that London and Paris had already been bombed. In our last few broadcasts of the evening, we told our listeners to tune in again at 6 a.m. next morning. From then on we broadcast continuously, in Arabic, English, and French, warnings to keep away from all areas in Port Said north of certain named streets. Those who could not get away should gather on the ground floor of their houses, or in cellars if they had any. This was a calculated risk for our own troops. It enabled the defenders to deduce that a seaborne attack was coming in. Orders had been given that the guns of the supporting naval ships were only to open fire if the enemy fired first, and that guns of 6-inch or larger calibre were not to be fired at all. In fact, the air was so cluttered up with priority signals that these orders did not reach the naval commander, Admiral Holland-Martin, until after the fighting was over; but fortunately he had anticipated them, and given identical orders off his own bat. The landings actually took place at 6.45 a.m., three-quarters of an hour after our first warnings.

I flew over next day, taking with me a French officer, Captain Laperroussas, who had been born and bred in Tunisia and was bilingual in French and Arabic. Finding that there were various useful things that could be done only on the spot, I decided to leave him behind in Port Said; and I find recorded in my little black note-book a plaintive request in French in his own handwriting for one of his colleagues in Cyprus to send over his small-kit for him. I set in train various operations designed to combat Cairo Radio's appeals for a strike among the Port Said workers, and had some success initially. I wandered around the streets chatting to the locals in my modest Arabic, and found them waving and welcoming. The chief concern of most of them was whether they would get their jobs back: they had been unemployed ever since the closure of the Canal, and were near starvation point. At this stage we were being regarded as liberators, and not as horrid imperialist bullies. I saw General Hughie Stockwell, the overall land commander, who was enjoying himself, apart from the fact that the order: – "Stop!" had been flashed from London just when Ismailia, whose garrison was reported to have vanished, was on the point of falling. I called on the Governor – Mahmoud Riad, but not the Mahmoud Riad who later became Foreign Minister – who was under house arrest and as unhappy as one would expect. He answered with reluctance such questions as I put to him: had our broadcasts been heard? Had people acted on them? I had the impression that he was worried about his future standing with Nasser, in case he was deemed not to have defended the place with enough resolution, even though he was merely the civil Governor. He admitted that our broadcasts had been heard, but was obviously unwilling to risk being quoted as conceding that we had tried to minimise casualties. I liked him, and reckoned that he was behaving with dignity and propriety in an unenviable situation. When I asked whether there was anything I could do for him, he brightened and suggested a list of British friends whom he would like told of his safety: it was headed by General Sir Richard Hull, who until a few months before had been the last British commander in Egypt: some distant cousins of mine who used to live in Alexandria were also included. This unexpected link made him more friendly, and me the more reluctant to press him.

Thereafter I divided my time between Cyprus and Port Said, keeping a room in The House of the Palm, a boarding house near the Greek Cathedral. I explored the town thoroughly, and found there had been hardly any damage except to the wooden bathing-huts on the beach, some of which had been full of ammunition – these were all burnt out; to a small area in the old Arab town; to a block of flats behind the Governorate, where a small party of Egyptian soldiers had fought stoutly; and to Navy House and the Customs Shed, where, being unable to get away because they were surrounded by water, a party of police had held out to the end. I was able to confirm that our broadcasts had been heard and acted on, but had to accept reproof from both the Greek and Italian Consuls for not having used their languages as well. I was convinced in those first few days, and remain so, that civilian casualties had been minimal.

One of my broadcasts had got me into trouble, and I was sent home to explain myself, and to help with the preparation of answers to Parliamentary Questions about it. The offending passage ran something like this. "Soldiers of the Egyptian Army! You know that we have no quarrel with you. You know also that we are attacking no civilian targets. We hear that, knowing this, your tanks are taking refuge in villages, confident that our aeroplanes will not attack those villages. But that turns those villages into military targets, and soon we shall be obliged to bomb those tanks." We went on to suggest that the best thing for them to do would be to slip into plain clothes, go home, and make the tanks go away. This was construed, by various members of Parliament, as a threat to attack villages, which I suppose is a reasonable construction to put on it. The real object, of course, was to undermine the confidence of the soldiers, and I feel no qualms about it: it still seems to me rather subtle. But there were many people in Britain who were genuinely shocked by the whole intervention. One woman M.P. declared in the House of Commons the following year that she had been ashamed to call herself British while on a visit to Egypt, and had passed herself off as Norwegian. (A few years later, she was made a Companion of Honour.) The B.B.C. conceived itself to be morally bound to give maximum publicity in all its services, including its Arab service, to criticism of the operation, within Britain and without. A furious British Ambassador in one of the Middle East posts sent a telegram: – "Why bother to knock out Cairo Radio when the B.B.C. is doing its work for it?"

I was only in London for a couple of days before I was turned round and whizzed out again in company with Sir Walter Monckton. Cairo claims that the civilian death-roll in Port Said ran into many thousands had rattled the Government, who decided to send out Monckton, lately Minister of Defence but now Paymaster-General, on a one-man enquiry. For a few brief hours it was to have been me: a silly idea, as obviously the hostiles would have considered me committed to the hilt; so it was to be Monckton, with me to hold his hand and make the local arrangements. I had never met him before, and met him only once afterwards; but during those three or four days that we were together I found him one of the most impressive men I had ever met. He took down all the statements in note form in his own hand in pencil in a series of huge black note-books, using the right-hand page only: his entries filled the first line, and subsequently trailed away across the page, until the bottom line had only a word or two in it. He was courteous and gentle throughout, even with the angriest of witnesses. I thought and think that he gave too much credence to those who claimed that the casualties had been high. There had certainly been a macabre pile-up of corpses for several days at the cemetery at the western end of the town; but the cemetery was on the road towards Gamil airfield where the airborne troops had landed, the grave-diggers had all run away, and the normal death rate in the city of 180,000 inhabitants, especially when most of them lived on a low standard anyway and had earned no wages for many months, must have been high: by which I mean that not all those deaths were likely to have been due to the hostilities. There was a still later and more leisurely investigation by Sir Edwin Herbert, the then President of the Law Society. My own conviction is that a figure of 600 civilians dead as a direct result of the assault would be well in excess of the truth.

Port Said was much the same in most ways since I had left it a few days before. General Hughie Stockwell was still driving himself around in his Land-Rover, chucking sweets to the children, and indulging in his favourite pastime of teasing the Russian Consul by merely following him about. He had put a guard on the Consulate, and given the serjeant in charge a camera, telling him to photograph the Consul every time he went in or out: this was in no way putting restrictions on the Consul's movements or freedom of action, but it made him unaccountably shy. Before I went home for the first time, I dropped in on the General to take a drink off him, and asked whether he'd like me to ring up his wife when I got back; I had known them both in the far-off days when I had been A.D.C. to Wavell. His headquarters were in the comfortable Canal

Company offices and he was sitting on a sofa. He swung up his
legs so that he was lying at full length, with his head on a
cushion and his whisky-and-soda in his hand; and said: – "Yes,
tell her I'm having a hell of a rough time."

But in other ways Port Said had changed. A chill had come
over it. Everybody knew we would shortly be leaving. Those
who had shewn friendliness were looking nervously over their
shoulders in case they should soon be denounced by their
neighbours for having done so. The first United Nations
troops, Danes and Norwegians, had already arrived in their
blue-painted tin hats, and were looking about them curiously.
It was as though the leaves were falling from the trees, except
that most of us thought at that stage that the United Nations
were taking over the Canal for good, which seemed an accep-
table solution.

I returned to London with Monckton to help write his report,
and while there received a signal not to come back to Cyprus.
My branch was being broken up. I asked to be allowed to come
and preside over its death-bed, but this was thought unnecessary, and Michael Wingate Gray administered the last rites. We
were going out with a whimper, but it might have been worse:
there could have been a major bang.

Even now I do not understand why there was such a furore
about the Franco-British intervention, or why some people still
talk about what they call "Suez" *tout court*, with a sense of
shame. It is often cited as the supreme, undisputed example of
moral depravity on the part of a Government, and of that
Government as dragging our country with it into disgrace. I
can understand the indignation of the passionate pro-Arab,
though most people with an informed affinity with the Arab
world dispute that the Egyptians are Arabs. I can understand
the indignation of the out-and-out pacifist, for whom nothing
can ever justify a resort to force. I try to understand the indignation of those who believe that all such disputes should be
submitted to the United Nations, though I find this more
difficult: by what stretch of the imagination can they persuade
themselves that the French and British owners of the Canal

would have got a fair hearing there? Even if after protracted litigation at the International Court at the Hague the verdict had gone in our favour – and most international constitutional lawyers seem to think it would – can they imagine Colonel Nasser accepting it, or the United Nations enforcing it? The facts are clear. The Canal belonged to the British and French until 1968, and the Canal Zone was evacuated by British troops less than three months before its seizure, in the understanding, freshly reiterated by Nasser, that this position was accepted. Everybody I know who has met Nasser tells me that he is charming. The fact remains that the seizure of the Canal was as cynical a piece of double-crossing as any in history.

Those who have doubts about the legal and constitutional position, or the efforts made by the British and French to avoid the ultimate step, should read the chapter entitled "My Suez Story" and the legal opinion of Professor A. L. Goodhart quoted there in Sir Robert Menzies's book *Afternoon Light*.* I would go so far as to say that nobody is qualified to pronounce on the morality of the proceedings who has not steeped himself in this chapter. Menzies is in my view one of the great men of this century, and if that view were ever to falter, five renewed minutes in his company would dispel any doubt. He himself is a professional constitutional lawyer of the first rank, and he happened to be in London on political business as Prime Minister of Australia at the moment when the Canal was sequestrated. He tells in his book how Eden (Prime Minister) and Selwyn Lloyd (Foreign Secretary) were themselves uncertain about the legal position, though in none about the moral; and how he agreed to appear on television in Britain and state his legal opinion.

In the small hours of the 22nd August, in the American Ambassador's sumptuous house in Regent's Park in London, Menzies allowed himself to be persuaded by Foster Dulles, Eden and Lloyd to head a small committee to go and reason with Nasser. The other four members were a Swede, a Persian, an Ethiopian and an American. They were beginning to have

Afternoon Light: Cassell: 1967: pp. 152-3.

some hopes of reaching an agreement with Nasser when President Eisenhower at a press conference said that the United States were "committed to a peaceful settlement of this dispute, nothing else." From that moment, as Menzies puts it, "at a time when silence would have been golden, the President of the United States, by speaking, relieved us of whatever chance – and a very slim chance it was – we had of success." This single sentence from Eisenhower was the green light for Nasser. At a subsequent meeting in Washington, months later, Menzies ventured to reproach Eisenhower for this ill-timed and disastrous remark. Eisenhower replied: – "When a press conference is held, the democratic process requires that questions should be answered." I am not competent to rate Eisenhower as President, but I have an unhappy feeling that this single remark counts heavily against him, revealing as it does a want of awareness of the weight which must attach to any words from the President of the United States.

All that was now a matter of history, and so was the invasion itself. The troops came back, and the many reservists among them returned to civil life. For myself there was to be a change of scene. During the planning period for "Suez," I had been told by the C.I.G.S., Sir Gerald Templer, that I was to be switched from my Highland Territorial brigade to a Regular one stationed at Dover: it was actually one of those which took part in the Port Said landings. I was delighted, as I was beginning to get bored with the almost undue amount of leisure which went with the Territorial job; and still more delighted when I heard that a close friend of mine was about to take over the division in which my new brigade was. Our friendship remains completely unimpaired, but unfortunately we disagreed with each other from the outset about tactical matters. I think the difference in our views stemmed probably from our different experiences in the war: my belief was that he had learned nothing since Anzio, and his that I had learned nothing since Burma; but I repeat that it moulted no feather from our friendship. After eighteen months came the news that my brigade was to be disbanded as one of the economy cuts; and I learned from my general that he was recommending me, not for the promotion which I hoped I was now due for, but for employment in the War Office, still as a brigadier.

I was now forty-seven, and seemed to be treading water so far as advancement was concerned. I had had a splendid innings, but I reckoned I was getting stale: so I sent in my papers. I was interviewed by both Sir Gerald Templer and Sir Hugh Stockwell, who had just become Military Secretary. Both suggested that I should change my mind and stay on, but I suddenly found that I was in no sort of doubt. The time had come for me to hang the trumpet in the hall.

I retired without rancour, and without any sort of chip on my shoulder. I had behind me twenty-eight years which I would not willingly have spent in any other profession. None other could have afforded me so much variety or interest; and my heart never ceased to bleed for those of my contemporaries who had been condemned to spend those years in bowler-hats, instead of in balmorals or their equivalent. I had also had another life in parallel, based on a secure and happy family background, of country life, travel, sailing, writing, and of friendships with people who had nothing to do with the Army.

I never consciously chose to follow the profession of arms: my father and I without discussion had tacitly assumed that I would do just that. It is odd to think how nearly I became a Grenadier like my father and grandfather: I would have been proud indeed, but my life would have been different. I would have hated soldiering in London and its environs, and I am glad to have spent so much of my life with Jocks. Somebody once said that The Black Watch was more like a religion than a regiment; I certainly always thought of myself as being in The Black Watch rather than in the Army, even though through no fault of my own I spent nearly three-quarters of my service away from it. Perhaps this concept was almost too strong in me; yet it was Wavell, whose total time with it was much the same as mine, who said: "The Regiment is the foundation of everything."

To echo something I have said already, all my memories

were precious; not all of them were happy. No soldier can avoid sustaining casualties in the field, and wondering whether with greater skill he could have kept them lower. An inability to accept casualties without too much self-reproach has been the Achilles heel of many a commander at every level. And no soldier whether in war or peace can avoid becoming embroiled in difficult decisions which may cause him days, or even months, of worry. Sometimes a downward loyalty may conflict with an upward one: I have found myself in trouble several times fighting a senior on behalf of a junior. But although I have often been at odds with the Army, I have never fallen out of love with it.

The death sentence on my brigade had been pronounced in the spring of 1958, and the execution was planned for December, so I had a few months in which to plan my foreseeable future. It would be made up of nine months in the year writing books, on the small property near Kilkerran which my wife and I had bought soon after our marriage; and three travelling abroad as a special correspondent for *The Sunday Times*. It never crossed our minds that not far ahead lay a future wholly unforeseen, of five blissful years in New Zealand. Meanwhile, I prepared for my first assignment as a journalist: a journey to Algeria, where among other contacts I had many French Army friends.

We had been almost two years in Dover. We had enjoyed getting to know the townspeople, prowling round the docks and exploring the nooks and crannies and dungeons of the Castle. I planned to travel to Algiers by way of Paris; and, abandoning my wife and son for the time being, had booked a passage on the cross-Channel ferry. My Camp Commandant had arranged this as his last service to me; but I was puzzled when he insisted that I must be on board three-quarters of an hour before the advertised time of sailing. My wife and I went down to the ship that drizzly December morning, and found that a cocktail party had been surreptitiously organised for us in one of her lounges. The joint hosts were British Railways, who owned the vessel; the Mayor and Corporation of Dover;

and the officers of the Garrison. This was fast running down, but the two remaining battalions out of the three were the Gordons and the Camerons: Regiments which I had known all my service, and which up to this final day had been under my command.

We had several drinks, and bade farewell to each other. My wife and my hosts went ashore, and the Captain asked me on to the bridge, whence I waved to my friends on the quay. As we cast off and began to move, I made to go below; but the Captain said: "Wait a bit." We gathered way, and began to steam out into the harbour towards the misty Channel. I glanced up at the Castle, which I had known ever since dining there with the Seaforth Highlanders twenty-five years before; but it was in cloud. Suddenly all the ships in harbour began giving me a toot on their sirens. This for me was almost the last straw, but there was another to come.

On the very end of the breakwater, bearded, dripping wet, clad in the kilt, stood Pipe-Major Macrae of The Queen's Own Cameron Highlanders, playing for all he was worth the old tune of farewell: –

> *Happy we've been a' thegither,*
> *Happy we've been ane and a';*
> *Happy we've been a' thegither:*
> *Sorry that ye're gaun awa'.*

INDEX